Whispers in the Dark

The Fiction of
LOUISA MAY ALCOTT

Whispers in the Dark

The Fiction of
LOUISA MAY ALCOTT

Elizabeth Lennox Keyser

The University of Tennessee Press
Knoxville

Frontispiece. Louisa May Alcott.
Courtesy of the Louisa May Alcott Memorial Association (Orchard House).

The paper in this book meets the minimum requirements of the
American National Standard for Permanence of Paper for Printed
Library Materials. ∞ The binding materials have been chosen
for strength and durability.

Library of Congress Cataloging in Publication Data

Keyser, Elizabeth Lennox, 1942-
      Whispers in the dark: the fiction of Louisa May Alcott / Elizabeth Lennox Keyser.
         p.   cm.
      Includes bibliographical references and index.
      ISBN 0-87049-809-6 (cloth: alk. paper)
      1. Alcott, Louisa May, 1832-1888—Criticism and interpretation.
2. Feminism and literature—United States—History—19th century.
3. Women and literature—United States —History—19th century.
4. Children's stories, American—History and criticism. I. Title.
PS1018.K48 1993
813'.4—dc20   93-17587
                                                            CIP

For Marshall

Contents

Acknowledgments

I would like to be able to name all the friends and family members who, over the years, have contributed indirectly but importantly to this project. However, for fear of omitting someone, I will limit my acknowledgments to those who have materially assisted me.

Modern editors of Alcott's work, such as Claire Booss, Sarah Elbert, Joel Myerson, Daniel Shealy, Elaine Showalter, and, above all, Madeleine Stern, have greatly facilitated studies such as mine. And, as I hope my notes will indicate, I am also considerably indebted to other Alcott scholars.

Despite the work of Alcott editors, many materials remain unpublished. A National Endowment for the Humanities Travel to Collections grant enabled me to examine manuscripts in the Houghton Library of Harvard University, and I am grateful to it and to the Alcott family, as represented by John Pratt, for permission to quote from these. I would also like to thank the New York Historical Society and the Louisa May Alcott Memorial Association (Orchard House) for permission to use photographs from their collections as the cover and frontispiece, respectively, of this book. The Macmillan Company kindly granted me permission to reprint material from my previously published essay, "'The Most Beautiful Things in All the World'? Families in *Little Women*" in *Stories and Society: Children's Literature in Its Social Context*, edited by Dennis Butts (London, 1992).

A 1984 NEH Summer Seminar, conducted by Elaine Showalter, helped launch me on the writing of this book. The feminist scholars whom I met in that seminar have encouraged me over the years, both in their correspondence and by the example of their own publications.

Lynette Carpenter, Beverly Lyon Clark, Robert Dawidoff, Lois Kuznets, and Judith Messick read portions of the manuscript at one stage or another. Elaine Hedges, Leslie Mitchner, and Daniel Shealy all read drafts of the entire manuscript, and their suggestions have substantially improved it. Since I came to Hollins College in 1988, members of the Faculty Writing Workshop have read and commented on various chapters. While I have not invariably heeded their strictures, I have always valued their good-humored support.

I wish to thank the University of Tennessee Press for its prompt attention to my manuscript and its patience in awaiting revision. Special thanks are due Carol Orr, formerly of the press, whose friendly interest in my work over the years encouraged me to submit it there.

No one has helped me more materially with this project than Cynthia Obrist. A research grant from Hollins College enabled me to employ her in the final preparation of the manuscript. Not only has she transferred the entire book to computer disk; she vows to wean me away from the thirty-five-year-old manual typewriter on which I composed it.

Mr. Knightly, in reproving (and *im*proving Emma), tells her: "This is not pleasant to you, Emma—and it is very far from pleasant to me; but I must, I will,—I will tell you truths while I can, satisfied with proving myself your friend by very faithful counsel, and trusting that you will some time or other do me greater justice than you can do now." At last I can do justice to my friend Marshall Waingrow, who, no matter how unpleasant for both of us, insisted on telling me truths about my manuscript, from which I concede it has benefited.

Introduction

Because her subject matter was drawn—of social necessity—from the world of women in which she lived as an unmarried daughter of a bourgeois family, because she addressed herself to the stages of women's lives—as young girls, mothers, matrons, in families, in the domestic sphere—her paintings are easily mis-recognized. Instead of being seen as a radical critique of dominant ideologies, they are used as confirmation of them.

> Rozsika Parker and Griselda Pollock,
> *Old Mistresses* (41)

What Parker and Pollock write of Mary Cassatt may with equal validity be said of her older contemporary, Louisa May Alcott. Not only have her depictions, like Cassatt's, often been misread and misappropriated; her stature as an artist of considerable range and, more important, depth is only now gaining appreciation. Alcott, of course, is best known for her series of books for young people, the first of which, *Little Women* (1868–69), has become a classic. Like Cassatt's canvases, Alcott's juvenile fiction foregrounds women and children in domestic settings, and such is the sentimental appeal of these portrayals that they have long been taken as wholehearted support for the prevailing ideology of Alcott's day—that of separate spheres for men and women. Within the past twenty years, however, scholars have begun to focus their attention on Alcott's works for adults. *Hospital Sketches* (a fictionalized account of her Civil War nursing experience), *Transcendental Wild Oats* (a burlesque of her father Bronson Alcott's utopian experiment at Fruitlands), *Work* (a novel for adults that recounts the author's brief careers as domestic servant, actress, seamstress, and governess as well as her near suicide), and *Diana and Persis* (a novella based on her sister May's experience studying art abroad) have served to remind us that the range of both Alcott's experience and her writing extended well beyond the "moral pap" she seemed content to purvey.[1]

But the reexamination of these adult texts is not sufficient to explain the current interest in Alcott, especially among feminist scholars. That interest has been kindled largely by the discovery of Alcott's anonymous and pseudonymous sensation fiction, first published prior to *Little Women* in the 1860s and reprinted by Madeleine Stern in the mid-1970s.[2] As David Reynolds has shown in *Beneath the American Renaissance,* antebellum America produced for a mass audience periodical and pamphlet fiction ranging from improbable adventure to violent pornography. Alcott's sensation fiction, however, seems to have an even greater affinity with that of her English contemporaries—Wilkie Collins, Charles Reade, and Mary Elizabeth Braddon. These writers, according to Winifred Hughes, created "a kind of civilized melodrama, modernized and domesticated—not only an everyday gothic . . . but also a middle-class Newgate, featuring spectacular crime unconnected with the usual criminal classes" (16). The discrepancy between what Stern calls the "hidden Louisa May Alcott," whose fiction abounds in madhouse scenes, mistaken identities, illicit passions, and ruthless heroines, and "the children's friend,"[3] as she came to be called, argues for an author not simply versatile but complex.

Most scholars now perceive a radical, visionary, or at least revisionary impulse in her fiction, but they disagree as to where and to what extent this impulse has been realized. Some believe that anonymity permitted what acknowledged authorship, especially of books for children, did not—the revolutionary rage and rebellion necessary to produce compelling work. These scholars value her career primarily for what it tells us about the constraints operating upon talented, ambitious women, especially women artists, in nineteenth-century America. Others feel that anonymity encouraged self-indulgence and escapism or, at best, provided catharsis, whereas the extraordinarily popular and lucrative children's fiction, if not great literature, enabled Alcott to promote reform and even envision a utopian society. In short, some would argue that the phenomenal success of *Little Women* doomed Alcott as both an artist and a feminist, others that fame provided her with both a winning form and a secure platform.[4]

The case for Alcott's programmatic feminism can readily be supported by biographical fact and fictional expression. Growing up in a reform-minded household and community, Alcott advocated suffrage and an active, independent life for women.[5] In *Little Women,* for example, Marmee believes it better to "be happy old maids than unhappy wives" (123), that women should "educate [themselves] to take [their] part in the world's work" (482), and that husbands have a place in the nursery (481). In *An Old-Fashioned Girl,* a female sculptor creates a figure she describes as "strong-minded, strong-hearted, strong-souled, and strong-bodied . . . larger than the miserable pinched-up woman of our day." And she refuses to put "a man's hand in hers" or "a child in her arms," because the woman of the future is "to stand alone" and "be something more than a nurse" (258). In *Work,* the heroine finds her calling as an advocate for women's rights and describes herself as "'strong-minded,' a radical, and a reformer" (437). In *Rose in Bloom,* the heroine declares that women, like men, have a duty to make something of their lives and that marriage, for women as for men, is only part of life (10). Finally, in *Jo's Boys,* Plumfield has evolved into coeducational Laurence University, one graduate has fulfilled her dream of becoming a doctor, and the March sisters' sewing circle, like Alcott's fiction itself, has become a forum for the discussion of women's issues.

Yet, though Alcott's domestic fiction may oppose one conventional view of women, its opposition is consistent with another. According to Nina Baym in *Woman's Fiction,* the term *domestic fiction* (often used interchangeably with *sentimental fiction*) has been applied to nineteenth-century American fiction, usually written by and appealing to women, that deals with social relations, is set in the home, abounds in domestic detail, and, while it may criticize prevailing domestic arrangements, views the ideal home as a model for society at large. Taking her cue from Baym, Frances Cogan, in a more recent study of this fiction as well as of contemporary advice books, argues that the Cult of True Womanhood—the notion of women as fragile, sexless, dependent, and self-denying—was opposed by what she calls the Ideal of Real Womanhood. Advocating "intelligence, physical fitness and health, self-sufficiency, economic self-reliance, and careful [combining love and prudence] marriage" (4), the Ideal of Real Womanhood corresponds to the program outlined in Alcott's domestic fiction.⁶ These two ideals—True Womanhood and Real Womanhood—correspond to the "angelic" and "practical" female exemplars identified by Reynolds in his study of the same literature (342). Both Cogan and Reynolds offer explanations for the dissatisfaction that many readers feel with Alcott's domestic fiction, whether for children or adults. Cogan argues that their emphasis on duty to others, especially one's family, "destroys any interpretation of these Real Womanhood writers as feminist" and leads critics to confound them with their rivals, the proponents of True Womanhood (5). Reynolds ultimately sees "moral exemplar feminism," even of the "practical" (i.e., "Real Womanhood") variety, as of lesser literary value and political effectiveness than what he calls "the literature of women's wrongs" (351). By implication Reynolds places Alcott's domestic fiction in the first category; he singles out her sensation masterpiece *Behind a Mask* as an example of the second (408–9).

Reynolds is representative of recent Alcott scholarship, which, since the reprinting of her sensation fiction, has gone far toward establishing her as an interesting and important writer. But he is also representative in his view that, with *Behind a Mask,* Alcott "reached a peak of literary complexity . . . but then willfully turned to the writing of more conventional children's literature" (419). Others would identify that peak as *Little Women*'s "great and unrivalled beauty" (Habegger 240) or "human complexity" (Langland 126), but most would see her at some point shortly before or after its publication in 1868–69 turning *to* the conventional and formulaic and turning *from* the darker or more problematic aspects of human, especially female, experience.

I see a longer trajectory for Alcott's career as a richly suggestive artist. Rather than abandoning a radical feminist critique for the creation of exemplary female characters, Alcott enables a critique of the exemplars themselves. On the surface level of the domestic fiction, Alcott advocates reforms in women's dress, education, entertainment, and employment that her readers (those sympathetic to the Real Womanhood ideal, at least) could accept, especially as she continues to suffuse the home in a rosy glow and to dignify women's work within it. Beneath the placid surface, however, the passions, antagonisms, and power struggles that complicate gender relations in the sensation fiction continue unabated and threaten to erupt. Other scholars have detected a residue of resentment and even rage in the domestic fiction but have attributed it to repression, ambivalence, and frustrated literary ambition. I credit Alcott's imagination, if not always her conscious intent, with more ideological consistency and artistic control. She may not have been subversive in Reynolds's sense of deliberately flouting convention or by deliberately planting keys for the decoding of her surface texts. Nevertheless, she does consistently supply the means of dismantling the system of values that her more or less conventional plots, characters, and narrators appear to support. Alcott's work, like that of more highly acclaimed American artists, "*allows for* a critique of the structure it exploits" (Modleski 1987, 309) or, in other words, "*readily allows—makes itself available to*—an oppositional reading" (Lubin 95, my emphasis).

Alcott's domestic fiction allows for a critique of conventional values largely through features it shares with her sensation fiction, features which in modern terminology bear the stamp of intertextuality and self-referentiality. Not only does Alcott's fiction, whether sensational or domestic, abound in allusions to other works of literature and art; her characters create texts, textiles, paintings, and sculptures, and, above all, enact plays that comment on the novels and stories in which they appear. Take, for example, "Patty's Patchwork" (1872), a children's story from the six-volume collection *Aunt Jo's Scrap-Bag*. In it ten-year-old Patty initially rebels against her socialization as a woman, represented by the tedious task of making patchwork. Only when her significantly named Aunt Pen shows her how the patches can, in the form of a diary, become a means of self-expression does Patty get caught up in her work. Into the quilt, then, goes Patty's life—her good intentions and tender feelings as well as her temptations and mischief, sorrow and rage. Before presenting the finished quilt to Patty's mother, Aunt Pen inscribes the few white squares with sententious verses, thereby transforming it from a diary into a "moral bed-quilt" (195) and Patty from an impulsive child into an exemplar or "comforter" (197). Yet Aunt Pen preserves its "puckered bits and grimy stitches" (208), evidence of the passion and pain that went into it. In effect, Aunt Pen plays editor to Patty's creation: she provides an improving gloss but declines to sanitize or smooth the text itself. Aunt Pen's editorial comments serve as unexceptionable morals for Alcott's (and her persona Aunt Jo's) own story; but Aunt Pen's editorial activity suggests that Alcott's imposition of such morals actually enables her to acknowledge the intractable material beneath them. The lesson for the reader, then, is as much one in subversive writing and reading as it is in domestic virtue, and, as such, it serves as a paradigm for Alcott's art.[7]

Alcott's own mother, by playing Aunt Pen to Louisa's Patty, may have inspired her characteristic practice of using one text to comment on—whether to camouflage or undercut—another. As biographers agree and as the autobiographical *Little Women* suggests, Alcott was extremely close to her mother, Abba, whom she resembled both physically and temperamentally. Alcott's father, the transcendentalist philosopher, educator, and founder of the short-lived utopian community Fruitlands, required his daughters "to keep their journals regularly, and although these were open to the inspection of father and mother, they were very frank, and really recorded their struggles and desires. The mother had the habit of writing little notes to the children when she wished to call their attention to any fault or peculiarity" (Cheney 1980, 23). Ednah Cheney and a more recent biographer, Madelon Bedell, imply that the "openness of communication" fostered by these journals more than compensated for "a certain denial of individual privacy" (M. Bedell 1980, 248).[8] Yet Louisa and her sisters were enjoined by their parents, as Patty was by Aunt Pen, to perform conflicting tasks: to create a candid, spontaneous record of their private feelings and to prepare for public scrutiny a register of their moral growth.

Abba Alcott's comments on Louisa's early journals indicate that she wanted her daughter to have an outlet for her emotions but urged—perhaps to forestall Bronson's criticisms of both mother and daughter—that they become increasingly edifying. On Louisa's tenth birthday, for example, Abba gave her a pencil case, "for I have observed that you are fond of writing, and wish to encourage the habit"; but she begins and ends the birthday note by exhorting Louisa to "be gentle with sisters, obedient to parents, loving to every one" and to "Go on trying . . . to be and do good" (Cheney 1980, 23). One year later, a year in which Louisa has recorded being sad and cross, not minding mother, hating a "fussy" piano teacher, and crying herself to sleep, Abba writes, at Louisa's invitation, "I like to have you make observations about our conversations and your own thoughts. It helps you express them and to understand your little self. Remember, dear girl, that a diary should be an epitome of your life. May it be a record of pure thought and good actions, then you will indeed be the precious child of your loving mother" (*Journals* 47). On the one hand, Abba praises Louisa's frankness, but on the other she implicitly threatens to disown the recorder of "impure" thoughts.

Louisa apparently responded to such mixed messages by continuing to express her angry feelings while supplying herself the moral commentary that would regulate them. At age twelve Louisa, after describing an angry outburst at her sister Anna, reproof by her father, and shame "over my bad tongue and temper," inscribed a poem that begins "The stormy winter's come at last" and concludes "With patience wait till winter is o'er, / And all lovely things return; / Of every season try the more / Some knowledge or virtue to learn." On reading this entry years later, Alcott added a wry comment: "A moral is tacked on even to the early poems" (*Journals* 54). Thus we have in Louisa May Alcott's childhood journals the stuff of her children's stories: a record of anger and resistance to authority, a gloss that transforms the record into an exemplum, and a perspective, often conveyed by still another text, that undoes the transformation.

As I will later discuss in chapters on individual works, texts that function as exempla within her stories or undo their exemplary nature often take the form of plays. To give here just two examples from Alcott's domestic fiction for adults: in *Work* the heroine begins her career as an actress and ends as a women's rights activist, but her recitation, in a domestic setting, of Portia's "pretty speech" committing her spirit to Bassanio serves to indicate her essential womanliness; in *Moods* the heroine's only "crime" is to live too much for and through others, but her chilling portrayal of Lady Macbeth and her own guilty sleep-walking imply that the surrender of power, for a woman, can be as great an evil as its usurpation. Alcott's heroines—whether domestic or sensational—frequently play Shakespeare's women characters, but they are just as likely to enact contemporary plays (such as Charles Reade's *Masks and Faces* in *Work*), fairy tales (such as "Cinderella" in *Little Men*), or melodramas (such as "The Witch's Curse" in *Little Women*) based on those the young Louisa wrote and staged.[9]

Still other theatrical performances in Alcott's fiction are literally wordless, consisting of tableaux vivants that, by alluding to familiar texts, comment on the action. By having Jean Muir, the heroine of *Behind a Mask*, pose as Judith beheading Holofernes, Alcott implies that her ruthlessness is justified. Similarly, by having the angelic Gladys, heroine of *A Modern Mephistopheles*, play not only Enid and Elaine but Vivien in scenes from *Idylls of the King*, Alcott renders her morally ambiguous. Finally, by having Laurie in *Jo's Boys* upstage Jo's domestic drama glorifying motherhood with his own tableau, *The Owlsdark Marbles,* Alcott hints at a darker side to life at Plumfield. Even in the rare works that do not feature theatrical performances, works of art function as tableaux.[10] Sculptures of Adam in "Psyche's Art," of Cupid and Psyche in *A Marble Woman* (where, at a masked ball, the hero plays Hamlet), of the Coming Woman in *An Old-Fashioned Girl,* and of Saul in *Diana and Persis* are only a few of the wordless texts that speak eloquently—although sometimes in different languages—to both characters and readers.

This special form of intertextuality—Alcott's use of a "play within the play"—also had its origins in the author's childhood. Stern, who gives a detailed account of Alcott's youthful dramatic activities and ambitions, writes that her "thrillers . . . had their source in the writer's early dramatic career," as did any story, such as *Little Women* or *Work,* that contained autobiographical elements (1943, 194–95). Karen Halttunen, while acknowledging the importance of Louisa's early playacting and writing, traces her inspiration to the allegorical dramas that Bronson Alcott improvised for his daughters (1984, 236). According to Halttunen, Bronson's dramas enforced self-control and female abnegation, but Louisa's adolescent melodramas, like the one the March sisters perform, permitted self-expression and masculine assertion. Later, as a fiction writer Alcott drew upon her experience both as an actress and as a dramatist. In her pseudonymous sensation stories, "villainous actresses and ex-actresses . . . use their dramatic skills to fulfill their selfish ambitions in flagrant defiance of the cult of domesticity" (240). But in her juvenile fiction, Halttunen argues, Alcott reverted to the moral allegories of her childhood, even adopting her father's favorite, *Pilgrim's Progress,* as a model. I would assert, however, that the plays within these "moral allegories" provide a vehicle for smuggling in the outlawed defiance. Halttunen's own discussion of Victorian parlor theatricals, in her book *Confidence Men and Painted Women,* demonstrates how Victorian Americans, by admitting theatricality into the home, tacitly acknowledged the theatricality, the artificiality, of the genteel life. Much as they, in enacting a charade or tableau vivant, expressed their self-consciousness about, even critique of, bourgeois values, so Alcott, by creating such scenes in her domestic fiction, acknowledged *its* duplicity—that her seeming idealization of the domestic realm, with its constraining roles for women, overlay a profound skepticism about the organization of domestic life.

Alcott seems to admit to such a stratagem in another *Scrap-Bag* story, "Mamma's Plot" (1873). In this innocent-appearing piece, a mother helps her daughter, Kitty, circumvent her headmistress's practice of reading and editing the students' letters home. By supplying Kitty with notepaper of different colors, each of which conveys a covert message, Mamma enables Kitty to indicate her desperate loneliness while writing, for her headmistress's eyes, that "our meeting will be the more delightful for this separation" (786).[11] Patty's Aunt Pen and Kitty's headmistress, as readers who render judgment and stand ready to edit another's work in the interest of propriety, correspond to the reading audience, editors, and publishers that Alcott, as a writer for the young as well as a Victorian woman writer, must satisfy. But Aunt Pen and Kitty's mother, as collaborators who understand the expressive possibilities of traditional tasks and conventional forms, suggest the mature artist, one who found ways to propitiate a conventional audience while still allowing her more rebellious self—Patty or Kitty—expression. There is, however, a subtle difference in their methodology: Aunt Pen permits spontaneous expression, then provides a cover to "lie under" (196); Mamma, as the word *plot* implies, encourages deliberate encoding. Regardless of Alcott's conscious intention, we can, by unraveling her cover stories, by attending to what has been edited over or edited out or encoded in the form of a play or other work of art, occupy the position of Kitty's mother—the audience for which and, ultimately, by which, subversive meanings are produced.[12]

At the end of "Mamma's Plot," Mamma writes "to madam and ''fessed,' like an honest mamma as she was." Madam, "when the matter was sensibly and respectfully put before her . . . saw the justice of it, forgave the little plot, and amazed her pupils by gradually omitting to watch over them as they wrote" (788). Ironically, as madam stops insisting on reading and approving her students' letters, she comes to appreciate the genuine qualities of those they voluntarily submit. And she finds herself no longer ridiculed and feared but respected and even loved. Alcott, in having Mamma confess and madam reform, seems to confess her own need for protective coloration and to ask her readers' understanding of it. If, in reading Alcott, we look beyond the exemplary texts that madam, in reading Kitty, initially looked *for*, we too will feel a closer kinship with the writer. And as madam comes to see in Kitty "one of her own little daughters, lost long ago" (789), so we will come to find in Alcott a lost foremother.

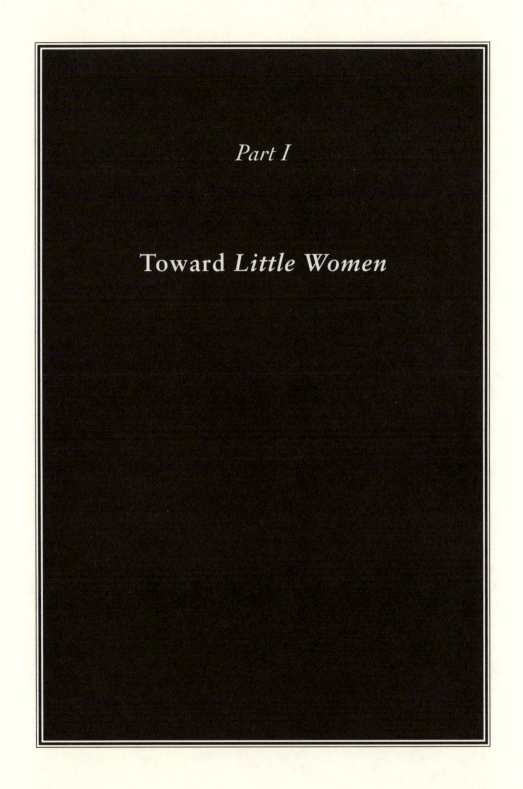

Part I

Toward *Little Women*

CHAPTER 1

"The Wrongs of Woman": "A Whisper in the Dark"

In the history of folktale and fairy tale, women as storytellers have woven or spun their yarns, speaking at one level to a total culture, but at another to a sisterhood of readers who will understand the hidden language, the secret revelations of the tale.

Karen Rowe, "To Spin a Yarn: The Female Voice in Folklore and Fairy Tale" (57)

The events of her past life pressing on her, she resolved circumstantially to relate them, with the sentiments that experience, and more matured reason, would naturally suggest. They might perhaps instruct her daughter, and shield her from the misery, the tyranny, her mother knew not how to avoid.

Mary Wollstonecraft, *Maria or The Wrongs of Woman* (31)

In an early sensation story entitled "A Whisper in the Dark," Alcott seems to have anticipated her fate as a lost foremother whose feminist voice would be barely audible to successive generations of readers. First published anonymously in the June 1863 issues of *Frank Leslie's Illustrated Newspaper* and reprinted posthumously in 1889 together with *A Modern Mephistopheles,* the story frames her career and underscores its continuity. Madeleine Stern, in her introduction to a new edition of *A Modern Mephistopheles,* speculates that the earlier story "had enough moral overtones for the author to acknowledge its authorship twenty-five years after she had written it" (xli), but all the sensation fiction, no less than the domestic, centers on love and marriage, and its heroines usually conform in the end or are punished for their rebellion.[1] So enslaved by love, sometimes to a much older man, are some of these heroines that at least one critic finds the sensation fiction "politically regressive," reveling in rather than challenging the unequal distribution of power between the sexes.[2] Eschewing the overt, if conventional, concern for women's issues of the domestic fiction, Alcott doubly camouflages the subversive implications of the sensation fiction. Not only are her sensation heroines subdued by love, like their domestic cousins, but Alcott's "obtrusive Gothic paraphernalia," as Stern has called it (xlii), assures the "total culture" that their rage and suffering are far removed from normal female experience. Yet this very paraphernalia can convey to "a sisterhood of readers" Alcott's indignation at their wrongs.

In "A Whisper in the Dark," Alcott uses two staples of Gothic fiction—the madwoman and the asylum—to represent the "wrongs of woman" in patriarchal society, the way in which women resist as well as collude with their oppressors, and the need for feminist consciousness and communication across generations. Her use of the asylum indeed constitutes such communication, for it alludes to Mary Wollstonecraft's *Maria or The Wrongs of Woman* and Charlotte Brontë's *Jane Eyre* and anticipates such works as Charlotte Perkins Gilman's "The Yellow Wallpaper" and Jean Rhys's *Wide Sargasso Sea*. Further, the story implies fundamental tenets of feminist theory: a woman's right to determine her own destiny rather than have it determined for her by a male-dominated society; the crucial connection between economic independence and self-determination; the role of male language and male science in imposing constraints and treating consequent complaints; and above all, the power of women to communicate with, inspire, and sustain each other even when reduced to seeming powerlessness. Alcott's "hidden language" enables her to speak to us even when her narrator/heroine, who develops a feminist consciousness under duress, recants upon her rescue and subsequent marriage.[3] It is tempting to see the narrator's recantation, like Aunt Pen's inscription on Patty's quilt, as Alcott's own rejection of sensation for domestic fiction, rebellion for conformity. But the narrator, like Aunt Pen, is a reader as well as a writer, and the texts that she reads, like Patty's quilt, comment on the text that she creates.

Sybil, the heroine, narrates her story after its events have been distanced by time. She begins with her discovery of a compact between her dead father and his foster brother, which stipulates that, when she comes of age at eighteen, she will marry the latter's son, Guy, thus entitling him to share the family estate and fortune. Not long before her eighteenth birthday, Sybil leaves the care of Madame Bernard, the woman who raised her, and accompanies her uncle to his present home, the family estate that will soon pass into her possession. There, upon meeting her moody but charming cousin, Sybil determines to wrest some power from the situation by making him propose out of love as well as necessity. But before she can complete her conquest, pecuniary difficulties force Guy's father to demand Sybil's immediate compliance with the compact. Having overheard her uncle admit to Guy that "the contract is not binding against her will" (550), Sybil resists the sudden pressure to marry. Her uncle, with whom she has flirted to make Guy jealous and who now thinks that she has some aversion to Guy, offers to marry her himself. While he has his arm around her, Guy enters and, believing Sybil to have accepted his father, denounces them both. Sybil, fearing that she has lost Guy forever, in part through her own willfulness, angrily rejects her uncle's renewed proposal, now worded as a command, and the ring he proffers. So violent becomes Sybil's resistance that her uncle's friend, Dr. Karnac, declares her mad and confines her in his asylum. There another female inmate attempts to communicate with Sybil, urging her to find something that she has hidden, then to flee before she too is driven mad. After the death of her fellow inmate, Sybil manages to escape and, on encountering Guy, learns that her uncle is now dead and that the woman who had tried to warn her was her mother, supposedly the victim of hereditary madness. A chastened Sybil consents to marry Guy, but though their marriage proves happy, she remains haunted by "that dead image of my mother . . . that spectral whisper in the dark" (575).[4]

The remarkable opening scene of "A Whisper in the Dark" illustrates the striking if superficial difference between Alcott's sensation stories and her children's fiction. Enclosed in a carriage on their way to the family estate, Sybil and her uncle (who remains nameless) engage in a contest of wills that foreshadows their later conflict. Sybil, having learned without his knowledge of the compact, tries to gain further information about his son, the man she is destined to marry. But her uncle, a cynical man of the world not unlike Charlotte Brontë's Rochester, easily evades her questions. Piqued yet "pleased by the approbation his eye betrayed," Sybil, "who felt her charms and longed to try their power," "kissed him daintily, and perched . . . upon his knee with most audacious ease" (538–39). To Sybil's consternation, he returns the dainty kiss with rough caresses, ignores commands to let her go, and threatens to tame her as he has tamed his son. Then in a passage that anticipates Sybil's later rebellion and its aftermath, she describes how he succeeds in mastering her: ". . . quite beside myself, I had suddenly stooped and bitten the shapely white hand that held both my own. I had better have submitted; for . . . his hand tightened its grasp, for a moment his cold eye glittered and a grim look settled round the mouth, giving to his whole face a ruthless expression that entirely altered it. I felt perfectly powerless. All my little arts had failed, and for the first time I was mastered. Yet only physically; my spirit was rebellious still" (539). Not content with physical mastery, however, her uncle then proceeds to master her psychologically: "he began to relate certain exciting adventures he had known abroad, lending to the picturesque narration the charm of that peculiarly melodious voice, which soothed and won me in spite of myself, holding me intent until I forgot the past" (539). He then completes his conquest by offering Sybil a "mildly aromatic" cigarette. "Slowly the narcotic influence of the herbs diffused itself like a pleasant haze" (539), and Sybil awakens to find her cheek "pillowed" upon her uncle's arm and to join him in "a French *chanson*" (540).[5]

No little woman would conduct herself as Sybil does, but her thoughts and behavior, until her rejection of her uncle's proposal, are stereotypically feminine. She never questions that her future lies in masculine hands, is easily seduced by "a bijou" of a room and "Parisian gifts," and preens before her mirror. While thus engaged, she overhears her cousin ask when he can "inspect our new ornament." Immediately "resolved to deserve his appellation," Sybil strikes a pose: "I possessed a pretty foot, therefore one little slipper appeared quite naturally below the last flounce of my dress. . . . My profile was well cut, my eyelashes long, therefore I read with face half averted from the door. The light showered down, turning my hair to gold. . . . after a satisfied survey, [I] composed myself with an absorbed aspect and a quickened pulse to await the arrival of the gentlemen" (542). Sybil, like most of Alcott's heroines, is a consummate actress. Her purpose is more innocent than that of the later sensation heroines, and her behavior more calculated than that of little women like Amy and Meg March, but her techniques are similar and similarly designed to captivate a male audience.

Motivated by youthful rebelliousness, a fondness for manipulating others, a young girl's romantic dreams, and, finally, a woman's need for love, Sybil fails to question patriarchal assumptions until, at her uncle's request, she peruses her father's will in which the terms of the compact are set forth. Then "a sudden bewilderment and sense of helplessness came over me, for the strange law terms seemed to make inexorable the paternal decree" (553). Finding herself entrapped in patriarchal language, Sybil begins to protest her entrapment in patriarchy itself. "What right had my father to mate me in the cradle? . . . No! I'll not be bargained away like a piece of merchandise, but love and marry when I please!" (554). Not long after uttering this "declaration of independence" (554),[6] Sybil further defies her uncle by hurling the ring he offers her against a mirror, thus shattering the image that hitherto had pleased them both. When Dr. Karnac concludes that she needs "much care, and should obey," Sybil's "patience gave out at this assumption of authority." Denying her kinship to her uncle, who "deserves neither respect nor obedience," she claims to be "the best judge of [her] own health" and, for the first time, declares that this "is my house . . . my room" (559). In one passionate outburst Sybil denies that gender is sufficient to compel respect or obedience, asserts her identity as a rational being, and insists on her right to property, privacy, and her own person. But such claims are considered further proof of madness, and the room of her own that Sybil has claimed promptly becomes a cell.

Sybil escapes the prison of her room only to be imprisoned in Karnac's asylum. Like Wollstonecraft's Maria, she awakens from a drugged sleep to find herself in unfamiliar surroundings. "A moment I stared about me bewildered, then hurried to the window. It was grated." She quickly discovers that, while she slept, her hair was cut: "There was no mirror in the room, but I could feel that it had been shorn away close about face and neck" (561). A female attendant finally responds to her cries of "impotent despair" and tells her that she has been sent there because she is ill. At first Sybil does not understand: "How can I be ill and not know or feel it?" But her attendant ominously replies, "You look it, and that's enough for them as is wise in these matters" (562). Dr. Karnac proceeds to treat her as male doctors have reputedly treated female patients: he "took an ungenerous satisfaction in annoying me by a display of power. He never answered my questions or entreaties, regarded me as being without sense or will, insisted on my trying various mixtures and experiments in diet, gave me strange books to read, and weekly received Hannah's report of all that passed" (565–66).[7] As Mary Wollstonecraft recognized in her *Vindication of the Rights of Woman*, the tyranny of the male doctor is but one form of the male tyranny from which "the greater number of female follies proceed" (318). These follies (in Sybil's case her violent rebellion followed by apathy) in turn are used to justify further tyranny or, at best, paternalism. Subjected to Dr. Karnac's treatment, it is little wonder that Sybil soon becomes "a shadow of my former self" (564).

Sybil's deterioration is anticipated early in the story by references to her mother.[8] Soon after arriving at her uncle's, she notices a miniature and is told that it is her mother's portrait. The face is that of a "spirited" and "passionate" woman, "but the whole seemed dimmed by age, the ivory was stained, the glass cracked, and a faded ribbon fastened it. My eyes filled as I looked, and a strong desire seized me to know what had defaced this little picture of the mother whom I never knew" (549). She asks her uncle if she resembles her mother and is told she is "a youthful image of her" (549). When Sybil asks where her mother is buried and expresses a wish to visit the grave, he answers portentously, "You shall someday, Sybil" (550). Later, having defied her uncle, Sybil is astonished at "the ruinous image the opposite mirror showed me. Everything looked blurred and strange" (558). The blurred reflection connects Sybil with the blurred likeness in the miniature and suggests that she, like her mother and perhaps most women in their society, will undergo diminution and distortion of identity. If she continues to rebel, her mirrorless cell warns, she will suffer its obliteration.

Once in the asylum, Sybil literally follows in her mother's footsteps. Many have commented on the role of Bertha Mason as Jane Eyre's double, for Jane paces the third story while Bertha runs backward and forward on all fours in the attic.[9] Sybil, for want of diversion, becomes obsessed with the inmate directly above her and eventually finds herself "pacing to and fro as those invisible feet paced overhead" (565). Sybil also hears the sound of singing and the rocking of a cradle: "night after night the steps kept time to mine, and the faint lullaby came down to me as if to soothe and comfort my distress" (567). On her eighteenth birthday, the day on which Sybil was to have come into her estate, her uncle visits her. "Hannah pointed to the carpet worn to shreds by my weary march, to the walls which I had covered with weird, grotesque, or tragic figures to while away the heavy hours, lastly to myself, mute, motionless, and scared" (568).[10] By reenacting her mother's experience, the once rebellious and volatile Sybil has been rendered meek and mute.

Eighteen years of solitary confinement have not entirely silenced Sybil's mother, who is still capable of uttering "a whisper in the dark." One evening Sybil, having walked in her sleep, awakens to find herself standing before her mother's door and hears a whisper at the keyhole: "Find it! For God's sake find it before it is too late!" (566) Sybil, however, does not know what she is supposed to find or how to find it and gives way to despair. Finally, on the night she has resolved to hang herself, she hears the whisper again, this time at her own keyhole: "The dog—a lock of hair—there is yet time" (569). This additional clue renews Sybil's hope, and after her unknown benefactor's death, she finds a "strange treasure trove" buried in the collar of the dead woman's dog. Tightly woven into the collar with a lock of the woman's hair,[11] Sybil's treasure consists of "two strips of thinnest paper, without address or signature, one almost illegible . . . both abrupt and disjointed, but terribly significant" (570). Their significance consists of the information that Sybil is not the victim of misguided and overzealous concern for her health but of a cold-blooded plot to destroy it. After deciphering these texts, Sybil feels "redoubled hatred and contempt for the men who could repay my girlish slights with such a horrible revenge" (571). "Redoubled hatred" results in redoubled vigilance, even ruthlessness, and when one of Dr. Karnac's chemical experiments produces an explosion, Sybil takes the opportunity to escape, abandoning a mortally wounded man in order to do so. Hannah's warning, "leave him at your peril" (571), suggests that women are conditioned to believe that they imperil themselves when they reject the role of nurturer, even if those they are asked to nurture have, as in this case, served as their jailers. Sybil, having been alerted by her mother to the masculine conspiracy against her, has no pity to spare for the dying man. The elaborately secreted notes and their effect upon Sybil imply that women can be victims of oppression and long to escape it but fail until they realize that their oppression is systematic.

Sybil's reunion with Guy and repudiation of her "folly" seem designed to satisfy the conventional reader's desire for a happy and edifying ending, but Alcott's language suggests a more subversive intent. Sybil, on fleeing the madhouse, first mistakes Guy for one of Karnac's henchmen: "a hand seized me, a voice rang in my ears, and with a vain struggle I lay panting in my captor's hold." Even when she recognizes him as her "surest refuge," her description of herself as "too weak for words," clinging to him "in an agony of happiness," implies a mute and passive dependency. Finally, Guy addresses her as "poor child," offering paternal protection in exchange for her newly won freedom (572). The dubious nature of that protection is indicated by parallels between the ending of Sybil's story and its beginning. Once again Sybil finds herself in a closed carriage with a male guardian, and once again, after their violent struggle, she allows herself to be soothed into forgetfulness. Perhaps most important, Sybil's reference to "the cordial of his presence" (572) connects Guy with his father's "narcotic influence."[12] Under this renewed influence, Sybil takes a distorted view of her previous experience: "I was taken to my future home, approved by my uncle, beloved by my cousin, and, but for my own folly, might have been a happy wife" rather than an asylum inmate (574). Yet Sybil's recantation, with its series of passive verbs, confirms her mother's "unerring instinct" (574)—that patriarchy entraps women not only physically but mentally; it limits not only their freedom of action but their freedom of thought and confidence in their ability to think. Patriarchy, by teaching women to love their oppressors, induces a kind of amnesia. Sybil's mother herself confesses longing for "the husband I have lost," but immediately, as though returning to reality, she writes, "stop! I must not think of those things or I shall forget" (570). Sybil, in her relief and gratitude on being reunited with Guy, and in repudiating her former protest as "folly," illustrates the insufficiency of isolated insights to transform consciousness and resist the power of custom and habit.

Sybil, as her name implies, is in a sense a prophetess, a harbinger of future change.[13] In a state of extraordinary excitement, she defies the pressure to conform to patriarchal expectations and in her rage manages to articulate the demand for certain rights that remain to be fully won. But every generation has had its sibyls. What women have lacked is communication and continuity of effort from one generation to another. Sybil's "strong desire . . . to know what had defaced this little picture of the mother whom I never knew" marks the awakening of her feminist consciousness. The very fact that Sybil has been separated from her mother since birth, has had no communication with her for eighteen years, and has been led to believe that she is dead symbolizes the way in which women are prevented from sharing and building on each other's experiences. Ironically, women, when silenced, when deprived of the opportunity to share (in the sense of communicate) experiences, doom others to share (in the sense of repeat) them. As Dale Spender has put it, "what we today have in common with women of the past is our experience of being silenced and interrupted; our experience of becoming a member of society in which women have no visible past, no heritage; our experience of existing in a *void*" (14). Alcott's description of the mother's notes— "without address or signature," "almost illegible," "stained," "worn," "feebly written," "abrupt," "disjointed," but nonetheless "a treasure trove"—aptly characterizes women's records of their experience, including in some ways the originally anonymous, recently discovered "A Whisper in the Dark."

Shortly before discovering these faded fragments of her heritage, Sybil seems, as she gazes at her mother's corpse, destined to share her fate. In fact, she momentarily wonders whether it is not her own dead body and she its disembodied spirit. Prior to that confusion of identities, she finds, on entering her mother's asylum cell, "a room like mine, the carpet worn like mine, the windows barred like mine; there the resemblance ended, for an empty cradle stood beside the bed" (569). The empty cradle, Sybil's cradle, powerfully represents the mother's silencing, but the resemblance does not, as Sybil initially thinks, end there. As she approaches the bed and lifts the cover, "the face I saw was a pale image of my own . . . and on the hand, still clenched in that last struggle, shone the likeness of a ring I wore, a ring bequeathed me by my father" (569–70). Later Sybil learns from Guy that her mother "had been melancholy mad" and her affliction concealed from Sybil, "lest the knowledge should prey upon my excitable nature and perhaps induce a like misfortune" (574). But the affliction concealed from Sybil lest she inherit it is not madness but, as Lynette Carpenter has persuasively argued, rebellion.[14] For how could one who, though dying, exerted such heroic effort to save an unknown woman have acquiesced in a compact that virtually deprived her own daughter of choice in the most important matter of her life? The identical rings worn by Sybil and her mother suggest that madness and subsequent enclosure is a patrilineal rather than a matrilineal legacy.

On her escape from the asylum, Sybil is still ignorant of her mother's story. What she learns of it, she learns from Guy; in other words, she receives the authorized or masculine version. No wonder, then, that she is unable to generalize on the basis of her own experience, which she regards (as Alcott allows her readers to regard) as an isolated phenomenon. The daughter's need to hear her mother's story from her own lips—or pen—in order to avoid repeating her mother's experience was recognized by Mary Wollstonecraft's heroine Maria, who gives us some notion of what Sybil's mother's youth might have been like. Maria, like Sybil, is drugged, and while she sleeps, her infant daughter is taken from her breast. On awakening the next morning in the "mansion of despair," Maria's first thoughts are of her child, and until she is led to believe that the child has died, "Her infant's image was continually floating on [her] sight" (23). Thus, "the events of her past life pressing on her, she resolved circumstantially to relate them, with the sentiments that experience, and more matured reason, would naturally suggest. They might perhaps instruct her daughter, and shield her from the misery, the tyranny, her mother knew not how to avoid" (31).[15] But even Maria, for all her experience of male tyranny, has been so conditioned to regard men as the natural protectors of women that she entrusts herself to Darnford, a fellow inmate, who, in the fragmentary conclusion of the work, eventually abandons her. By having her heroine flee from one asylum, the madhouse, to another, her lover's arms, Alcott, like Wollstonecraft, warns not only of the "wrongs of woman" but of the "mind-forged manacles" that prevent her from righting them.[16]

Sybil, echoing Jane Eyre, concludes her Gothic tale on a domestic note: "Home received me . . . Guy married me, and I was happy." But if the conventional ending seems to overlay the radical and subversive message of Alcott's story, the language used to describe Sybil's reconciliation with Guy serves to undercut the ending: "when all was told, when each saw the other by the light of this strange and sad experience—Guy poor again, I free, the old bond still existing, the barrier of misunderstanding gone—it was easy to see our way, easy to submit, to forgive, forget, and begin anew the life these clouds had darkened for a time" (575). The reference to "the old bond," the repetition of the word "easy," above all the verbs "submit" and "forget"—especially the latter with its echo of the mother's passionate "stop! I must not think of those things or I shall forget" and of the way Sybil's uncle on *their* carriage ride charmed her until she "forgot the past" (539)—all suggest that Sybil, not her author, has taken the easy way out. And Alcott further qualifies her happy ending by having Sybil admit that it is not as easy to forget the past as she had anticipated. After professing her happiness with Guy, Sybil admits that she still sees "that dead image of my mother," still hears "that spectral whisper in the dark" (575). Finally, Sybil's narrative, in which she carefully records her memory of the past, serves like Maria's to preserve it. Although Sybil mentions no daughters of her own, her tale seems designed to provide them with the education that she received, belatedly and in cryptic form, from her own mother.

"A Whisper in the Dark," though belonging to a very different genre from "Patty's Patchwork" and written much earlier in Alcott's career, has much in common with the children's story. Sybil, like Aunt Pen, reads another's text and conveys her interpretation of it by creating a text of her own. But though her text, like Aunt Pen's, would seem to distort the meaning of the first even in paying tribute to it, that primary text—blurred, smeared, begrimed, and puckered as it may be—continues to speak eloquently of female struggle and suffering. Both "A Whisper in the Dark" and "Patty's Patchwork" are as much about responding to texts as they are about creating them, and the whispered admonition "Find it" urges us to excel Sybil and Aunt Pen as readers and to find the muted message of rage and rebellion Alcott received from *her* mother. Louisa and Abba Alcott, like Sybil and her mother, were considered demented, dangerous, or demonic by the powerful male whose will they, however indirectly, opposed. During Louisa's turbulent adolescence, Bronson Alcott recorded in his journal: "Two devils, as yet, I am not quite divine enough to vanquish—the mother fiend and her daughter" (M. Bedell 1980, 244). Doubtless *this* journal entry, unlike Louisa's childhood ones, remained private, but Sybil's, and Alcott's, story provides a sufficient gloss. As Sybil inherited from her mother a spirit of rebellion that was never entirely extinguished, so Alcott inherited what Martha Saxton calls Abba's "melancholy and anger." But because, as we have seen, Abba also suggested a way of dealing with these emotions in writing, her maternal legacy did not prove "disastrous," as Saxton has argued (136); instead it proved even more liberating than Sybil's mother's notes, enabling Alcott to utter her own insistent whispers in the dark.[17]

CHAPTER 2

"Woman in the Nineteenth Century": Moods

The conflict between self and other thus constitutes the central moral problem for women, posing a dilemma whose resolution requires a reconciliation between femininity and adulthood. . . . It is precisely this dilemma—the conflict between compassion and autonomy, between virtue and power—which the feminine voice struggles to resolve in its effort to reclaim the self and to solve the moral problem in such a way that no one is hurt.

Carol Gilligan, *In a Different Voice* (70–71)

Now there is no woman, only an overgrown child. That her hand may be given with dignity, she must be able to stand alone.

Margaret Fuller, *Woman in the Nineteenth Century* (176)

Alcott's tendency to whisper her subversive messages was probably reinforced by the reception of her first domestic novel, *Moods* (1864). If "A Whisper in the Dark" appears to have been inspired by Mary Wollstonecraft, *Moods* offers more direct homage to Margaret Fuller, revising Hawthorne's negative portrayal of Fuller as Zenobia in *The Blithedale Romance*. In the sensation story, Sybil receives in cryptic form the advice that Wollstonecraft's Maria determines to communicate to her daughter; in the domestic novel, the heroine, Sylvia Yule, receives direct advice from a mother surrogate, Faith Dane, who, if not a portrait of Fuller, embodies her feminist ideas. Sylvia herself illustrates Fuller's claim that "Now there is no woman, only an overgrown child" and the disastrous consequences of such imma-turity. Sequestered from and denied meaningful work in the world, Sylvia inno-cently conceives a passion that, after her marriage to another, leads her to the verge of adultery. Perhaps because the book came literally too close to home in its treatment of unhappy marriage, Alcott was accused of suffering, like Sylvia, from maidenly ignorance while violating feminine decorum. For example, the young Henry James wrote in a condescending review: "The two most striking facts with regard to 'Moods' are the author's ignorance of human nature, and her self-confidence in spite of this ignorance" (223).[1] Even before James's review appeared, Alcott was disheartened by some readers' reactions. As she wrote in her journal: "I seem to have been playing with edge tools without knowing it. The relations between Warwick Moor & Silvia are pronounced impossible, yet a case of that sort exists in Concord" (147). In her correspondence about the book, in her preface to the 1882 edition, and in her revisions of the text itself, she alternately sheaths and draws, blunts and hones, her edge tools.[2]

In an 1865 letter Alcott responded to criticism by stressing Sylvia's "peculiar" nature and denying a "desire to settle or unsettle any question, to convince or convert any one to any theory whatever" (110).[3] And in her preface to the 1882 edition, Alcott wrote that her purpose was "to show the mistakes of a moody nature, guided by impulse, not principle" (225) rather than to present an argument for the dissolution of unhappy marriages. But in the letter Alcott virtually denies Sylvia's peculiarity by citing the grateful responses of "good women who have tried to do their [marital] duty & become meek martyrs instead of happy workers" (110). And in another letter regarding *Moods,* she confides, "Self abnegation is a noble thing but I think there is a limit to it; . . . half the misery of the world seems to come from unmated pairs trying to live their lie decorously to the end, & bringing children into the world to inherit the unhappiness & discord out of which they were born" (108).[4] In both editions of the novel, Alcott attributes Sylvia's moody or conflicted nature to her parents' unhappy marriage—a "tie that bound and burdened the unhappy twain" until, "worn thin by constant friction," it "snapped at last" (82–83). Sylvia inherits from her father "pride, intellect, and will; from her mother passion, imagination, and the fateful melancholy of a woman defrauded of her dearest hope" (84). Clearly, a society that encourages men to exercise "pride, intellect, and will" in the struggle for "profit, power, and place"

(83) and women to pin their "dearest hope" upon romantic love will produce self-divided children like Sylvia, "an enigma to herself and her life a train a moods" (84). And as Alcott's 1864 epigraph from Emerson suggests, to live life as "a train of moods . . . which paint the world their own hue" limits one's vision, entraps one in a narrow subjectivity.

A subplot omitted from the 1882 edition further indicates that moods are born of gender inequality and produce marriages doomed to perpetuate the cycle. In the opening chapter of the first edition, Adam Warwick attempts to break an engagement because he realizes that he is bound to Ottila, a seductive Cuban, only by sexual attraction. Accused by Warwick of having "a gifted but neglected nature" (9), Ottila begs him to help her "repair the faults of birth, education, and orphanhood" (10–11). Like Sylvia, Ottila is not only the product of a misalliance; she has no outlet for her energy and talent. As the narrator later comments, "set down in uneventful [or repressive] times, the courage, wit, and passion that might have served high ends dwindled to their baser counterparts, and made her what she was,—a fair allurement to the eyes of men" (99). Denied access to other sources of power, Ottila seeks sexual power over men, challenging Warwick to wage "the old war . . . which fills the world with *unmated pairs* and the long train of evils arising from marriages made from *impulse, and not principle*" (12, my emphasis). Here, in the language of both her 1865 letter and her 1882 preface, Alcott implies that moody or impulsive decisions produce further generations of "unmated pairs." In the earlier edition, Ottila's ill-considered attachment to Warwick anticipates what we later learn of Sylvia's parents and foreshadows Sylvia's own hasty marriage to Moor, one which, Alcott implies, is never consummated.

Alcott needed no literary models to help her connect unequal parents with moody offspring. As a child she witnessed her own parents wage "the old war," and it is probably no coincidence that her terse comment, "Moods began early," follows an entry from eleven-year-old Louisa's Fruitlands journal (51), written during that war's most bitter battle.[5] However, personal observations were no doubt reinforced by Margaret Fuller's impassioned plea for egalitarian marriage, parenting, and education. Fuller, who served for a time as Bronson Alcott's assistant at the Temple School, believed that "no age was left entirely without a witness of the equality of the sexes in function, duty and hope," but "when there was unwillingness or ignorance, which prevented this being acted upon, women . . .

made use of the arms of the servile,—cunning, blandishment, and unreasonable emotion" (172)—the very arms that Ottila takes up in her contest with Warwick. Further, when Man "educated Woman more as a servant than a daughter," he "found himself a king without a queen," and the "children of this unequal union showed unequal natures" (170), like those of Ottila and Sylvia. Earlier in her feminist treatise Fuller argues that were "Woman established in the rights of an immortal being," she would not be "perverted . . . into the belief that she must marry, if it be only to find a protector, and a home of her own." Neither would Man "by rash haste, lose the chance of finding a friend in the person who might, probably, live half a century by his side" (70–71). Husband and wife, rather than living as master and servant, guardian and ward, parent and child, would "assist one another to learn what is required for this sublime priesthood of Nature [parenthood]. But, for this, a religious recognition of equality is required" (72).

In addition to Fuller's discussion of egalitarian marriage, Alcott may well have been influenced by Hawthorne's *The Blithedale Romance* (1852). Ironically, the heroine Zenobia, whom many believe to be an unflattering if glamorized portrait of Fuller, bears a striking resemblance to Ottila or the "woman in the nineteenth century" that Fuller laments.[6] In pleading her case before Hawthorne's narrator, Miles Coverdale, Zenobia describes herself as "weak, vain, unprincipled, (like most of my sex; for our virtues, when we have any, are merely impulsive and intuitive,) passionate, too, and pursuing my foolish and unattainable ends, by indirect and cunning, though absurdly chosen means, as an hereditary bond-slave must" (822). Zenobia is a "hereditary bond-slave" in the sense that both Ottila and Sylvia are. The daughter of Fauntleroy, whose "whole being seemed to have crystallized itself into an external splendor," and a woman "whose nature was deeper than his own" but nonetheless subject to him, Zenobia was raised with "no adequate control, on any hand . . . and her character was left to shape itself" (791, 797). Unlike Zenobia, her half sister Priscilla seems all too content within "the sphere of ordinary womanhood," but she too "might be considered as the true offspring of both parents, and as the reflection of their [unhappy] state" (794). Both daughters of Old Moodie, as Fauntleroy comes to be called, are beset by moods that mystify the narrator. And both become enthralled, as Ottila and Sylvia do, with the same man, a reformer or philanthropist of magnetic power and almost ruthless dedication. A lifelong admirer of *The Scarlet Letter*,[7] to which she refers in *Moods,* and Hawthorne's neighbor for years in Concord, Alcott seems to have followed his lead in fictionalizing their transcendentalist associates. But whereas Hawthorne satirized the contradictions in social reform, including feminism, Alcott, like Fuller, emphasizes the centrality of feminism to any reform effort.

The seventeen-year-old Sylvia Yule, like Hawthorne's Zenobia and Jo March in *Little Women,* finds the "sphere of ordinary womanhood" constricting.[8] The daughter of a wealthy widower, Sylvia cannot, like her older sister Prudence, content herself with domestic activity and neighborhood gossip. Nor can she devote herself to art as her brother Mark attempts to do. She is roused from her ennui only by the return from abroad of their neighbor, the poet Geoffrey Moor, and the arrival of his friend, the reformer Adam Warwick.[9] Chaperoned by her brother, Sylvia accompanies Moor and Warwick on an idyllic river journey, during which she falls in love with Warwick—and Moor falls in love with her. Warwick, too, finds that he loves Sylvia; but thinking that Moor has a prior claim, and remembering Ottila's claim on him, he leaves without making a declaration. In his absence Sylvia, to please her family and assuage her loneliness, marries Moor and embarks on her wedding journey. Reencountering Warwick, who has now extricated himself from Ottila, Sylvia realizes that she has made a terrible mistake, but, settling down with Moor, she tries her best to act the part of a happy, devoted wife. Months later Moor, increasingly aware of Sylvia's distress but ignorant of its cause, invites Warwick and a female cousin, Faith Dane, to visit them. During this visit, Sylvia is tempted to leave Moor for Warwick but manages to resist the temptation. After the guests leave, however, Sylvia begins walking in her sleep, and the alarmed Moor finally forces her to confide in him. As a result the two separate, and Sylvia seeks advice from Faith, who for lack of a suitable partner has never married. She warns that Warwick's nature would submerge Sylvia's weaker one and urges her to be a friend but nothing more to both men. Moor and Warwick go abroad, where the latter engages in the Italian revolution. Sylvia, meanwhile, returns to her father's house, where her health gradually declines. When she realizes that she is dying, she calls Moor back to her, but they are reunited only after Warwick has sacrificed his life to save Moor's in a shipwreck, which, like the one that destroyed Margaret Fuller, ironically occurs within sight of land.

At the time Moor and Warwick enter her life, Sylvia is longing for male friendship, "because men go where they like, see things with their own eyes, and have more to tell" (25) than girls, who all seem "made on the same pattern" (24). Sylvia's moods express resistance to this pattern but provide no effective escape. She languishes in bed, then hurls Prudence's tonic—or prescription for life—out the window. She restlessly shifts the furniture about in a vain attempt to create a comfortable space for herself. She plants—then replants—a shrub, as though seeking more room and richer soil for her own roots. When allowed to accompany her brother, Warwick, and Moor on a river journey, Sylvia feels that she is both participating in the male world from which she has been excluded and receiving the affection that, as a motherless girl, she craves. Yet Sylvia's inclusion in this male party could serve as a paradigm for tokenism. Like Zenobia and Priscilla at Blithedale, Sylvia escapes the constraints of her society only to find them recreated in a seeming idyll.

Serving as "a smiling Silence for their figure-head" (33), Sylvia on the river journey is chastened for self-assertion and rewarded for self-abnegation. The day that she remembers as her happiest, she is repeatedly humiliated and finally humbled. Left under Warwick's protection because her brother and Moor plan to take "too rough a road for Sylvia" (42), she is first humiliated when the pretty basket she has made for berrying proves "graceful but unable to stand alone" (46). She is compensated, however, by Warwick's praise of her abstemiousness: "You are a true woman, Miss Sylvia, for though your palm is purple there's not a stain upon your lips, and you have neither worked nor suffered for yourself it seems" (49). A more severe humiliation comes when Sylvia insists on viewing a forest fire at close range, thus endangering both their lives. On rescuing her, Warwick advises that "obedience is an old-fashioned virtue, which you would do well to cultivate" (53). At the beginning of the day Sylvia boasted that she was "no helpless, fine lady" and could "walk, run, and climb like any boy," but by its end she has found it "pleasant to be the object of his care" (51, 56). Warwick, on his part, "found satisfaction in the knowledge of her innocent faith in him, the touch of the little hand he held, the sight of the quiet figure by his side" (56). Innocent, trusting, diminutive, and quiet, Sylvia now realizes that she, no more than her basket, can stand alone. When, near the end of their journey, she and her friends participate in a golden wedding celebration, she is undisturbed by the "patriarchal air" about the seemingly idyllic farm home or by the clear demarcation of gender roles within it. Nor does she discern the significance of "daughter Patience," the crippled and hopelessly dependent woman whose room, like the dying Beth's in *Little Women,* serves as the spiritual center of the household.

Sylvia views the river journey as a rite of passage, but her boast that "when I seemed most like a child I was learning to be a woman" (75) strikes the reader as ironic. For in her eagerness to prove herself a woman—gentle, trusting, docile, submissive, and self-forgetful—Sylvia abandons the quest for autonomy and fails to become an adult. Upon returning from the journey Sylvia tries "heartily to forget herself in others, unconscious that there are times when the duty we owe ourselves is greater than that we owe to them" (108). To Moor and her family, Sylvia's new submissiveness makes her seem more womanly and thus better qualified for the adult institution of marriage. Yet she remains the penitent, chastened child Warwick found so appealing. On the day of her wedding to Moor, a man whom she respects rather than loves, "her eyes wore the unquestioning content of a child who accepts some friendly hand, sure that it will lead it right" (117). Only after marriage does Moor realize, to his chagrin, that childlike dependency is a false sign of mature womanhood. On their honeymoon Sylvia continues to regard him as "protector, friend, and lover" in the sense of suitor (121), and, on their return to the Old Manse, she begins to languish. To cheer her, Moor improvises a "fireside fête" in which they both dress as children. Sylvia, her hair in tails and looking "about twelve," holds up a thin hand and says that, except for her wedding ring, "I should think I was little Sylvia again." Watching Moor whittle, whistle, and pop corn, Sylvia requests "a doll to match your knife" and accepts Tilly, a servant's child, as a "lovely plaything" (134–35). Just as the golden wedding was tarnished by the suffering of daughter Patience, an emblem of female passivity and helplessness, so the gaiety of the fireside fête is forced. Sylvia's masquerade as child exposes her more earnest masquerade as woman. And Sylvia is no anomaly but "woman in the nineteenth century" as described by Fuller or, as Zenobia contemptuously describes Priscilla, "the type of womanhood, such as man has spent centuries in making it" (739).

A sharp contrast to Sylvia, the child-woman, is Faith Dane, "a self-reliant soul" whom "solitude has led . . . to study and reflect upon the question toward which [her] thoughts inevitably turned" (181).[10] An aspect of this question becomes a subject of debate when Faith and Warwick visit the Moors. Sylvia's sister Prudence believes that "a pair once yoked should abide by their bargain, be it good or ill, and preserve the proprieties in public no matter how hot a hell their home might be for them and for their children" (146). Warwick, speaking indirectly to Sylvia, insists that the couple should acknowledge their mistake and separate. Faith, realizing that her words hold special significance for Sylvia and Warwick, urges that, if the husband is worthy of love, his wife "should leave no effort unmade, no self-denial unexacted, till she has proved beyond all doubt that it is impossible to be a true wife." Then, however, she has the "right to dissolve the tie that has become a sin, because where no love lives inevitable suffering and sorrow enter in, falling not only on the guilty parents, but the innocent children" (147). Speaking from her own experience as a child of such a union, Faith expresses Alcott's belief that there are reasonable limits to self-sacrifice, to patience, and that, in exceeding those limits, one becomes open to the charge of selfishness.

But in a society that offers women few ways of establishing selfhood, persistence in a loveless marriage can seem heroic self-assertion. Thus when Warwick later warns Sylvia, "it were more merciful to murder him [Moor] outright than . . . endeavor to perform as a duty what should be your sweetest pleasure" (157), she cites him as her model: "All my life I have desired strength of heart and stability of soul; may I not hope to earn for myself a little of the integrity I love in you? If courage, self-denial, and self-help, make you what you are, can I have a more effectual guide? You say you shall outlive this passion; why should not I imitate your brave example, and find the consolations you shall find?" (160) Sylvia's rhetorical questions convey Alcott's critique of transcendentalism—that in framing ideals for Man it was thinking only of men. Sylvia's determination to forge an identity through self-sacrifice is doomed to fail for the very reason that she clings to it: her circumscribed environment does not offer her the consolations that will enable Warwick to outlive *his* passion.

Both Warwick and Moor, despite their obvious differences, regard Sylvia as a child while desiring her as a woman. Faith Dane, who represents and speaks for mature womanhood, is not the object of desire. She both lacks the charm of an ingénue and expects more from men than does a girl like Sylvia. Thus Warwick, disappointing Moor's hopes and relieving Sylvia's fears, can avow: "Faith is no more to me, nor I to Faith, than the friendliest regard can make us" (156). A "touchstone to all who approached, forcing them to rise or fall to their true level" (144), Faith is too formidable a figure to find a mate even among the most liberated. Like Hawthorne's Hollingsworth and Coverdale, who compete for the "gentle parasite" Priscilla rather than Zenobia, Alcott's heroes are attracted to "an overgrown child" rather than a woman like Faith, who has proven that she can "stand alone." But Alcott's heroine is made of sterner stuff than either Priscilla, who marries Hollingsworth, or Zenobia, who, in a twisted allusion to Fuller's death by water, immediately drowns *herself* when spurned by him. To Sylvia's credit, she at least comes to recognize the necessity of performing the task that Fuller and Faith enjoin—that she "put from her the press of other minds, and meditate in virgin loneliness" (Fuller 121).

Margaret Fuller foresaw the day when "Apollo will sing to his lyre what Vulcan forges on the anvil, and the Muse weave anew the tapestries of Minerva"— a day, in other words, when the feminine and masculine in both male and female natures will be reconciled (118). Geoffrey Moor and Adam Warwick are Fuller's Apollo and Vulcan. As Faith sums them up: in Adam "the head rules, in Geoffrey the heart. The one criticises, the other loves mankind" (180). Moor, as Faith realizes, possesses feminine traits that women must learn to modify, including the capacity to idolize their loved ones and sacrifice themselves for them. Prior to meeting Sylvia, Moor possessed "no longing . . . so strong as that for a home, where he might bless and be blessed in writing that immortal poem a virtuous and happy life" (85). In his waiting posture[11] he is, like Sylvia herself, expecting someone else to give shape and meaning to his existence. Moor's feminine traits as well as Sylvia's muselike nature are revealed in the diary he leaves her upon their separation. In it Sylvia reads of "her chameleon self, etched with loving care, endowed with all gifts and graces, studied with unflagging zeal, and made the idol of a life" (175–76). Warwick, on the other hand, possesses masculine traits that women should develop but to a more moderate degree. As Faith warns, Warwick "clings to principles; persons are but animated facts or ideas; he seizes, searches, uses them, and when they have no more for him, drops them like the husk, whose kernel he has secured" (180). Just as Zenobia predicts for Priscilla "a melancholy lot" with Hollingsworth, "sitting all alone in that wide, cheerless heart" (824), Faith compares Sylvia, should she marry Warwick, to a "woodbird mating with an eagle . . . striving to fill and warm the wild eyrie" (181).

Sylvia's task is not, as she thought, that of choosing between the two men but that of striking a balance between heart and head, the Muse and Minerva within herself. "Owing to the unequal development of her divided nature" (106)—the preponderance of Muse over Minerva—neither Apollo/Moor nor Vulcan/Adam can help her. Recognizing the wisdom of Faith's analysis, Sylvia tells Moor: "I cannot be your wife, I ought not to be Adam's; but I may be myself, may live my life alone, and being friends with both wrong neither. This is my decision; in it I believe, by it I will abide" (184–85). While it could be argued that Sylvia has simply substituted reliance on Faith for reliance on Moor or Warwick, Faith—as her allegorical name implies—represents Sylvia's own inner wisdom, the Minerva aspect of her nature invoked for the first time. Sylvia regards Faith's word as "the law by which I will abide," but Faith gently corrects her: "You shall be a law to yourself, my brave Sylvia" (182). Faith, who takes the place of the mother Sylvia has lacked, is a repository of those values that Sylvia, if she is to become an autonomous adult woman, must now internalize. Combining as she does the intellectual strength of Warwick with the "woman's heart" of Moor, Faith softens her stern advice with "the motherly embrace, the silent shower, the blessed balm of sympathy which soothed the wounds it could not heal" (183).

Sylvia's wounds, far deeper than those inflicted by Faith's words, finally prove incapable of healing. Determined though she is to live apart from Moor and Warwick, her indoctrination in self-sacrifice—especially on behalf of the men closest to her—prevents her from developing her own life. She returns to the patriarchal home that has irremediably injured her, and "Intent on making her life a blessing, not a reproach to her father, she lived for him entirely" (190). Like daughter Patience, of the golden wedding idyll, and like Beth in *Little Women,* Sylvia, as her strength fails, becomes the spiritual center of the family, "taking unsuspected thought for the comfort or the pleasure of those soon to be left behind, so tenderly, that she could not seem lost to them, even when she was gone" (213). Contemporary readers subscribing to the True Womanhood ideal perhaps found Sylvia "strengthened, purified, and perfected by the hard past, the solemn present" (213), but the language of the final paragraphs implies her regression. Sylvia is described as awaiting death much as she earlier awaited marriage—with "the weary yet happy look of some patient child waiting for its lullaby." "Cradled on the heart that loved her best," she is literally carried off to bed—her deathbed, as it proves—by her husband. The terms used to describe this convey-ance, at the end of which Moor finds that "the morning had already dawned," aptly characterize the "little journey," "silent passage," and "short pilgrimage" of her life

(216). Following immediately upon a description of the moonlit river journey as painted by Sylvia's brother, these terms further connect her patriarchal initiation into life with its tragic waste and brevity.

Although Sylvia finally fails of the androgynous development exemplified by Faith, both Alcott's heroes approximate it. The most powerful symbol of their transformation is the book "Alpen Rosen," a collection of Warwick's essays and Moor's poems. This joint effort—like its title—suggests that each has become more androgynous and thus a more complete human being. Moor, the rose, has borrowed strength from Warwick, the mountain, who in turn has acquired sweetness: "Warwick's rugged prose gathered grace from Moor's poetry, and Moor's smoothly flowing lines acquired power from Warwick's prose" (194). The penultimate chapter further conveys the theme of transformation and release. Just as Faith serves as an alter ego for Sylvia, the Minerva aspect that she must strive to integrate, so Warwick represents qualities that Moor must incorporate as well as the male love of mastery that he must reject. Warwick's injury and eventual death signify the modification of "a man's nature" that, as Moor warns Sylvia, "is not forgiving like a woman's and . . . harbor[s] impulses you know nothing of" (170). After suffering an injury in the Italian revolution (a struggle in which Margaret Fuller was also engaged), Warwick confides to Moor that the "restless, domineering devil . . . was cast out" and that "a new spirit entered in and took possession" (203). This new spirit leads Warwick to sacrifice his life for Moor, a reversal of roles that suggests the latter's more complete humanity as well. The hard, demanding, imperious egotism that Moor himself occasionally revealed, especially in his merciless response to Sylvia's confession, has died, but his womanish softness has been infused with Warwick's masculine strength. Hawthorne, by modeling his heroine on Fuller, then having her drown herself out of disappointed love, mocks the notion of female self-reliance, or at least Fuller's. Alcott, by having one of her heroes face with equanimity a death similar but unsought, pays tribute both to Fuller's androgynous ideal and to her unfailing courage.

Alcott's dialogue with and debt to Hawthorne, as well as her commemoration of Fuller, culminate in a remarkable passage at the end of *Moods*. In an apocalyptic dream Sylvia envisions herself as part of a vast throng awaiting in shadowy silence the end of the world. Suddenly a light breaks, a sea rolls slowly toward them, and "million upon million vanished with longing eyes fixed on the arch of light through which the ebbing sea would float them when its work was done." Sylvia, like the rest, loses her fear, "for I seemed such an infintesimal atom of the countless host that I forgot myself." After glimpsing "a benignant face" through the "soft glimmer," she awakens with a "joyful yearning" for the promised oblivion (211). Following as it does Warwick's heroic death by drowning, the vision calls to mind Margaret Fuller confronting inevitable death at sea. But the vision also points to the contrast between Sylvia, passively watching others die and awaiting death herself, and Warwick, whose "resolute will" saved his companions and "fought against the elements as if they were adversaries of mortal mould" (206). The most striking part of the dream, however, is the phenomenon that presages the breaking of the light: "In that universal gloom and stillness, far above me in the heavens I saw the pale outlines of a word stretching from horizon to horizon. Letter after letter came out full and clear, till all across the sky, burning with a ruddy glory stronger than the sun, shone the great word Amen" (210). To Alcott's contemporaries such typology would serve to vindicate Sylvia's withdrawal from the world and eventually from life itself. But the similar vision of Hawthorne's Dimmesdale is attributed to the "highly disordered mental state" of one "rendered morbidly self-contemplative by long, intense, and secret pain" (252). Thus the resemblance between Dimmesdale's "immense letter,—the letter A,—marked out in lines of dull red light" (252) and Sylvia's "great word Amen" identifies not only his actual with her contemplated adultery but also his self-delusion with her self-denial.

As if to prepare the reader for this allusion to Hawthorne, Alcott two chapters earlier explicitly compares her heroine with his:

As Hester Prynne seemed to see some trace of her own sin in every bosom, by the glare of the Scarlet Letter burning on her own; so Sylvia, living in the shadow of a household grief, found herself detecting various phases of her own experience in others. She had joined that sad sisterhood called disappointed women; a larger class than many deem it to be, though there are few of us who have not seen members of it. Unhappy wives; mistaken or forsaken lovers; meek souls, who make life a long penance for the sins of others; gifted creatures kindled into fitful brilliancy by some inward fire that consumes but cannot warm. (190)

The narrator goes on to except Sylvia from "the melancholy chorus" once she finds, in living for her father, "a purpose that took her out of herself" (190). Yet what is that purpose if not a penance for the sins of others? In retrospect, the *narrator's* purpose seems less to distinguish Sylvia from "the melancholy chorus" of "disappointed women" than to help the reader more fully appreciate her membership in that chorus. In *The Scarlet Letter,* if not in *The Blithedale Romance,* Hawthorne went on to envision a life for his heroine independent of both husband and lover, a life not unlike the one that Faith Dane elects to live. Although Alcott did not envision such a life for Sylvia, *Moods*—no less than *Woman in the Nineteenth Century*—demonstrates the need for alternatives to muselike wife- and daughterhood.

Alcott's reference to Hawthorne's adulteress allies Sylvia with passionate heroines, the great female "sinners" of male-authored tragedy and melodrama. Perhaps Alcott, in revising the novel years later, realized that such allusions made the sensational subplot, with its implied parallel between Ottila and Sylvia, unnecessary. One minor episode from the 1864 edition, preserved in the 1882 edition, seems to anticipate the course of Alcott's career, a course epitomized by the omission of Ottila from the 1882 *Moods*. In this episode Sylvia's brother Mark enters two of his paintings in a local exhibition and is chagrined "to find Clytemnestra disposed of in a single sentence, and the Golden Wedding lauded in a long enthusiastic paragraph" (103). Mark's father explains, much as Mr. March explains to Jo in *Little Women,* that "the work which warms the heart is greater than that which freezes the blood" (104). Mark contends that the Golden Wedding is "a daub compared to the other," but, upon witnessing the public's decided preference for his domestic scene, utters an irreverent "Hang Clytemnestra!" (104) and prepares to capitalize on his unexpected success, so much like that of *Little Women.* This episode thus dramatizes Alcott's own preference for "the lurid style," as she called it,[12] and the commercial value of the sentimental and domestic. It also, however, exemplifies the technique that she would come to rely on as she abandoned sensational for children's literature—that of alluding to the absent passions so as to suggest their ineluctable presence. Significantly, in the 1882 *Moods* Sylvia, "with a dagger in her hand," has become the model for her brother's Clytemnestra (234).

In fact, Sylvia in the 1882 edition takes on the siren qualities of both Clytemnestra and Ottila. The allusion to Sylvia as Clytemnestra begins a chapter added to the later version in which Warwick first observes her perched upon a rock, singing as the tide rises around her. Rather than attempting to lure a lover, however, Sylvia is pining for her long-dead mother, a casualty, like Cytemnestra's daughter, of the marital battleground. After Warwick, in a foreshadowing of subsequent events, saves Sylvia from drowning, she resolves to avoid the cave from which he rescued her, as well as the cliff, on which she feels exposed, and, instead, to frequent a sunny nook somewhere between them. Later, in another added scene, Sylvia serves as camp-side entertainer on the river journey, performing roles from Shakespeare for an admiring male audience. Like Zenobia, who "was fond of giving . . . readings from Shakespeare" (725), Sylvia gives a performance that both foreshadows and precipitates events to come. Just as Zenobia's "wild, spectral legend" alludes to Priscilla's past and future enslavement,[13] so Sylvia plays female characters—Ophelia, Lady Macbeth, and Juliet—whose lives have fateful parallels with her own. Only when, dressed as a "saucey lacquey," she plays first Rosalind and then, "with quick changes of voice and manner," Orlando does she briefly integrate the conflicting sides of her nature (245). Warwick, watching, regards her acting as "a safer vent" than "melancholy dreams or daring action" (244), the feminine and masculine extremes represented by the cave and cliff, but he fails to see that some power to act in the world is as necessary for Sylvia as for himself.

Not only is Sylvia more like the heroines of Aeschylus, Shakespeare, and Hawthorne in the 1882 edition, but Warwick, like their heroes, is more implicated in her fate. In still another added passage Adam Warwick, the prophet and exemplar of Emersonian self-reliance, contributes to Sylvia's failure to develop that quality. The morning after the golden wedding celebration, for which Warwick had donned the clothes of the elderly patriarch, he delivers a patriarchal sermon. Like Hawthorne's reformer Hollingsworth, who at Eliot's pulpit dispenses "a treasury of golden thoughts" (737), Warwick delivers an impromptu assault "upon established customs, creeds, and constitutions" (254). Unlike Hollingsworth, who when pressed condemns "all the separate action of woman" as "false, foolish, vain, destructive of her own best and holiest qualities" (739), Warwick lists among other evils "the false public opinion that grants all suffrages to man and none to woman yet judges both alike" (254–55). But the effect of Warwick's sermon on Sylvia is as disturbing as the effect of Hollingsworth's on Zenobia. The latter, rather than resenting her lover's diatribe, is chastened; and Sylvia, rather than inspired to action, is confused. For while Warwick warns Moor that he is too "enamored of self-sacrifice" (253) and recommends living "a little for yourself . . . else the feminine in you will get the uppermost" (254), he urges Sylvia to forget *her*self in work, which, given the lack of choices for women at the time, can only mean devotion to the very domestic duties from which he would liberate Moor. Later Sylvia confides to Moor: "Mr. Warwick has pulled my world to pieces, but has given me no other, and I don't know where to look" (256). And Warwick, as well as Moor, begins to fear "that in handling this young soul they might have harmed it, as even the most careful touch destroys the delicate down on the wing of the butterfly, that is its symbol" (258). In this passage so reminiscent of Hawthorne, we see that Warwick's own sin is the unpardonable one—that of tampering with the soul of another.

The most dramatic difference between the two versions of *Moods* is the ending. Sylvia does not develop greater independence in the 1882 edition, but she does live and, after a year's separation, returns to her husband. In order to prepare for their reconciliation, Alcott makes many minute and subtle changes in the text. For example, Faith now claims that marriage is "the most beautiful and sacred relation . . . for our best training and mutual happiness," provided that it be a relation of "mutual fitness" (271). And she exhorts Sylvia to "love and live for Geoffrey" during their separation (272). The reunion of Moor and Sylvia, though prepared for, is less satisfying than the brave stand Sylvia takes initially in the first edition and, in some ways, less satisfying than her decline and death.[14] In the revised edition an ironic parallel develops between Sylvia and her sister Prudence, who in both editions feels herself displaced by the prodigal daughter and consequently agrees to marry Gamaliel Bliss, a widower with nine children. When Sylvia expresses her incredulity, Prudence assures her, "I tried to love him, and I did not fail" (193). In the 1882 edition Sylvia too feels displaced when, upon the death of her father, her brother and his wife take up residence in the family home. At this point Sylvia, having tried to love *her* husband, decides that *her* efforts have succeeded and returns with him to the Old Manse. The ending of the first edition, however regressive for Sylvia, is uncompromising, for in it she, unlike Prudence, cannot will herself to love her husband and content herself with domestic busyness.

Nevertheless, there are signs in the ending of the 1882 edition that Alcott meant to portray some growth in Sylvia, or at least her own hope for a feminist future. In this edition it is not Sylvia who dies but her father, whose misalliance was largely responsible for Sylvia's. His death, together with the birth of Sylvia's niece and namesake, seems to represent the death of the old patriarchal order, the arrival of a new dispensation, and the rebirth of Sylvia herself. Similarly, Sylvia's return to the Old Manse, despite its disturbing parallel with Prudence's marriage, is described in positive terms. As a bride Sylvia in the 1882 edition left housekeeping duties to a housekeeper. The assumption of such duties, then, can be interpreted as the casting off of girlhood and the acceptance of adult womanhood, including adult sexuality. Finally, subtle changes in the description of a painting— Sylvia's brother's rendering of the river journey—suggest Alcott's androgynous vision of a more egalitarian world. In the first edition a dying Sylvia contemplates the portrayal of Warwick at the helm, herself "a quiet figure . . . couched under the green arch" (216). In the later edition the same picture at the Old Manse has replaced "Correggio's Fates" (231) or "the weird Sisters" (279), which, rather than the misogyny that conceived them, Sylvia has long feared and blamed. This version of the river journey, moreover, portrays Warwick's "vigilant expression" as "touched by the tender magic of the new sentiment for which he had found no name as yet" and Sylvia as "not asleep, but just waking" (279). As she turns from the painting, her face is described as possessing "a look Adam might have owned, so full of courage, hope, and ardor was it" (280).[15] This final chapter, reentitled "At Last," now seems to predict a new order—one in which women will awaken to their powers and men be "touched by a tender magic." In a letter to her father, written six months before her death, Alcott remarked of Emerson: "Pity he could not get a little nearer to people & let them love him. Like Hawthorne he seems like a beautiful soul in prison trying to reach his fellow beings through the bars, & sad because he cannot" (321). As Margaret Fuller forecast in *Woman in the Nineteenth Century*, the old Adam—the masculine nature that undervalues the things of the heart and home—must die if men are to escape their prison, but the strengths of that nature must live on, in men and women alike.

Alcott, by providing a conventional happy ending in 1882, may not have blunted or sheathed her "edge tools" so much as refined them. Another refinement is her preface to the revised *Moods*, where, in what I take to be a strategic move, she presents the book as both juvenile literature and juvenilia. As mentioned earlier, Alcott tries to defuse her explosive material by asserting that the theme is not marriage but "the mistakes of a moody nature.... Of the former subject a girl of eighteen could know but little, of the latter most girls know a good deal; and they alone among my readers have divined the real purpose of the book." Here Alcott attempts to place the novel among those for which she has been acclaimed—her girls' books—and to pass it off as essentially the product of an eighteen-year-old.[16] She persists in the first strategy by desiring "to give my first novel ... a place among its more successful sisters" and by hoping that "the young people will accept the amendment" of the new, happier ending. And she pursues the second in deliberately confounding the heroine's immaturity with that of the youthful author: "At eighteen death seemed the only solution for Sylvia's perplexities; but thirty years later ... my heroine meets a wiser if less romantic fate than in the former edition" (225).[17] Finally, Alcott ingratiates herself with the reader by purporting to regard *Moods* (as well as her other works) as Jo March comes to regard the "little stories" she produces for a "charitable world": "Hoping that ... the elders [among her readers] will sympathize with the maternal instinct which makes unfortunate children the dearest, I reintroduce my first-born to the public which has so kindly welcomed my later offspring" (225–26). In this way Alcott can avert the contradictory charges leveled at the first edition—the charges that its author was both unmaidenly and ignorant of the world. As a "girl" of eighteen, the author was innocent of any deep purpose, and as the loving mother of many offspring, she possesses all the wisdom of experience, not to mention all the maternal virtues.

But the preface to *Moods* is more than a disingenuous disclaimer such as Hawthorne appended to *The Blithedale Romance*,[18] for it contains a subversive subtext, a restatement of the very theme it seemingly denies. In contending that "a girl of eighteen could know but little" of marriage but a "good deal" of moods, Alcott indicts her society for keeping girls in ignorance of the nature of marriage and their own sexuality; "a girl of eighteen" *should* know more of marriage than did Sylvia Yule. Further, by suggesting that her girl readers "know a good deal" of Sylvia's moods and mistakes, Alcott makes her heroine representative, not peculiar. They too, the author implies, suffer Sylvia's ennui, her lack of opportunity and direction, as well as her dependency. They too are doubtless products of unequal marriages, conflict-ridden homes. No wonder that they, like the martyred women Alcott refers to in her correspondence, "divined the real purpose of the book" and thanked her for it. The 1882 edition of *Moods* is, then, much like

Patty's patchwork quilt: the preface, like Aunt Pen's writing on the quilt, serves to sanitize and simplify the work of a younger, more romantic and rebellious artist, while allowing the original grime and puckers to remain. And Alcott, in introducing *Moods* as her firstborn and by stressing its kinship to its sisters, also points to a family likeness among her progeny, however different their features may appear.

Far from being deterred by the novel's mixed reception, Alcott was inspired to treat the same theme almost immediately. In her February 1865 journal entry we find a comment on *Moods*—"some fear it isn't moral because it speaks freely of marriage"—followed by a reference to her latest work: "Wrote a new Novelette for Elliott 'A Marble Woman' & got $75 for it" (139). Though masked in pseudonymity and dressed in sensational garb, *A Marble Woman* is a reworking of *Moods* that looks forward to *Little Women.*

CHAPTER 3

"The Seduction of Daughters" or "The Sins of the Fathers": A Marble Woman or The Mysterious Model

The seduction of daughters is an abuse which is inherent in a father-dominated family system; we believe that the greater the degree of male supremacy in any culture, the greater the likelihood of father-daughter incest.

> Judith Herman and Lisa Hirschman,
> "Father-Daughter Incest" (263)

He looked as if he might just have stept out of a picture, and, in truth, was likely enough to find his way into a dozen pictures; being no other than one of those living models, dark, bushy bearded, wild of aspect and attire, whom artists convert into Saints or assassins, according as their pictorial purposes demand.

"Miriam," whispered Hilda, a little startled, "it is your Model!"

> Nathaniel Hawthorne, *The Marble Faun* (867)

A Marble Woman or The Mysterious Model, like *Moods,* deals with a motherless adolescent girl involved in ambiguous relationships with two much older men. Like the earlier sensation story "A Whisper in the Dark," it offers a sustained critique of the patriarchal model of gender relations that mystifies and immobilizes women. And like *Moods,* though in more cryptic form, it advocates replacing that model with one more egalitarian and androgynous. Drawing upon the myth of Amor and Psyche, the story of Pygmalion and Galatea, and, as its title suggests,

Hawthorne's *The Marble Faun* (1860), Alcott's bizarre melodrama implies that both violence and sterility result from men's efforts to mold women in a vain effort to shape themselves.

As in *Moods,* the eighteen-year-old heroine, Cecilia Stein, is tormented by her love for two men—her guardian, the sculptor Bazil Yorke, and his supposed model, known only as Germain. The story opens with Yorke's adoption of Cecilia, then twelve years old, in accordance with her dying mother's wish. Reluctantly accepting this responsibility, he secretly determines to mold Cecil, as he calls her, into a beautiful but passionless young woman, in part to avenge himself upon her mother, who rejected him in order to marry another man, in part to protect them both from the pain he has come to associate with passion. The first five years of their relationship pass quietly; Cecil not only serves as model for Yorke in his tower studio but becomes an accomplished sculptor herself. But then three events conjoin to awaken Cecil from her childlike innocence. First, she receives a passionate embrace from a cloaked figure whom she mistakes for Yorke; then her neighbor, a young man named Alfred, proposes marriage, forcing her to choose between him and her guardian; and finally, the subjects she and Yorke are modeling, a Cupid and a Psyche, enlighten her as to her growing love for Yorke. True to his original purpose, however, Yorke makes Cecil promise to abandon all thoughts of love, and, as token of her acquiescence as well as her chagrin, she destroys her Cupid.

As though to test Cecil's self-control, Yorke invites to the house Germain, whose sinister appearance had frightened Cecil as a child and whose embrace she had mistaken for Yorke's. But on witnessing the affinity Cecil now feels for the gentle, cultivated man, Yorke arbitrarily forbids her to see him again. When Germain later enters the house and pursues Cecil to the tower studio, Yorke violently repels him, damaging his Psyche in the struggle. Eventually Yorke, on the pretext of silencing rumor and being better able to protect her, proposes to marry Cecil, with the stipulation that they continue their relationship of guardian and ward. Thus Cecil more deliberately than Sylvia makes a mock marriage, and just as Sylvia, forced to feign devotion, becomes a sleepwalker, so Cecil, forced to feign indifference, resorts to opium.

Yorke, oblivious to Cecil's suffering, is at first content with their passionless "marriage" and proud to display Cecil as if she were one of his statues. But on overhearing two men characterize him as a Pygmalion who lacks "the art of warming and waking his Galatea" (455),[1] Yorke becomes as obsessed with eliciting Cecil's passion as he has made her determined to conceal it. After discovering her opium addiction, he takes her to the shore to recover, then to a beautiful new home. In his efforts to rouse her from her lethargy, he even encourages visits from Germain, but these, ironically, convince Cecil that Yorke is incapable of jealousy and hence does not love her. Finally, at a masquerade ball, Yorke trades his Hamlet costume for Germain's domino and attempts in vain to wrest from Cecil the secret of her emotional life. Maddened by what he misinterprets as Alfred's renewed attentions to Cecil, Yorke later in the evening loses all control. Germain intervenes just in time to prevent Yorke from hurling Alfred to his death, much as Donatello in *The Marble Faun* hurls Miriam's model. Cecil, shocked but gratified at this revelation of jealousy, feels for the first time secure in Yorke's love but elicits a confession only after the dying Germain reveals to her what Yorke has always known—that he is her father, a fugitive from justice who long ago committed a crime of passion such as that from which he has saved Yorke.

As in "A Whisper in the Dark," Alcott uses the Gothic machinery of a highly implausible and melodramatic story to make a number of telling points about the nature of patriarchy. Yorke's behavior in regard to Cecil, behavior that he believes to be dictated by their peculiar circumstances, is, as he himself later acknowledges, self-defeating from beginning to end. Yet this behavior corresponds to that of fathers, husbands, guardians, and protectors of women in patriarchal society. The silence, obedience, and self-control that Yorke enjoins on the child Cecil—and Warwick on the adolescent Sylvia—are conventional feminine virtues, and the passionlessness he later encourages was also part of the prevailing ideology.[2] The master-ward relationship, which persists even after marriage, and the elaborate mask that Cecil must wear, both in public and in private, point to women's dependent status and the ensuing need to conceal their natural impulses. The Psyche that Yorke molds, using Cecil as a model, represents the way in which patriarchal culture would construct woman so as to immobilize her, and Yorke's carefully ordered and guarded home, which is nonetheless haunted by the presence of Germain, suggests the seemingly impenetrable fortress of patriarchy, ironically endangered by the very father it is designed to protect. The symbiotic but stormy relationship between Germain and Yorke exposes male self-division and its disastrous consequences, though Germain's timely intervention, confession, and death, like Warwick's transformation and sacrificial death, make wholeness seem possible. Finally, the concealment of Germain's identity from Cecil signifies, like Sybil's separation from her mother, the need for women to reclaim their past and recognize the truths of their own nature. In regard to these themes, the characters' names are richly suggestive: the father's, August Stein, of sovereignty and stone; the father surrogate's, Bazil Yorke, of monasticism and monarchy; and the daughter's, Cecilia Stein, of sainthood, blindness, and music as well as stone. But the father's alias, Germain or german, means full kinship—a relationship based on recognition and reciprocity.

Alcott, as though to emphasize the deprivation that Cecilia will suffer, begins the story by contrasting Yorke's home with one in which a woman is the guiding spirit. Cecil, on being sent to Yorke, is "ushered . . . into a city garden, where a few pale shrubs and vines rustled in the wind. . . . nothing was in bloom, and the place had a neglected air" (408). But as she waits, Cecil is invited by a "rosy, bright-eyed boy about her own age" to join him on the wall between Yorke's cheerless garden and the "blooming plot" next door (408). At the mention of her "mamma," Cecil gives way to tears but is comforted, not only by Alfred but by his mother, whose smiling face she sees in the "window of the adjoining house" (409). From the bright garden and smiling maternal face, Cecil turns to a gloomy house governed by a stern "master." Yorke's forbidding manner discourages the expression of emotion. Thus Cecil repeatedly controls her impulses—to cry for her dead mother, to cry out at the appearance of "a strange uncanny face" at the window, to question Yorke about his "mysterious model," and to raise her face for a goodnight kiss. She does not even protest his attempt to deny her gender by calling her Cecil rather than Celia, her mother's name for her. Her only consolation for these spoken and unspoken prohibitions is Yorke's tower studio, a seductive but ultimately life-denying version of the female garden next door: "A smiling woman seemed to beckon her, a winged child to offer flowers, and all about the room pale gods and goddesses looked upon her from their pedestals with what to her beauty-loving eyes seemed varying expressions of welcome" (414). Cecil quickly makes herself at home among this "gathering of ghosts" (414), and within five years she has become one of them: "Colorless, like a plant deprived of sunshine, strangely unyouthful . . . as beautiful . . . and almost as cold" (418).

Alcott's description of the sculpture studio as garden suggests her indebtedness to Hawthorne's "Rappaccini's Daughter" as well as to *The Marble Faun*. Cecil, like Beatrice Rappaccini, becomes adept in her guardian's line of work. Her mother, a former pupil of Yorke's, taught her how to model clay and called her "little Bazil" (415). Five years later she has indeed become a diminutive version of the sculptor, creating a minor counterpart—"a little Cupid exquisitely carved in the purest marble"—of his masterpiece, "a lovely, Psyche-bending form" (418).[3] The image of two sculptors working side by side, collaborating on complementary projects, could serve as a paradigm of gender equality, but Cecil's work is as ancillary as that of Beatrice in caring for her father's plants. When Yorke asks what prompted her to mold the figure, she answers, "Your making Psyche suggested Cupid. . . . I could not do a large one, so I pleased myself with trying a little winged child with the bandage and bow" (422). Her failure to make a full-sized Cupid, a fitting mate for Yorke's Psyche, recalls the limitations ascribed to women artists—their tendency to imitate, their lack of ambition, and their willingness, like Hawthorne's Hilda, to become mere copyists or miniaturists. Cecil's Cupid also expresses her immature conception of love and inability to imagine a love between equals. Yet her juvenile Cupid, like Alcott's own juvenile works, is subtly subversive. Like Beatrice Rappaccini's tender nurture of her voluptuous sister plant, Cecil's modeling of Cupid, "just drawing an arrow from his quiver" (418), betokens the failure of a masculine attempt to "repress all natural emotions" (422).

Yorke's own statue, for which Cecil has served as model, is as ironic as Cecil's is subversive. The Psyche, bending "with her graceful hand above her eyes, as if she watched her sleeping lover" (418), exposes his self-serving view of woman—not performing heroic labors but gazing rapt upon the man she loves. Yet Yorke portrays Psyche at the moment in which she dares to look at her hitherto unseen lover and learn the truth about him, the moment that sets her upon her journey and inspires her heroic feats. Cecil, like Psyche, becomes conscious and is no longer content with what Erich Neumann calls "imprisonment in the patriarchate."[4] When Yorke bids her "be what I would have you," she inquires in a tone of nascent rebellion, "A marble woman like your Psyche, with no heart to love you, only grace and beauty to please your eye and bring you honor . . . ?" Yorke, realizing that "he had worked out his design in stone, but not yet in that finer material given to him to mold well or ill," answers, "Yes, I would have you beautiful and passionless as Psyche, a creature to admire with no fear of disturbing its quiet heart, no fear of endangering one's own" (425). Like Rappaccini, who asks the dying Beatrice if she would "have preferred the condition of a weak [or normal] woman, exposed to all evil, and capable of none" (which, of course, is exactly her condition in relation to her father), Yorke wants Cecil, as much for his sake as her own, to be "as terrible as [she is] beautiful" (1005).

Yorke's failure to fashion either himself or Cecil according to his design is further signified by the return of Germain, whose passionate intensity suggests the primitive beneath man's veneer of civilization. Germain, in the violent crime he once committed, in his early sinister appearance, and in the damage that his forcible intrusion does to Yorke's Psyche, seems allied with Miriam's model, a disruptive, demonic force. Yet her model's moral ambiguity is implied by his "reputation of unusual sanctity" (1213), his burial among the Capuchins, and the belief of some that he was "endeavoring to prevail on any unwary visitor to take him by the hand, and guide him out into the daylight" (878). Serving as model for both saints and assassins, he is also associated, through his "goat-skin breeches" (875), with the comparatively innocent "faun," Donatello, the descendant of a prehistoric race. But Donatello, after slaying the model and retreating to his ancestral tower, loses his connection with the Golden Age, including his capacity for pleasure. The tower to which he resorts, like the one Yorke (and Hawthorne's Hilda) inhabits, seems to represent not only man's disconnection from the natural world but his vain attempt to dissociate himself from his instinctual nature. For all that he has lost, however, Donatello has gained something: his fall into civilized manhood has given him ascendancy over woman. Miriam, who once treated him with amused and affectionate tolerance, has become his adoring and abject slave.

Most obviously, of course, Germain mirrors the incestuous nature of Yorke's feelings for his adopted daughter. And here again a kinship with *The Marble Faun* becomes apparent. Both Hawthorne's heroines are associated with Beatrice Cenci, an infamous patricide and probable incest victim. The saintly Hilda, having copied Guido's Beatrice, is horrified to observe her friend Miriam's face assume the same expression. But later, after witnessing the violent death of Miriam's model, Hilda glances in a mirror and finds "Beatrice's expression . . . depicted in her own face" (1022). Still later an artist's sketch of Hilda is said to have been suggested by the same portrait, and she mysteriously disappears when an errand for Miriam takes her to "the paternal abode of Beatrice, the gloomy old palace of the Cencis" (1176). Shortly before her reappearance, her lover Kenyon, on finding the remains of a statue, ponders, "I seek for Hilda, and find a marble woman! Is the omen good or ill?" (1206) In a sense, Hilda *is* a marble woman even before her abduction and imprisonment in a convent, where she is "watched over by such a dear old priest" (1241). A "daughter of the Puritans," as she calls herself (896, 1153), Hilda is unable to sympathize either with Beatrice or with Miriam, who, to escape the persecution of her "model"—a depraved, demented, Man-Demon (and, as we are led to believe, her "destined husband," "the representative of another branch of her paternal house" [1211])—willed, if she did not engineer, his death.

By associating his heroines with Beatrice Cenci, Hawthorne attributes their crimes and limitations to the patriarchal power that Miriam resists and Hilda worships. Similarly, Alcott uses the incest motif to expose the illegitimate power one sex wields over another—by arresting women's development, exploiting their dependency, and, when all else fails, reverting to physical force. In "A Whisper in the Dark," Sybil's uncle, the most sinister of Alcott's seductive father figures, turns her innocent flirtation into a virtual rape. Later, when she refuses to become his daughter by marrying his son, he tries to coerce her into marriage with himself. In *Moods*, Geoffrey Moor and Adam Warwick, though as idealistic as Sylvia's uncle is cynical, prefer a formless creature whom they can mold and master to their peer in maturity and intellect. Sylvia turns to Moor for mothering, to Warwick for mentoring, but neither can resist the erotic opportunity afforded by these childlike appeals. Finally, in *A Marble Woman*, Yorke treats the beautiful young woman who loves him and whom he eventually marries as a daughter, pupil, or ward; Germain treats his daughter as the object of romantic love and desire. Both, by confounding their protective paternal instincts with their passionate impulses, epitomize the way in which men simultaneously deny and gratify their sexual feelings and exercise power over those whom they need not treat as equals.[5]

Germain is the outlawed passion that legitimates male domination of women. Yorke initially uses Germain's presence in his house as a rationale for repressing the child Cecil, for enjoining her to silence and unquestioning obedience. Later, when threatened by her awakening sexuality, he treats Germain's visit as a rite of passage, an opportunity for her to acquire "womanly accomplishments" and assume her role as "little mistress of the house" (427). He insists that she gather

her "dark locks plainly back into a knot" (427), urges her to "control herself" (429), and flashes her warning signs throughout the evening. By the time of her wedding, Cecil "seemed to have grown a woman . . . calm as the marble Psyche that adorned an alcove." The statue, for which Cecil posed as model, has now become *her* model of adult womanhood. And that model is associated with the other model, Germain, who "glided in unannounced . . . and placed himself in the shadow of the draperies that hung before a deep window" (448). Although his presence momentarily threatens her composure, his presence in her life from the beginning has made it proof against that threat. Dying, Germain tells Cecil that her mother's love "would have saved us both" by preventing his crime of passion; Cecil he praises for having proven his "saving angel" (503–4). Thus Germain reveals at least one motive force behind patriarchy: men, in attempting to dominate and master women, to shape them into little women who can influence *them* and appeal to their better nature, are actually trying to master themselves.[6] As Kenyon says to Hilda, "Were you my guide, my counsellor, my inmost friend, with that white wisdom which clothes you as with a celestial garment, all would go well" (1236).

The beheading of Yorke's Psyche, like the destruction of Cecil's Cupid, indicates that efforts to repress female sexuality and thus contain, compartmentalize, and safeguard male sexuality injure both women and men. Not only is Psyche beheaded; Yorke himself is crushed by her fall. Later, as he views the mended statue, he marvels, "I never thought my Psyche [or conception of womanhood] would cause me so much suffering" (438). But rather than heed this warning, he attempts once more to imprison Cecil/Psyche in Amor's cave. To protect her from the importunate Germain, Yorke insists that Cecil remain indoors during his convalescence. Even after their marriage, he does not allow her to leave the house alone: "I think you will tell me like an obedient little wife, and ask me prettily to go with you or for you" (452). Cecil, to avoid Yorke's disapproval, colludes in her own imprisonment. Her mending of the Psyche constitutes, as Jeanne Bedell has noted, an effort at self-repression (12). After the wedding ceremony, she quickly changes from her bridal dress into a "plain gray gown" and retreats to the tower studio, the bastion of reason and self-restraint that Germain attempted to take by storm. But the passionlessness and passivity enjoined on Cecil, while designed to perpetuate Yorke's absolute control (she continues to call him "master," at least in private), actually undermines it. As Cecil in a rare rebellious mood reminds him, "your will is not my law, because though my husband before the world, you are only my guardian here" (453).[7] Upon overhearing himself described as a Pygmalion unable to animate his statue, Yorke demands that Cecil imitate Mrs. Vivian, a radiant bride, who obviously dotes upon her husband. Both to retain his power over Cecil and to demonstrate his prowess before the world, Yorke desires to arouse Cecil's passion without having to meet her emotional needs or acknowledge the existence of his own. In other words, he would like to be a kind of unmoved mover. Cecil can only thwart him by numbing her emotions, and, when that fails, assuming the immobility of death.

Like her breaking of the Cupid, Cecil's opium addiction both suppresses and constitutes rebellion. Yorke himself first prescribes laudanum, which her mother also took for relief from pain, when Cecil, restless from enforced inactivity, finds it impossible to sleep. Sustained but secret use then enables her to be as Yorke would have her—docile, childlike, and passive. Craving for the drug, however, finally leads her to defy his orders and leave the house in search of it. That night the overdose that enables her, as Mrs. Vivian, to gratify his vanity also robs him of his triumph. Before the evening is over, Cecil, under the drug's influence, escapes in sleep the unbearable pain of having to display in public emotions she must not express in private. After the near-fatal overdose exposes her addiction, Dr. Home says significantly to Yorke, "a woman's reasons for such freaks are many" (461).[8] Cecil, like Beatrice Rappaccini, unwittingly discovers, then deliberately seeks, immunity, conformity, and oblivion in the narcotic proffered by her father/lover. But she also, like Hawthorne's heroine, takes revenge. Beatrice, after quaffing the deadly potion that would supposedly purify her, reproaches both Dr. Rappaccini, who has subjected her to his chemical experiments, and Giovanni, who, by administering another drug, would reverse the effect. Of her father she inquires, "wherefore didst thou inflict this miserable doom upon thy child?" and of Giovanni, "was there not, from the first, more poison in thy nature than in mine?" (1005) Cecil's self-administered doses and their near-fatal consequence similarly condemn as deadly her guardian's prescription for life.

As her resemblance to a statue suggests, the conflicting demands placed upon Cecil—for marble repose and human vivacity—approximate what Hawthorne portrays as the near-impossible and perhaps inhuman demands placed upon the

art of sculpture.[9] The miracle of the Faun is that the artist "succeeded in imprisoning the sportive and frisky thing, in marble" (861). But, as the word *imprisoning*
implies, sculpture is a "fossilizing process," a "frozen art." Miriam points out that
"a painter never would have sent down yonder Faun out of his far antiquity, lonely
and desolate" (866) but would have portrayed him in relationship to others and his
environment. The narrator contends that clay models are superior to marble statues
because the latter are not the sculptor's work but "that of some nameless machine in
human shape," the ignorant artisans who actually chip the marble (949). Although
they seem to liberate "the figure . . . imbedded in the stone" (948), that very illusion
suggests to Miriam a deterministic view of life: "As these busts in the block of marble
. . . so does our individual fate exist in the limestone of Time. We fancy that we carve
it out; but its ultimate shape is prior to all our action" (949). And marble busts, the
narrator reflects, far from conferring immortality on their subjects, "measure the
little, little time, during which our lineaments are likely to be of interest to any human
being" (951). Thus Miriam concludes that "it will be a fresher and better world, when
it flings off this great burthen of stony memories" (952) and that "sculpture has no
longer a right to claim any place among living arts" (955).

Yet Miriam well understands the perennial appeal of sculpture, an appeal it
shares with the model of passionless womanhood. As she says to the sculptor
Kenyon, "You turn feverish men into cool, quiet marble. What a blessed change
for them!" (952). Hilda's "small, beautifully shaped hand, most delicately sculp-
tured in marble" (952) and kept in a precious antique box, epitomizes her cloistered life and Kenyon's chaste, undeclared passion for her. Yet it keeps that passion
alive and perhaps provides a more exquisite pleasure than would a reciprocal
relationship. Kenyon's ambitious model of Cleopatra, combining "the repose of
despair" with "latent energy and fierceness" (957), is designed to do for generations of men what Hilda's hand does for Kenyon: "Soon, apotheosized in an
indestructible material, she would be one of the images that men keep forever,
finding a heat in them which does not cool down, throughout the centuries" (958).
Hilda's hand and the Cleopatra both represent the contradictory demands that
men make of sculpture and of women: that they cool, control, and purify men's
passions so that those passions may be safely indulged and perpetuated. Even
Kenyon comes to see the self-defeating nature of his art. Once joyfully united with
Hilda, he models a "beautiful little statue of Maidenhood" but refuses "to im-

prison [its] airy excellence in a permanent material" (1164). Similarly, by not chipping the face of Donatello entirely out of the marble in which it is embedded, Kenyon succeeds in posing "the riddle of the Soul's growth" (1170). And although his masterpiece is finally freed "from the imprisoning stone" (1166), Kenyon expresses the irreverent desire "to hit poor Cleopatra a bitter blow on her Egyptian nose," a blow, Hilda adds, that "all statues seem doomed to receive" (1167).

Yorke's disillusionment with *his* art, especially with the marble woman he has made of Cecil, is signified by his willingness to tolerate Germain for her sake. Clearly, Germain represents a crucial part of both male and female nature, a part from which Yorke has estranged himself and tried in vain to estrange Cecil. Inimical to Yorke's Psyche, to whom he delivers the inevitable blow, Germain has the power to animate Cecil, who "could not dislike [him], in spite of mystery, violence, and unmistakable traces of turbulent life" (469). But until his identity and kinship are acknowledged, Germain remains a threatening and divisive presence, as Yorke discovers the night of the masquerade ball. Yorke's ambivalence about acknowledging his connection with Germain is represented by their exchange of costumes. On the one hand, Yorke, in discarding his Hamlet costume to assume Germain's domino, expresses a desire to associate himself with Germain. Further, his rejection of the Hamlet role signals his readiness to forgo his self-protective contempt for female "frailty." On the other hand, Yorke's deceptive use of Germain's domino in order to extort a confession from Cecil is Hamlet-like and recoils upon him, for the misleading responses he elicits lead him to the brink of madness. While Yorke's assumption of Germain's identity prompts him to violence and thus would seem to justify his banishment, Germain's timely intervention suggests that, far from being inherently destructive, the force he represents, if recognized and incorporated rather than repudiated or merely appropriated, can be saving.

Cecil's growing intimacy with Germain, alternately encouraged and discouraged by her husband, indicates that she too will come to terms with what he represents. In "At Last," the final chapter of the 1882 version of *Moods,* Sylvia seems to have been infused with some of Adam Warwick's energy. So too in the final chapter of *A Marble Woman,* also entitled "At Last," Cecil, by fully recognizing and accepting her father, reclaims the heritage of power and passion that she and her sex have traditionally been denied: "the one word 'father' had unlocked her heart, and all its pent-up passion flowed freely now that a natural vent was found" (501–2). Germain, in telling his story to Cecil, demonstrates the destructiveness of both unbridled male passion and the denial of passion to women. Cecil's mother, by insisting that Yorke keep Cecil from her father or even knowledge of him, helped perpetuate the patriarchal tyranny from which she would have protected her daughter. Conversely, Cecil's acceptance of the father, and the father's legacy, frees her from her status as perpetual daughter. Cecil, fearing that Yorke will attempt to separate her from her dying father, insists that she will "cling through everything" to Germain, "for you have no right to take me from him" (506). Paradoxically, Cecil's assertion of her right signals the end to the passive aggression that began with the breaking of her Cupid. Only when unable to demand their rights, when constrained to obey, do women, like Cecil, obey with such a vengeance.

The final scene, in which Cecil and Yorke together witness the death of Germain, points once again to his dual function in *A Marble Woman*—as an emblem of patriarchal power and as the hope of liberation from it. With Germain's confession and death dies the hidden, and thus the most powerful, pretext for the exercise of patriarchal power—a power that, as Yorke admits, tries in the name of justice to visit the sins of the mother upon the daughter (507), makes the home a prison, and forces women, both in private and in public, to play a part and deny their true selves. For Germain's death signifies the death of the instinctual, the irrational, and the passionate as something outside the self—something that men can erect towers against and shield women from. In both the revised *Moods* and *A Marble Woman* the surviving couple mourns but profits from the sacrificial death of the more aggressive hero. Cecil and Yorke, kneeling together beside the dying Germain, acknowledge their kinship with and indebtedness to him; Cecil blesses him "for saving me to be your happy wife," whereas Yorke, after confessing his emotional torment, blesses Germain for seeing his folly and saving him from himself (511). That which, its dangers exaggerated, shrouded in mystery, and concealed, erupts in male violence and justifies female repression can—when confronted, acknowledged, and embraced—effect psychic wholeness and reciprocal relationships. It only waits, like Miriam's model, to be "guided out into the daylight."[10]

Miriam believes her model to possess a secret that would place her "at the head of modern art; the sole condition being agreed upon, that she should return with him into his sightless gloom, after enriching a certain extent of stuccoed wall with the most brilliant and lovely designs. And what true votary of Art would not purchase unrivalled excellence, even at so vast a sacrifice!" (879) Alcott's critics have attributed her power, at least in the sensation fiction, to a similar source, the dark male figure that haunted her dreams during a near-fatal bout of typhoid fever but whom she believed in retrospect to have been her anxiously attending mother.[11] Moreover, it is as though Alcott, having been tormented like Miriam, adopted Hawthorne's heroine as her model of the female artist whether Gothic or domestic. Miriam sees her "lay figure," the dummy she drapes when painting fabric, as a type of womanhood—harmless, "pliable," ornamental, a "poor puppet" having "nothing on earth to do" like "nine women out of ten" (885–86). Yet Donatello, on first glimpsing the dummy, sees a feminine counterpart of Miriam's model, "a woman with long dark hair, who threw up her arms, with a wild gesture of tragic despair, and appeared to beckon him into the darkness along with her" (885). This radical discrepancy, like that between Alcott's dream figure and its reality, is reflected in Miriam's work. One series of sketches embodies the "idea of woman, acting the part of a revengeful mischief towards man": "Jael, driving the nail through the temples of Sisera," Judith beheading Holofernes, and "the daughter of Herodias, receiving the head of John the Baptist in a charger" (887–88). A second series consists of "domestic and common scenes, so finely and subtly idealized that they seemed such as we may see at any moment" but all presenting "a truer and lovelier picture of the life that belongs to woman, than an actual acquaintance with some of its hard and dusty facts could have inspired" (888–89). As though to comment on the unreality of these scenes "a figure was pourtrayed apart . . . and in every instance . . . the face and form had the traits of Miriam's own" (889–90).

Alcott's masterpieces of the late 1860s, *Behind a Mask* and *Little Women,* bear an uncanny resemblance both to Miriam's "lay-figure" and to her diverse productions. In *Behind a Mask,* which many consider the most brilliant of the sensation stories, Alcott presents "woman, acting the part of a revengeful mischief towards men."[12] The heroine, Jean Muir, is a professional actress, adept at portraying "the life that belongs to woman," a life devoted to decoration and service, but like Judith, whom she plays in a tableau vivant, she seeks liberation and revenge. In *Little Women,* Alcott's first and most famous juvenile novel, she presents Miriam's "domestic and common scenes . . . finely and subtly idealized."

The March sisters, under the direction of their devoted mother, go through the stages of a woman's life that Miriam depicts—courtship, marriage, motherhood. They perform many parts and assume varied duties, developing the "pliable disposition" incumbent upon them as little women. Yet just as Jean, for all her mischief, is a mistress of the domestic arts, so the little women remain haunted and haunting. As we shall see, Germain is very much present as the villainous or demonic but also the creative side of the heroine, Jo March—a side represented in a milder way by her "selfish" sister, Amy, and by her rebellious male friend, Laurie. This side may be repressed by the exemplary mother, Marmee, and be all but imperceptible to the reader, but Alcott, no less than Miriam, insinuates herself into her idyll as though to undermine its portrayal of domestic bliss.

CHAPTER 4

"The Second Sex":
Behind a Mask or
A Woman's Power

Woman plays the part of those secret agents who are left to the firing squad if they get caught, and are loaded with rewards if they succeed; it is for her to shoulder all man's immorality: not the prostitute only, but all women who serve as sewer to the shining, wholesome edifice where respectable people have their abode. When, thereupon, to these women one speaks of dignity, honor, loyalty, of all the lofty masculine virtues, it is not astonishing if they decline to "go along." They laugh in derision particularly when the virtuous males have just reproached them for not being disinterested, for play-acting, for lying. They well know that no other way out is open to them.

Simone de Beauvoir,
The Second Sex (578–79)

Insignificant as this action was, it spoke very plainly. It spoke very plainly of ever-recurring fears—of fatal necessities for concealment—of a mind that in its silent agonies was ever alive to the importance of outward effect. It told more plainly than anything else could have told how complete an actress my lady had been made by the awful necessity of her life.

Mary Elizabeth Braddon,
Lady Audley's Secret (197)

Alcott's 1866 sensation story *Behind a Mask or A Woman's Power,* published a year after *A Marble Woman* and two years before *Little Women,* is doubly self-referential, for in it Alcott not only writes again from "behind the mask" of her pseudonym A. M. Barnard but, more important, anticipates the direction her career is about to take. Jean Muir, the heroine, is an older, more cynical version of the ingénues Sybil, Sylvia, and Cecil. At thirty, the age of Sylvia's mentor, Faith Dane, Jean uses her skill as a professional actress to impersonate the child or marble woman the younger heroines actually become. As the narrator of *Moods* comments in regard to Sylvia, "Men seldom understand the subterfuges women instinctively use to conceal many a natural emotion which they are not strong enough to control, not brave enough to confess" (139). Jean, however, only pretends to employ these subterfuges, hoping that men will be so complacent upon recognizing them that they will fail to detect the deeper game in which they are but diversionary tactics. Both Jeanne Bedell and Judith Fetterley argue that Jean Muir's economically motivated impersonation of "a clever, kindly little woman," as she is called, ironically, by one of her victims, anticipates Alcott's strategy in *Little Women* and its sequels (8; 1983, 1). The parallel between Jean and Alcott, however, goes beyond their ability to play Lady Tartuffe, as Jean styles herself, for the purpose of achieving worldly success. For just as the unmasking of Jean Muir serves primarily to expose the ugly features of patriarchy and Jean's consummate skill in confounding it, so the recent unmasking of Alcott as Jean's creator enables readers to discern more clearly the feminist features and subtle artistry of her children's books.

Like a number of Alcott's works, including "A Whisper in the Dark," *Behind a Mask* is indebted to *Jane Eyre.* The story opens with the Coventry family— consisting of the invalid Mrs. Coventry, her sons, Gerald and Edward, her daughter, Bella, and her niece Lucia, who is engaged to Gerald—awaiting the arrival of Bella's new governess, Jean Muir. Their discussion, as they wait, recalls the way in which the haughty Ingram family discusses their former governesses in *Jane Eyre.* The cynical elder brother, Gerald, professes "an inveterate aversion to the whole tribe" (3) and predicts that the governess will try to "bewitch" Edward. Shortly thereafter Jean arrives, dressed like her prototype, Jane Eyre, in a "plain black dress, with no ornament but a little silver cross at her throat. Small, thin, and colorless she was, with yellow hair, gray eyes, and sharply cut, irregular, but very expressive features" (6). Like Jane, she is not yet twenty and "without a relation in the world" (5), but she immediately pleases Mrs. Coventry with her air of "meek obedience" and intrigues the rest with her "curious mixture of command and entreaty" (6–7). The reader, though, soon learns that she is in fact a divorced former actress of thirty who views her employment as a last opportunity to do what Jane Eyre did—enchant and marry a wealthy master. Here she has three prospects: the vulnerable, impetuous younger son; the cool, detached heir to the estate; and its present master, their elderly uncle, Sir John Coventry.

Jean quickly ensnares the younger brother, then disarms the suspicious Gerald by appealing to him for protection from Edward's passionate importunity. Her professed need is rendered convincing when Edward, in a jealous passion, wounds Gerald, whom he now regards as a rival. Jean also seeks protection from Gerald's friend Sydney, with whose family she was previously engaged. But far from fearing the violence of Sydney's love, Jean actually fears his efforts to prevent the Coventrys from being duped as he was. As Jean confides in a letter to her friend Hortense, to whom she writes throughout her stay at the Coventrys': "Sydney was more wily than I thought. All was going well, when one day my old fault beset me, I took too much wine, and I carelessly owned that I had been an actress. He was shocked, and retreated. I got up a scene, and gave myself a safe little wound, to frighten him. The brute was not frightened, but coolly left me to my fate" (97). Jean finally succeeds in seducing Gerald, who is closely guarded by Lucia, after she participates in a series of tableaux vivants, including a romantic scene opposite him. Having gotten Edward a commission in the army, ostensibly to protect him and Jean from each other but really to eliminate his rival, Gerald recants his former harsh words about governesses and proposes to Jean himself. Jean tentatively accepts his offer, but when Edward, having learned of her past from Sydney, threatens to expose her, she appeals to the affection she has assiduously cultivated in his uncle, Sir John. Edward makes good his threat by reading to the family the letters Jean wrote to and Sydney purchased from Hortense. But by then Jean has obtained her object and become Lady Coventry.

Critics of *Behind a Mask* and of another novel that doubtless inspired Alcott, Mary Elizabeth Braddon's *Lady Audley's Secret* (1862),[1] have pointed out that the careers of Jean Muir and Lucy Grahame, the governess who becomes Lady Audley, expose the contradictions and dangers inherent in the Cult of True Womanhood.

At several points in *Behind a Mask* the narrator, or one of the characters, recites a virtual litany of the womanly virtues possessed by Jean Muir. In the opening scene, Jean demonstrates her accomplishments by performing at the piano, her delicacy by fainting, and her "modest, domestic graces" by preparing and serving tea (8).[2] The impression that she leaves upon Edward is that of a pathetic but charming "little woman" (11). Jean goes on to win Mrs. Coventry with her "unobtrusive and retiring" manners and Sir John with her "respectful deference and . . . graceful little attentions . . . paid him in a frank and artless way." And she forces both Lucia and Gerald to admit that she is "meek, modest, faithful, and invariably sweet-tempered" (25). Later the infatuated Edward repeats his version of the litany to Gerald, dwelling on her "unsuspected kindness," her "faithful care," "sisterly interest," "gentle attentions," "sweet forbearance," and "friendly counsel, sympathy, and regard" (36–37). Thus Jean proves herself, like Miriam's lay figure, "a lady of exceedingly pliable disposition." She serves as nurse to the mother, instructor and role model to the daughter, entertainer and confidante to the brothers, companion to the uncle. But as Judith Fetterley observes, in order to analyze the needs of every person in the house, the little woman must be supremely conscious; thus, ironically, the innocence, simplicity, even stupidity imputed to her is in fact incompatible with her role (1983, 6). To please everyone with the apparent artlessness Sir John so much admires, Jean must be, as she is at the keyboard, a "perfect mistress of her art" (6).

According to Fetterley and to Karen Halttunen, works like *Behind a Mask* demonstrate the way in which the Victorian Cult of True Womanhood actually encouraged women to subvert it. Passionlessness, as we saw in *A Marble Woman,* was thought to ensure woman's moral superiority and hence her reforming or at least restraining influence upon men, but it becomes for Jean an instrument of ambition and revenge. As Halttunen writes, Jean Muir "commands total sway over the lives of others by means of a monstrous perversion of the sentimental concept of woman's influence. Whereas influence works through sincere affections, Muir's power operates through calculated deception; while influence is the product of loving self-denial, Muir's power stems from selfish ambition. Most important, although the sentimental woman exercises influence through her vulnerability, Muir seizes power through her complete immunity to emotion" (1984, 241). Passionlessness was thought to exempt women from certain temptations, including the temptation to resist patriarchal authority, but in Jean's case it only removes her scruples. While sentiment of the sort that kept women self-denying and vulnerable was thought to be compatible with, even dependent upon, passionlessness, Jean's "immunity" frees her to affect whatever sentiment serves her interest.[3] Yet Jean is not completely "immune to emotion," and in fact she brilliantly exploits her very real susceptibility. As Fetterley remarks, "Implicit in Jean's fainting, as in her entire handling of the performance situation, is the imagery of victimization" (1983, 8). Fetterley makes explicit what in *Behind a Mask* is implicit: men have no sympathy with victims of patriarchy such as the destitute, disreputable, and aging actress Jean truly is, but they do sympathize with and derive erotic gratification from the sufferings of young, well-born, and attractive victims such as Jean appears to be.

During her conquest of the male Coventrys, Jean repeatedly enacts scenes designed to pique their curiosity, enlist their sympathy, and inspire their passion. The morning after her arrival Jean arises early to explore the grounds of the estate. Sensing the approach of Sir John, whom she had not met the night before, "her whole air changed, she pushed back her hat, clasped her hands loosely before her, and seemed absorbed in girlish admiration of the fair scene" (13). When he greets her cordially, she apologizes for intruding and professes to have believed the master away. Pretending to take Sir John for his steward, she then expresses her admiration for the estate and for the reputation of its owner so as to flatter him without appearing to do so. When he finally confesses his identity, she affects to be "overcome with girlish confusion" (15). That evening Jean makes another move in her campaign against Sir John and at the same time gains revenge for his condescending treatment—his slight change in manner on discovering her to be the governess and his overheard remark that she is "not exactly a beauty, but accomplished and well-bred, which is better for one of her class" (23). After contriving that he witness through the window "a pleasant little scene" in which she reads aloud to Bella in her melodious voice, Jean mystifies him by bursting into tears as soon as Bella leaves the room. All night he "puzzled his brains with conjectures about his niece's interesting young governess, quite unconscious that she intended he should do so" (24).

Jean uses the same tactic, the assumption of a secret sorrow, in giving the coup de grâce to Sir John Coventry after Edward threatens to expose her. She begins this last campaign by telling Sir John that she must go away because now Gerald, like Edward before him, has fallen in love with her while her heart belongs to another. But Sir John, conscious of the disparity between his actual and her pretended age, is slow to arrive at the conclusion she desperately wishes him to draw—that she is in love with himself. At this point Jean's dilemma and its resolution illustrate how the sentimental ideal of womanhood demands an opposing shrewdness, for she finds a clever way to reveal her love without "overstep[ping] the bounds of maiden modesty" and thus jeopardizing his regard. When Sir John goes to his desk to write a letter recommending Jean as governess to another family, she notices a miniature portrait of Sir John: "Affecting unconsciousness [of his covert glances], Jean gazed on as if forgetful of everything but the picture, and suddenly, as if obeying an irresistible impulse, she took it down, looked long and fondly at it, then, shaking her curls about her face, as if to hide the act, pressed it to her lips and seemed to weep over it in an uncontrollable paroxysm of tender grief" (80–81). By simulating the emotion that Jane spontaneously displays at the prospect of parting from Rochester, as well as feigning an attempt to conceal that emotion, Jean is finally able to reap Jane's reward.

It is a tribute to Jean's skill as an actress that Gerald, though he suspects her from the first of having designs on Edward, becomes as much a dupe as Edward or Sir John. When Jean faints, shortly after her arrival, Gerald sardonically remarks, "Scene first, very well done" (7). The next morning Jean tames the spirited horse that Edward is so proud of, causing Gerald to warn his brother: "Not a bad move on her part. . . . She must be an observing as well as an energetic young person, to discover your chief weakness and attack it so soon" (19). Ironically, Jean uses the same tactics on Gerald that she used on Edward's horse—luring him to her while pretending to ignore him. Gradually, Jean becomes the angel in the Coventry house, creating "a happy circle" from which only the suspicious Gerald and the jealous Lucia are excluded. Bella's study becomes the center of the household, where Edward, Mrs. Coventry, and Sir John gather to hear Jean's songs and stories. But the family shrine becomes a private stage upon which Jean performs not so much to those within the room, who in fact become her supporting cast, as to those outside it. "Before long Coventry fell into a habit of strolling out upon the terrace of an evening, and amusing himself by passing and repassing the window of Bella's room" (26). Almost imperceptibly Gerald is drawn out of his role as reluctant spectator and into that of romantic lead opposite Jean Muir.

Jean effects this transformation by appealing to closely related aspects of Gerald's nature: his love of power and his latent sensuality. First, she flatters his masculine pride by confiding in Gerald as master of the house and by exhorting him to act more like one. On the one hand, Jean acknowledges Gerald as her master with a "sweet, submissive intonation . . . expressive of the respect, regard, and confidence which men find pleasantest" (44); on the other hand, she reminds him of his neglected duties: "He saw his fault, regretted it, and admired the brave sincerity of the girl in telling him of it" (31). Jean's "witchery," a word both Rochester and Gerald use to describe the mysterious charm of Jane and Jean, actually consists, like Jane's, of a meekness that flatters male vanity and a frankness that, because a legitimate if unconventional exercise of woman's edifying influence, seems not to challenge but rather to confirm masculine authority. Such witchery, however, in fact enables female mastery.

Like Jane Eyre, Jean is adept at playing little woman and sexual temptress simultaneously. And in this regard she approximates the impossible ideal that identifies women with the art of sculpture. In a remarkable episode Alcott communicates Jean's—and her own—understanding of Victorian eroticism. Gerald, having been wounded by his jealous brother, lies passive while Jean bathes his face, smoothes his hair, sings to him, and finally, on the pretext of inducing sleep, massages his hand. In order to do so, Jean "sat down behind the curtain and remained as mute and motionless as a statue . . . soon a subtle warmth seemed to steal from the soft palms that enclosed his own, his heart beat quicker, his breath grew unequal, and a thousand fancies danced through his brain" (40). Mute, motionless, and statuelike, Jean arouses Gerald while keeping her own sexuality curtained or masked. Warmly sympathetic with human suffering yet coolly oblivious to passion, Jean allays Gerald's suspicions and enables a guilt-free response. Not coincidentally, Jean finally seduces Gerald by means of a tableau vivant, an art form that, as its name suggests, shares the paradoxical attributes of sculpture. As Jean, playing a Puritan maid, embraces Gerald, her Cavalier lover, to protect him from the Roundheads, he feels an emotion foreshadowed by his sickroom sensations. Hitherto he had been "quite unconscious of the power which a woman possesses and knows how to use." Now, "a maiden heart throbbing against his cheek, for the first time in his life he felt the indescribable spell of womanhood."

Jean, in turn, "felt his hands tremble, saw the color flash into his cheek, knew that she had touched him at last, and . . . rose . . . with a sense of triumph which she found it hard to conceal" (53). Frozen into immobility in her role as Puritan maid, Jean is decorative and decorous but nonetheless provocative of sexual desire.

Gerald's posture in the two scenes described above, reclining and clinging as a woman comforts and protects him, points to an interesting feature of Alcott's work—the frequent reversal of gender roles for the purpose of exposing women's plight.[4] From the beginning Jean is the adventurer, intent on making her fortune; Gerald and Edward—like Sybil's cousin Guy, Geoffrey Moor, and Laurie in *Little Women*—are waiting for something or someone to give direction to their lives. Edward, the younger son, must wait for Gerald to obtain him a commission. As Bella reminds Gerald, "he chafes and is unhappy being dependent on you. Mamma and I don't mind; but he is a man, and it frets him" (21–22). While Bella's comment ostensibly distinguishes between male and female natures, it also serves to remind us that most women are in the position that Edward finds intolerable. In fact, Edward's infatuation with the older woman, Jean Muir, resembles the infatuation of Sylvia Yule with the older man, Adam Warwick; both Edward and Sylvia are susceptible to romance for lack of any other preoccupation. As Gerald says of Edward, "What could you expect of a romantic boy who had nothing to do but lose his heart to the first attractive woman he met?" Jean, in rejoining, seems to speak for women as much as she does for Edward: "If the 'romantic boy' had been allowed to lead the life of a man, as he longed to do, he would have had no time to lose his heart" (30–31).

Gerald, even more than Edward, seems to mirror the plight of Victorian women. Although he is the elder son, thus heir to the estate, he is as lethargic as his brother is restless. He admits that energy is attractive but protests "how the deuce *can* a man be energetic, with nothing to expend his energies upon?" (22). Gerald also lacks energy because, like Bazil Yorke and Cecil Stein, he is sexually repressed. In another scene reminiscent of *Jane Eyre,* Jean analyzes Gerald's character much as Rochester, disguised as a gypsy fortune-teller, analyzes Jane's. Just as Rochester tells Jane, "You are cold, because you are alone: no contact strikes the fire from you that is in you" (173), Jean tells Gerald that "under the ice I see fire, and warn you to beware lest it prove a volcano." Gerald, caught off guard, then confesses in such a way as to ally himself not only with his brother but with

Jean as well: "You are right! I am not what I seem, and my indolent indifference is but the mask under which I conceal my real self. I could be passionate, as energetic and aspiring as Ned, if I had any aim in life" (56–57). Jean, with her "fatal power of reading character" (56), unmasks Gerald as a kind of marble woman.

Jean Muir's name and that of her rival, Lucia Beaufort, suggest that women must not only immure their feelings but defend themselves against various slights, insults, and wounds. The beautiful Lucia fails to hold Gerald largely because she cannot conceal her love for him and her jealousy of Jean. She cannot feign the indifference, even contempt, that Jean feels for him and hence uses to attract him. When Gerald finally asks to be released from their engagement, Lucia retreats to her room; only Jean knows "in her own woman's heart how deeply Lucia's must have been wounded" (85). Jean's understanding of Lucia is based upon experience. The night of her arrival, Jean, on retiring to the privacy of her room, "half uncovered her breast to eye with a terrible glance the scar of a newly healed wound" (12). The wounds alluded to throughout *Behind a Mask* come to symbolize the wrongs of women, wrongs that they cannot protest but must conceal—or can only protest by doing themselves further harm.

Significantly, Jean refers to her wound when, in the process of seducing Gerald and protecting herself from exposure by Sydney, she deplores women's powerlessness. After telling Gerald that she attempted suicide to escape Sydney's efforts to coerce her into marriage, Jean appeals to him for protection: "If he menaced my life, I should not fear; but he menaces that which is dearer than life—my good name. A look, a word can tarnish it; a scornful smile, a significant shrug can do me more harm than any blow; for I am a woman—friendless, poor, and at the mercy of his tongue" (59). Although Jean lies about her relationship to Sydney and brilliantly turns his threats to her own advantage, she accurately portrays her vulnerability—and that of most women. The wound, though not inflicted to escape Sydney but to prevent him from escaping *her*, indicates that women must immolate themselves in order to propitiate men. Gerald, when he is wounded, insists on having Jean nurse him, because "she understands wounds better than anyone else in the house" (38). Thus he unwittingly connects the wounds that women inevitably suffer with their "natural" talent for binding the wounds of others.

Jean survives her wounds and even triumphs because her art enables her to disguise even as she expresses her true self. For example, Lucia's unbecoming jealousy gives Jean a chance to feign magnanimity: she piques Gerald's interest by consistently avoiding him, then when he presses for an explanation, she, with seeming reluctance, admits that she is trying to spare Lucia. But Lucia's jealousy also affords Jean an opportunity to express pain, indignation, and anger. As she explains to an astonished but admiring Gerald, "when I can bear no more, my true self breaks loose, and I defy everything. I am tired of being a cold, calm machine; it is impossible with an ardent nature like mine" (45). While this outbreak is finely calculated, it nonetheless protests the need for such unremitting calculation. Paradoxically, Jean is most herself when assuming what she pretends to be an unfamiliar role—that of actress. Prior to her tableau with Gerald, Jean plays Judith opposite a friend of his (who coincidentally resembles Sydney) in the role of Holofernes. As the curtain opens, Jean, with darkened skin and hair, startles the viewers with her transformation. "Hatred, the deepest and bitterest, was written on her sternly beautiful face, courage glowed in her glance, power spoke in the nervous grip of the slender hand that held the weapon, and the indomitable will of the woman was expressed." The narrator comments that it "was not all art: the intense detestation mingled with a savage joy that the object of her hatred was in her power was too perfect to be feigned" (51).[5] Jean resembles Judith in her determination to inflict rather than suffer wounds, and just as Judith resolved to "make my deceitful words to be their wound and stripe" (9:13), so it is primarily through words that Jean effects her triumph.

Jean Muir's art, her duplicity, as Fetterley and others have recognized, anticipates Alcott's in her children's fiction. As though to suggest a parallel between herself and Jean, Alcott makes her heroine a writer as well as an actress. Adept at intercepting letters and replacing them with forgeries, Jean boasts to her confidante, Hortense, "I can imitate almost any hand" (100). More important, she can assume almost any tone. Her masterpiece, in response to "a passionate appeal" from Edward, is "written with consummate skill" and filled with "wise argument, gentle reproof, good counsel, and friendly regard" (67). But while Jean is enjoining self-sacrifice upon one audience, and hence concealing her subversive motives, she is revealing those motives and relieving her genuine feelings to another. As Edward explains to his family upon exposing Jean, "There was a compact between the two women, that each should keep the other informed of all adventures, plots and plans, and share whatever good fortune fell to the lot of either of them. Thus Jean wrote freely." These letters convince the horrified Coventrys that Jean possesses "the art of the devil" (97).[6]

Edward, on exposing Jean, claims that "her own letters convict her" (97), but the purpose they ultimately serve is that of convicting the Coventrys themselves. Jean's letters to Hortense convey the unvarnished truth about every member of the Coventry family, and what begins as a revelation of Jean's character becomes an indictment of their own. Jean describes "the indolence of Monsieur the young master," who lets Lucia "worship him, like an inanimate idol as he is" (98). She depicts Sir John's worship of property—"His estate is his idol" (99)—and birth. And she boasts of having exploited the snobbery of both men by pretending to be of noble blood: "both felt the most chivalrous compassion for Lady Howard's daughter, though before they had secretly looked down on me, and my real poverty and lowliness" (100). During Edward's reading of the letters, all are mortified, but Lucia and Gerald have to suffer Jean's contempt for "this lover who has proved himself false to brother, mistress, and his own conscience" (101). Although Jean wrote the letters for her own amusement and relief, as a kind of salve for her secret wound, she could have contrived no better revenge on the Coventrys. Too late to prevent her marriage to Sir John, Edward, in his effort to unmask Jean, strips the mask from his kinsmen and himself, exposing "what fools men are" (101).

The rediscovery of Alcott's sensation fiction, the removal of the pseudonymous mask she wore so long, corresponds to the discovery of Jean's letters. Both Jean, as little woman, and Alcott, as the creator of little women, are revealed as consummate actresses—the one posing as angel in the house, the other as angel in the house of fiction. Jean, on her arrival at the Coventrys', insists on making tea for the family out of ostensible eagerness to "assume my duty at once, and serve you all. I understand the art of making people comfortable in this way" (8). Just as Jean hides self-interest behind a mask of duty, lulls her audience into complacency, and sustains an institution—the family—at which she looks askance, so Alcott seems to have catered to a reading public whose values she pretended to share or adopted under duress. Thus both Jean and her creator are accused of betraying their sex; but whereas Edward would convict Jean of betraying the values of True Womanhood, some would convict Alcott, in *Little Women* and its sequels, of betraying her feminist values.[7] Such a reading gains further credence from the nature of Jean's triumph, for the prize she wins, marriage to Sir John Coventry, condemns her to play in earnest the part she assumed in bitter jest. As though genuinely convinced of her unworthiness to marry Sir John, Jean takes "upon herself the vows of a wife with more than a bride's usual docility" (95) and "solemnly" promises the Coventrys to devote herself to his happiness. The removal of Jean's ironic mask, then, seems to predict Alcott's rejection of pseudonymity and the freedom it offered; Jean's transformation from sensation to domestic heroine seems to predict Alcott's corresponding change in genre; and Jean's exchange of irreverent audacities for conventional pieties seems to herald the platitudinous prose some readers deplore in *Little Women.*

Jean's final words in *Behind a Mask,* however, suggest an unregenerate nature: "Pausing an instant on the threshold before she vanished from their sight, she looked backward, and fixing on Gerald the strange glance he remembered well, she said in her penetrating voice, 'Is not the last scene better than the first?'" (104). Alcott's children's fiction may not be "better" than her sensation fiction, but it is no anticlimax. Just as Jean's letters enable the Coventrys, in retrospect, to see how she manipulated her domestic role, so *Behind a Mask* should alert us to the subversive potentiality of domestic fiction. In her last letter to Hortense, Jean writes: "Wishing to bring Monsieur's affair to a successful crisis, I got up a theatrical evening and was in my element" (100). This one sentence sums up Jean's economic necessity, her opposition to patriarchy, her creative energy, and her artistic self-fulfillment. In the context of a private home, a home in which she holds a precarious and menial position, Jean nonetheless exercises her talents and expresses her emotions. So too Alcott would find her element, become "a perfect mistress of her art," by getting up theatricals—and other subversive entertainments—within the domestic realm of children's fiction. Lucia cannot believe a woman wrote Jean's letters, nor could she believe that the frail, pallid governess was capable of portraying the fiery Judith; knowing that Alcott wrote *Behind a Mask,* we should be less incredulous to find a subversive artist in the guise of "the children's friend."

CHAPTER 5

"Portrait(s) of the Artist": Little Women

It was all very well to insist that art was art and had no sex, but the fact was that the days of men were not in the same way fragmented, atomized by indefinite small tasks. There was such a thing as woman's work and it consisted chiefly . . . in being able to stand constant interruption and keep your temper. Each single day she fought a war to get to her desk before her little bundle of energy had been dissipated, to push aside or cut through an intricate web of slight threads pulling her in a thousand directions.

May Sarton,
Mrs. Stevens Hears the Mermaids Singing (18)

My ideals of art are those with which marriage is perfectly incompatible. Success—for a woman—means absolute surrender, in whatever direction. Whether she paints a picture, or loves a man, there is no division of labor possible in her economy. To the attainment of any end worth living for, a symmetrical sacrifice of her nature is compulsory upon her. I do not say that this was meant to be so. I do not think we know what was meant for women. It is enough that it *is* so.

Elizabeth Stuart Phelps,
The Story of Avis (69–70)

Jean Muir's ability to ingratiate herself with the adolescent Bella and her mother anticipates Alcott's phenomenal success in *Little Women* (1868–69), the book that has kept her reputation alive throughout the twentieth century. Paid to educate, edify, and entertain the daughter of the household, Jean transforms dull lessons into lively fun, gently corrects breaches of propriety, and encourages plenty of fresh air and exercise as well as conventional occupations such as needlework. In the evenings she captivates the whole family by singing, playing, reading aloud, and telling stories. Little wonder that Bella "soon adored her" and Mrs. Coventry comes to trust her (25); together they enable Jean to infiltrate the patriarchal family, disruption of which has been her object from the outset. Mrs. Coventry at last comes to understand her purpose, for as Edward reads aloud Jean's letters, she "clasped her daughter in her arms, as if Jean Muir would burst in to annihilate the whole family" (102). Yet despite this understanding, she, no more than Bella, can wholly condemn Jean. After the governess's exposure, "Bella half put out her hand, and Mrs. Coventry sobbed as if some regret mingled with her resentment" (104). Bella's previous admiration for Jean as Judith—"Oh, isn't she splendid?" (61)—suggests that she extends her hand not to the defrocked governess but to the daring insurgent. Alcott's splendor as a juvenile writer, I would argue, derives from just such insurgency.

Jean Muir provided Alcott with a model when, two years later, she was asked by Thomas Niles of Roberts Brothers to produce a "girls' story," but *Little Women* had other precursors.[1] "A Modern Cinderella" (1860) and "Psyche's Art" (1868), both based on the Alcott family, also deal with the conflict between art (or some other fulfilling occupation) and life as constituted by romantic love and domestic responsibility.[2] *Little Women,* though it finally becomes Jo's story, contains portraits of all four Alcott sisters: Meg March, like Anna Alcott, is domestic; Jo, like Louisa, is a tomboy and writer; Beth, like Elizabeth, is frail; and Amy, like May, is charming and artistic. "A Modern Cinderella" seems to have been written as a tribute to Anna Alcott, for the self-centered literary and artistic sisters, Diana and Laura, are subordinated to Nan, called "little woman" and "Martha" by her father and "my 'angel in the house'" by the hero, modeled on Anna's husband, John Pratt. "Psyche's Art" was perhaps designed as a similar tribute to May Alcott, though her name is given to the dying sister of the heroine, who is called Psyche, Bronson's name for Elizabeth.[3]

Although the number of sisters in these stories varies from two to four, certain elements remain constant: in each a sister (Beth, Nan, Psyche) sacrifices her own interests to those of her family; in each one or more sisters (Jo, Diana and Laura, Psyche) learns to put "that humbler and more human teacher, Duty" before "the goddess Beauty" ("Cinderella" 286); in each a sister (Beth, Nan, May) sickens, Nan and Beth as a result of their sacrifices. Finally, as the artists learn to subordinate their needs to those of their families, their art becomes less heroic and ambitious, more domestic and humble: Diana resolves to "turn my books and pen to some account, and write stories of dear old souls like you [the hero] and Nan" (292); Jo likewise writes homely stories about ordinary people, and like Psyche, whose sister also dies, she resumes her art at the urging of the family, finding in it solace for her grief.[4] The lesson of these female artists, then, appears to be the lesson that Alcott supposedly learned: to subordinate their needs for artistic expression to the needs of their families and to use their artistic talents for the benefit not only of their own families but of the family as an institution.

The lesson in "Psyche's Art," however, is ambiguous. As though anticipating the furor over her refusal in *Little Women* to marry Jo to Laurie, Alcott equivocates as to the fate of Psyche and her fellow sculptor, Paul Gage: "Those who prefer the good old fashion may believe that the hero and heroine fell in love, were married and lived happily ever afterward. But those who can conceive of a world outside of a wedding-ring may believe that the friends remained faithful friends all their lives, while Paul won fame and fortune, and Psyche grew beautiful with the beauty of a serene and sunny nature, happy in duties which became pleasures, rich in the art which made life lovely to herself and others" (226). Of course one might argue that the ending Alcott obviously prefers is itself ambiguous. Is Psyche's art— "the art which made life lovely to herself and others"—her sculpture or merely the feminine art of pleasing and serving?[5] From what Psyche tells Paul in the final scene, the latter appears unlikely. Although her mother believes that she has forsaken sculpture, Psyche assures Paul that "when my leisure does come I shall know how to use it, for my head is full of ambitious plans, and I feel that I can do something now" (225). In other words, a year's devotion to domestic responsibility has served to confirm her commitment to her art. But what then do we make of the disparity between Paul's career and Psyche's? Is hers a minor talent exercised for the pleasure of a private audience—domestic, decorative, gratifying in its modesty and lack of pretension? Is Psyche resigned to view her art as an extension of the domestic sphere rather than as an alternative to it?

Psyche learns that a life of artistic achievement cannot be gracefully combined with a life of domestic responsibility. But she also learns that domestic life can offer a humanizing vision as well as legitimate subjects for art. At first she tries to employ her sister May as a model, but the dying child's fretfulness soon forces Psyche to acknowledge the opposition between her role as artist and that of caregiver. But while May obstructs Psyche's progress in one way, she facilitates it in another, for her inability to pose, to become an object, forces Psyche to see her more clearly than she has seen anything before. When, after May's death, Psyche resumes her work, she produces something "lovely in its simple grace and truth." This figure, "a child looking upward as if watching the airy flight of some butterfly which had evidently escaped from the chrysalis still lying in the little hand" (222), is most obviously a tribute to May and represents her soul's release. On another level, however, it represents the release of Psyche's creative spirit from its uneasy alliance with domesticity, though she has learned from domestic experience to see things whole.[6] "Psyche's Art," then, shows how temporary immersion in family life, such as Alcott herself often experienced, can serve to warn the female artist of the dangers of lifelong commitment to that sphere.[7] At the same time, it suggests how the traditional experiences of women can enrich their art.

"Psyche's Art" begins "once upon a time," as does a brilliant self-reflexive passage in *Little Women*. In an early chapter entitled "Burdens," Mrs. March, or Marmee, tells her girls a story that is the book in microcosm:

"Once upon a time there were four girls, who had enough to eat, and drink, and wear; a good many comforts and pleasures, kind friends and parents, who loved them dearly, and yet they were not contented." (Here the listeners stole sly looks at one another, and began to sew diligently.) "These girls were anxious to be good, and made many excellent resolutions, but somehow they did not keep them very well, and were constantly saying, 'If only we had this,' or 'if we could only do that,' quite forgetting how much they already had, and how many pleasant things they actually could do; so they asked an old woman what spell they could use to make them happy, and she said, 'When you feel discontented, think over your blessings, and be grateful.'" (Here Jo looked up quickly, as if about to speak, but changed her mind, seeing that the story was not done yet.)

"Being sensible girls, they decided to try her advice, and soon were surprised to see how well off they were. One discovered that money couldn't keep shame and sorrow out of rich people's houses; another that though she was poor, she was a great deal happier with her youth, health, and good spirits, than a certain fretful, feeble old lady, who couldn't enjoy her comforts; a third, that, disagreeable as it was to help get dinner, it was harder still to have to go begging for it; and the fourth, that even carnelian rings were not so valuable as good behavior. So they agreed to stop complaining, to enjoy the blessings already possessed, and try to deserve them, lest they should be taken away entirely, instead of increased; and I believe they were never disappointed, or sorry that they took the old woman's advice."

"Now, Marmee, that is very cunning of you to turn our own stories against us, and give us a sermon instead of a 'spin,'" cried Meg.

"I like that kind of sermon; it's the sort father used to tell us," said Beth, thoughtfully, putting the needles straight on Jo's cushion.

"I don't complain near as much as the others do, and I shall be more careful than ever now, for I've had warning from Susie's downfall," said Amy, morally.

"We needed that lesson, and we won't forget it. If we do, you just say to us as Old Chloe did in Uncle Tom,—'Tink ob yer marcies, chillen, tink ob yer marcies,'" added Jo, who could not for the life of her help getting a morsel of fun out of the little sermon, though she took it to heart as much as any of them. (58–59)

Marmee's story incorporates the experiences that her daughters have already related and thus recapitulates the chapter it concludes. It also embodies the same theme and employs the same method as the book as a whole: as *Little Women* continues, the four girls learn, under Marmee's tutelage, to moderate their longings and aspirations, to resign themselves to or content themselves with the choices available to them; and just as Marmee moves from the girls as individuals to the girls as a group and back again, so Alcott devotes a chapter to each in turn, then a chapter to the entire family, and so on throughout the book. Finally, Marmee's story and her daughters' responses to it suggest Alcott's relationship with her audience. It engages the girls' attention because, for all its "spin" or fairy-tale elements, it recognizably depicts the teller's and the listeners' lives. But their different reactions to it indicate different ways of reading the larger story. Simple Beth is content with what she takes to be a patriarchal sermon. Pleasure-loving Meg feels somewhat betrayed to find an exemplum masquerading as entertainment. Rebellious Jo attempts to subvert the sermon with blackface humor but, by alluding to *Uncle Tom's Cabin,* she inadvertently likens the girls and their mother to slaves. Thereby, Alcott invites at least some among her readers to transform the larger story into a different kind of sermon, a vehement protest against servitude and oppression.[8]

As Amy Lang writes of *Uncle Tom's Cabin,* "home [or the domestic sphere] fails as a *viable* alternative to this world because it is, finally, a contingent sphere, shaping itself in response to the male world outside it" (53). From the very first page of *Little Women,* Alcott makes clear the contingent nature of the March home. The novel opens with the March sisters preparing to sacrifice Christmas presents for themselves in order to purchase gifts for their mother, Marmee. But this sacrifice is not entirely self-initiated; it is prompted by Marmee's belief that "we ought not to spend money for pleasure, when our men are suffering so in the army" (7). In other words, this sacrifice within the home is exacted by the actions of men outside it. Later in the chapter the girls receive a letter from their absent father, a Union army chaplain, exhorting them to "fight their bosom enemies bravely, and conquer themselves so beautifully, that when I come back to them I may be fonder and prouder than ever of my little women" (16). This letter prompts Marmee to recommend that the girls play in earnest their childhood game of Pilgrim's Progress. She reminds them of how they used to "travel through the house from the cellar, which was the City of Destruction, up, up, to the housetop, where you had all the lovely things you could collect to make a Celestial City" (17). When twelve-year-old Amy claims to be too old for such games, Marmee reproves her: "We never are too old for this, my dear, because it is a game we are playing all the time in one way or another. . . . see how far on you can get before father comes home" (18). Marmee's words imply not only that life is a spiritual journey but that women's pilgrimage is merely a game, an imitation of men's, and that it takes place within the confines of the home for the purpose of winning male approval. Women can expand their constricted sphere only through the exercise of their imaginations, as when the March girls divide the sheets they are sewing into continents and "talked about the different countries as they stitched their way through them" (19).

Playing, pretending, acting—these activities loom large in the lives of the March girls and would seem to offer compensation for and temporary liberation from poverty, irksome tasks, and, above all, the constricting roles of little women.[9] Jo complains, "I can't get over my disappointment in not being a boy" (10), but her dramas allow her to play "male parts to her heart's content" (25). Even Jo's plays, however, serve to suggest the girls' entrapment. In "The Witch's Curse" Jo plays both the hero and the villain, an indication not only of her longing for male freedom and her major role in the larger drama of *Little Women* but also of her self-divided nature. Meg, the most conventional of the girls and the quickest to reprove Jo, plays both the witch, whose curse destroys the villain, and Don Pedro, "the cruel sire," whose patriarchal authority would thwart the hero. The casting of the youngest, Amy, as the heroine and her wooden performance in that role indicate its unchallenging and stultifying nature. Finally, Beth plays a "stout little retainer" (29), the part she habitually assumes in the March household, but also an ugly black imp, which implies a darker side to the retainer role. The futility of Jo's efforts to simulate the male world from which she is excluded becomes apparent at a meeting of the girls' Pickwick Club. When Jo recommends admitting Laurie, the boy next door, Meg and Amy object: "We don't wish any boys; they only joke and bounce about. This is a ladies' club, and we wish to be private and proper" (131).

By learning to make believe and play various parts, the girls are rehearsing for the games and roles they will, as Marmee says, be playing all their lives. Significantly, conventional Meg, not passionate Jo or stubborn Amy, is described as the most accomplished actress. Although she professes to be too grown-up to continue acting in Jo's productions, she is simply ready to play the part in life assigned her, a part for which, more than her self-assertive sisters, she has a talent. Yet all the girls, whether reluctantly or enthusiastically, must rehearse their lines in a domestic script. In a sense they are always on stage, performing for a male audience, for as Laurie tells Jo, "sometimes you forget to put down the curtain . . . and, when the lamps are lighted, it's like looking at a picture to see the fire, and you all round the table with your mother" (65).

A party scene early in *Little Women* points up both the opposition between

Meg and Jo, implied by their adversarial roles in "The Witch's Curse," and the nature of the part that Meg is eager to play—that of "a real lady." Meg, concerned that Jo's party dress is scorched in back from standing too close to the fire, warns her to "sit still all you can, and keep your back out of sight" (34). Because Jo has soiled her gloves, and because, according to Meg, "a real lady is always known by neat boots, gloves, and handkerchief" (37), she must wear one of Meg's, even though her hand is larger and will stretch it, while carrying one of her own. Girls like Jo, who burn their frocks and soil their gloves, who, in other words, are too full of passion and life, must acquire the art of concealment. But that art, uncomfortable in itself, can lead to further suffering. Meg, whose "tight slippers tripped about so briskly that none would have guessed the pain their wearer suffered smilingly" (38), pays for her dubious pleasure with a sprained ankle. Before Meg's accident, however, Jo meets Laurie, forgets the need to conceal her dress, and dances a spirited polka. But her few moments of exhilaration simply sharpen the images of pain, concealment, and constriction. Thus her comment on the evening, "I don't believe fine young ladies enjoy themselves a bit more than we do," can be read ironically, as can the narrator's aside, "And I think Jo was quite right" (45).

Such ambiguity is typical of Alcott's narrator even when she seems to be affirming the life of selfless service and patient, silent suffering. In one of the many passages that have been read as "a sweet sermon on self-sacrifice," the narrator seems to glorify Beth's passive, retainer role: "There are many Beths in the world, shy and quiet, sitting in corners till needed, and living for others so cheerfully, that no one sees the sacrifices till the little cricket on the hearth stops chirping, and the sweet, sunshiny presence vanishes, leaving silence and shadow behind" (53). Yet "silence and shadow" seems as much a description of the living Beth, the black imp, as of the void left by her dying. Marmee's moralistic judgments are similarly undercut by the situations that prompt them. The chapter "Burdens," which culminates in Marmee's "sermon," contains stories of women's ignorance, passivity, vulnerability, and dependence. Jo discovers that she is lucky, because, unlike her crotchety Aunt March, she can appreciate the magnificent library "left to dust and spiders" since her uncle's death. Meg concludes that she is luckier than the wealthy family she serves as governess because she hasn't "any wild brothers to do wicked things, and disgrace the family" (56). Amy stops envying a friend when that friend is punished in a most humiliating way for having made a caricature of the schoolmaster. And Beth marvels at the goodness of Mr. Laurence, who presented a big fish to a poor woman unable to feed her family. Each girl recognizes her comparative good fortune, and Marmee, by emphasizing their blessings, reinforces their complacency. But the stories themselves tell of women's intellectual and economic deprivation and their vulnerability to disgrace and humiliation. Thus in a sense Marmee's "sermon" can be read as a "spin," a glossing over of women's plight that, as Meg suggests, turns their own stories against them.[10]

While Jo is privileged compared with her Aunt March, her very privilege—her ability to penetrate male preserves such as her uncle's library—leads to conflict between her androgynous nature as mirrored by Laurie and her feminine role as modeled by Meg and Marmee. Confined, almost imprisoned, in the big house next door, Laurie is freed by Jo in a reversal of the Sleeping Beauty tale. In boldly entering the house that she regards as "a kind of enchanted palace, full of splendors and delights," and by confronting gruff old Mr. Laurence, Jo seems to be appropriating male power and freeing a part of her own nature. In fact, the shabby old brown house containing the five women—what Mr. Laurence calls "that little nunnery over there" (75)—and the stately but lifeless stone mansion containing Laurie, his grandfather, and his tutor, John Brooke, can be seen as representing feminine and masculine spheres. Jo and Laurie, whose friendship brings the spheres into contact and thus enlarges both of them, seem to make up a whole, androgynous person; Jo's nickname expresses her longing for masculine freedom and independence, whereas Laurie's nickname, "Dora," and even "Laurie" itself suggest the feminine in his nature, the kinship with his artist mother. Although Jo draws him into the March girls' charmed circle,[11] she also brings out the manliness in "Teddy," as she alone calls him, for as Mr. Laurence observes, "she seemed to understand the boy almost as well as if she had been one herself" (70).

Androgynous as he is, Laurie, like Jo, finds his entrapment in gender-role stereotypes especially galling. Laurie's "castle in the air" is "to be a famous musician . . . never to be bothered about money or business" (177). But Laurie's grandfather equates business with masculinity and Laurie's interest in art and music with effeminacy. Ironically, Mr. Laurence's efforts to ensure that his grandson prove his manhood by taking over the family business keep Laurie as sheltered from the world as any girl. In a sense Laurie, like Guy in "A Whisper in the Dark" and the Coventry brothers in *Behind a Mask*, exemplifies (as the reversal of the

Sleeping Beauty tale suggests) not only the masculine plight but the feminine. Like a woman, he is dependent on and subservient to a patriarchal figure, who in turn depends upon his subject for love. As Meg tells Laurie when he is encouraged by Jo to rebel: "you should do just what your grandfather wishes. . . . As you say, there is no one else to stay with and love him." We are told that Laurie "had a young man's hatred of subjection" (180), and we are left to infer that it is no more natural or legitimate than Jo's.

Laurie and Jo enable each other to temporarily escape entrapment in gender-role stereotypes. From their first meeting Laurie allows Jo to be her full self and offers her the male camaraderie for which she has always longed. In nominating Laurie for membership in the Pickwick Club, Jo argues that he will "give a tone to our contributions, and keep us from being sentimental" (132), and once admitted he inspires her to revise "her own works with good effect" (134). Laurie not only accepts, encourages, and provides a model for the development of Jo's masculine side; he also elicits and nurtures the feminine. On Jo's first visit to the "enchanted palace," she enters like a male hero but presents herself to Laurie as a nurse. Later, when Beth lies critically ill, Jo, despite her belief that "tears were an unmanly weakness" (97), allows herself to break down in Laurie's presence and be comforted by him. And though Jo's bracing companionship has tended to make him more manly, Laurie has learned, through contact with the feminine household, how to offer maternal support. In words that recall Marmee's on another occasion, he says, "I'm here, hold on to me, Jo, dear," and silently strokes "her bent head as her mother used to do" (228). In short, the friendship of Jo and Laurie seems to provide the best of both spheres—masculine strength and freedom from sentimentality with feminine sympathy. Later, when Jo, for reasons she finds difficult to explain, rejects Laurie's proposal of marriage, she feels "as if she had stabbed her dearest friend; and when he left her, without a look behind him, she knew that the boy Laurie never would come again" (455). The description of this parting makes it clear that Jo has betrayed not only a friend but a crucial part of herself that she cannot hope to recover. In refusing to marry Jo to Laurie, Alcott conveys her recognition that in society as it was then constituted such androgynous wholeness as would have been theirs—and as she had symbolically envisioned in *Moods* and *A Marble Woman*—was impossible.

The boy in Jo, as represented by Laurie, is successfully opposed by Meg, Beth, and Marmee. Meg and Jo, as the two eldest sisters, have a special relationship rather like that of Jane and Elizabeth Bennet in *Pride and Prejudice*. But unlike Austen's heroines, Alcott's are always at odds. Jo's "good, strong words, that mean something" are "dreadful expressions" to Meg (48); Jo enters the "enchanted palace" for the first time partly because she loves "scandalizing Meg by her queer performances" (61). Jo in turn is scandalized rather than delighted when, breaking in on Meg and her suitor John Brooke, she finds "the strong-minded sister enthroned upon his knee, and wearing an expression of the most abject submission" (286). In Jo's play, we remember, Meg plays the witch and Don Pedro, the symbol of patriarchal authority. In her unquestioning submission to that authority and in her affinity for the traditional female role, she does represent a curse and a threat. Like the benign witch in the play, Meg opposes what to her seems villainous or shocking in Jo, but, like Don Pedro, she also opposes what is heroic and creative. She does not realize that to subdue the one is to stifle the other. As the model lady, wife, and finally mother, Meg embodies the patriarchal pattern imposed on women that Jo wants desperately to escape.

Meg, while much tamer than Sybil, Sylvia, and Cecil, is akin to those adolescent heroines. The description of her simultaneously enthroned and submissive after accepting John's proposal reminds us of the illusory sense of power that Sybil sought in courtship, and the image of her perched upon his knee suggests that marriage will perpetuate her childhood as it did Sylvia's and Cecil's. Just as Sylvia "seemed most like a child" when "learning to be a woman," so Meg's initiation into womanhood coincides with a retreat into childhood. As a house guest of the worldly Moffats, Meg suddenly finds herself regarded as a marriageable young woman. In order to deny rumors about her and Laurie, she protests that he "is only a little boy" and that "it is quite natural that we children should play together" (112). Trying to decline the offer of a low-cut gown, Meg claims that "my old dress ...does well enough for a little girl like me" (113). Forced to wear the sophisticated and revealing costume, Meg survives the evening by imagining herself "acting the new part of fine lady" (116). Like Cecil after the ball at which she impersonates a radiant bride, Meg goes to bed "feeling as if she had been to a masquerade" (120). Afterward a chastened Meg confesses to Marmee that she has been "a silly little girl," but Jo rightly recognizes that, compromised, contrite, and childlike as she is, "during that fortnight her sister had grown up amazingly, and was drifting away from her into a world where she could not follow" (122).

Jo wishes that "wearing flatirons on our heads could keep us from growing up" (252), but the only apparent alternative to adult womanhood and the childlike submission it entails is to remain genuinely childlike, as Beth does. Lacking both Meg's willingness to conform and Jo's will to resist, Beth simply remains fixed in her role as "Little Faithful." In one of the many significant juxtapositions in *Little Women,* Beth enters the "Palace Beautiful" shortly after Jo's first visit to the "enchanted palace." But whereas Jo enters boldly, without a formal invitation, Beth creeps in only after being assured that no one will see her. She is as drawn to the grand piano as Jo is to the library, but Mr. Laurence, recognizing that her timidity almost cancels out her pleasure, provides her with a "cabinet piano" so that she can remain at home. Yet, despite her meekness, "over her big, harum-scarum sister Beth unconsciously exercised more influence than anyone in the family" (54). Jo refers to Beth as her "conscience," and when she rests her head on Beth's hood "the submissive spirit of its gentle owner seemed to enter into Jo" (229). As Jo's conscience, Beth, as in the play, is both Jo's retainer and her black imp. Her model of submissiveness is more subtle and insidious than Meg's because Jo is not aware of a need to struggle against it.

Marmee, who admits to being "angry nearly every day of my life" (101) and who has "never enjoyed housekeeping" (141), teaches, ironically, the self-repression that Beth alone has completely achieved, as well as the feminine and domestic virtues so easily acquired by Meg. When Jo asks how she has learned to "keep still" when angered, Marmee explains that Jo's father made "it easy to be good" (101–2). But Marmee's later advice to Meg on the necessity of controlling her temper so as not to provoke her husband's suggests that men do not so much make it easy to be good as demand it.[12] Despite her tacit admission of women's subordinate position in marriage, Marmee insists that "To be loved and chosen by a good man is the best and sweetest thing which can happen to a woman" (123).[13] By virtually denying her daughters other choices and by repressing the parts of themselves that would make other choices available, Marmee keeps her daughters dependent, undeveloped, diminutive—like Beth, who literally fails to attain adulthood.

Marmee allows, even encourages, the girls' childish dependency, but she would deny the child who seeks her own gratification. Amy, the "spoiled" baby of the family, is to Jo's chagrin the most insistent in her claim to adult privileges.[14] When Amy wheedles Meg and Jo to let her accompany them to the theater, Jo refuses, calling her a little girl and a baby. Amy warns that Jo will be sorry and promptly destroys Jo's "loving work of several years" (96). Jo is unable to forgive her and later, when Amy tags after her and Laurie, spitefully neglects to warn her of the thin ice through which she falls. In excluding, punishing, and nearly killing Amy, Jo seems trying to rid herself of the needy, greedy, demanding, and childish nature that nonetheless drives one to adult achievement and the achievement of adulthood. The destruction of Jo's book and her agony of remorse after the accident suggest, like Bazil Yorke's attempts to banish Germain, the futility and danger of denying one's natural impulses.[15] Just as Amy was the heroine in Jo's play, the issue at stake between the hero and the villain, so she seems to represent something crucial in Jo's nature, something toward which Jo is deeply ambivalent. Unfortunately, Jo and Marmee see this episode as calling for more repression rather than for a recognition of the feelings that prompted it.

Jo, unlike her sisters, consciously aspires to independence, but she internalizes her mother's values to the point that she cannot seek it without guilt. Jo views the publication of her first story as the first step in realizing "the dearest wishes of her heart"—"to be independent, and earn the praise of those she loved" (194). But the two wishes are conflicting, if not incompatible: to achieve independence she will have to assert herself in such a way as to incur blame; and to win the praise of those she loves best, she will have to curtail, or at least modify, her striving for independence. When Meg is staying with the Moffats, she slips Marmee's note "into her pocket as a sort of talisman against envy, vanity, and false pride" (109). Similarly, Jo pins Marmee's note "inside her frock, as a shield and reminder, lest she be taken unaware" (151). Jo must guard against her emotions at all times; otherwise she will disappoint her mother and, through her, her father. When, upon his return, Mr. March praises Jo, causing her to blush with pleasure, it is for having become "a young lady who pins her collar straight, laces her boots neatly, and neither whistles, talks slang, nor lies on the rug, as she used to do" (274)—in short, a lady as defined earlier by Meg.

Meg's marriage, as described in part 2 (originally entitled "Good Wives"), exemplifies the constriction—physical, mental, and emotional—to which even Jo finally adapts. The lawn of Meg's home, which she calls "my baby-house," is "about as big as a pocket-handkerchief," and her dining room is described as a "tight fit" (301, 297). Just as Meg earlier had to smile although her slippers pinched her feet, so now she must gracefully, even gratefully, accept her cramped and narrow lot in life. While John takes "the cares of the head of a family upon his shoulders" (338), Meg's greatest challenge is the making of jelly. Her failure touches off the one quarrel we witness between John and Meg, during which she declares, "I'm away—sick, dead, anything" (343). Rash as these words sound, the imagery surrounding Meg's marriage does indeed suggest a living death. After the birth of her twins, Daisy and Demi, Meg complains to Marmee that she is "on the shelf." Marmee, as an exemplar of "real womanhood," exhorts Meg not to "shut yourself up in a bandbox because you are a woman" (482) but to enter, at least through reading and conversation, her husband's sphere and teach him how to help in her own. Although John succeeds in teaching *her* how to cope with their son, Demi, years of little womanhood have ill prepared Meg to share John's world of ideas, and she soon decides "that politics were as bad as mathematics" (489). After a few such "domestic experiments," Meg learns "that a woman's happiest kingdom is home"—"the sort of shelf on which young wives and mothers may consent to be laid, safe from the restless fret and fever of the world, finding loyal lovers in the little sons and daughters who cling to them" (491). The image of the shelf, the passive verb "laid," and the idea that children are the most appropriate lovers for women all imply that marriage arrests female development.[16] Just as the title of part 1, "Little Women," suggests that adolescent girls should be miniature adults, so the eventual extension of that title to part 2 suggests that "good wives" should remain little women or girls.

Meg's "loyal lovers," Daisy and Demi, perpetuate the gender stereotypes Jo tries in vain to escape.[17] At three, Daisy begins to sew and "managed a microscopic cooking-stove with a skill that brought tears of pride to Hannah's [the Marches' servant's] eyes, while Demi learned his letters with his grandfather" and "developed a mechanical genius which delighted his father" (566). Whereas Daisy demands a "needler," Demi actually tries to construct a sewing machine. Furthermore, in their relationship to each other they reflect the age-old stereotypes: "Demi tyrannized over Daisy . . . while Daisy made a galley-slave of herself, and adored her brother, as the one perfect being in the world" (567). Daisy is so angelic, such a perfect little woman, that she reminds her family of Beth. "Her grandfather often called her 'Beth,' and her grandmother watched over her with untiring devotion, as if trying to atone for some past mistake, which no eye but her own could see"

(568). Her eye fails to detect that in rewarding Beth, and now Daisy, for angelic or slavish, self-abnegating behavior the family fails to prepare them for full participation in the adult world. Ironically, it is Jo, not Daisy, who eventually succeeds Beth as "angel in the house," for in evading Laurie, she walks into the very domestic trap she had sought to avoid. Encouraged by Marmee, who believes that Jo and Laurie "are too much alike, and too fond of freedom" (407), Jo goes to New York, where, just as she is getting a taste of independence, she finds in Professor Bhaer that "something sweeter" than freedom that Marmee had wished for her (408).

Whereas Laurie had always encouraged Jo's writing without attempting to direct it, Jo's parents and, later, Professor Bhaer, are as ruthless as her opportunistic editors. While still at home Jo frequently falls into a "vortex" of creativity and, after earning several checks for her stories, begins "to feel herself a power in the house" (333). But although she enjoys both the process and the proceeds of her writing, it does not, as she had hoped, bring her the unqualified praise of those she loves. The process disturbs Marmee, who always "looked a little anxious when 'genius took to burning,'"[18] and when her sensation story wins a cash prize, her father says, "You can do better than this, Jo. Aim at the highest, and never mind the money" (332). Perhaps Jo's earnings disturb her father for the very reason they delight her: "She saw that money conferred power." But she tries to reconcile her unwomanly desire for power with her duty, as a woman, to be selfless: "money and power, therefore, she resolved to have, not to be used for herself alone, but for those she loved more than self" (425). Not content to dictate Jo's attitude toward her writing, her parents intervene in the writing process itself. In order to accommodate their criticisms of her first serious novel, Jo "laid her first-born on her table, and chopped it up as ruthlessly as any ogre" (335). Later the newspaper to which she takes her sensation stories asks her to edit out all moral reflections, causing her to feel "as a tender parent might on being asked to cut off her baby's legs in order that it might fit into a new cradle" (428). Jo's work, no less than Meg's life, must adjust itself to a "tight fit," and the strikingly similar passages equate her parents' moral with her publisher's amoral influence.

Although Professor Bhaer is described as a "genial fire" (431), he too throws a damper on Jo's creative powers. Bhaer, like John Brooke, is a tutor, and his relationship with Jo, like John's with Meg, begins in German lessons, a return for Jo's mending of his socks. For Christmas, Bhaer gives Jo what he calls a "library" between two "lids," an edition of Shakespeare, which he takes from its "place of honor, with his German Bible, Plato, Homer, and Milton"—patriarchal works and authors all. Bhaer, in giving her Shakespeare, professes to hope that "the study of character in this book will help you to read it in the world and paint it with your pen" (422–23). But as Virginia Woolf points out in *A Room of One's Own,* women cannot write like Shakespeare until, freed from the fetish of chastity, they are allowed to experience life as Shakespeare and other male authors have done (48–52).[19] Jo, under the stimulus of her sensation writing, has begun to free herself and to experience life, at least vicariously: "as thrills could not be produced except by harrowing up the souls of the readers, history and romance, land and sea, science and art, police records and lunatic asylums, had to be ransacked for the purpose" (430). As a result, Jo begins to catch "glimpses of the tragic world which underlies society," but the narrator, like Professor Bhaer, reproves her for "beginning to desecrate some of the womanliest attributes of a woman's character" (430). After Bhaer, in disgust, burns a sheet of the *Weekly Volcano* for which Jo writes, she rereads her work, feeling as though she is wearing "the Professor's mental or moral spectacles" (438). He is soon satisfied to see that Jo has "stood the test" and "given up writing" (440).

Professor Bhaer saves Jo from "the frothy sea of sensational literature" (429) only to plunge her into a slough of creative and personal despond. Having sacrificed the *Weekly Volcano* and the vortex of creativity to Bhaer's "genial fire," Jo goes on to sacrifice "my boy," as she calls Laurie, to "my Beth" and, later, "my Professor." Her reasoning—"you'd hate my scribbling, and I couldn't get on without it" (449)—seems disingenuous, for Laurie, who greeted the sale of her first story with a "Hurrah for Miss March, the celebrated American authoress!" (188), has always championed her writing. Indeed, in rejecting Laurie, Jo feels much as she did when editing her work against her better judgment—"as if she had murdered some innocent young thing, and buried it under the leaves" (450). And in turning from Laurie to her dying sister, it is as though she chooses to wed death rather than life. Jo and Beth's time together at the shore is described as a honeymoon: they are "all in all to each other . . . quite unconscious of the interest they excited in those about them" (457). Beth lies with her head in Jo's lap, and Jo's arms "instinctively tightened their hold upon the dearest treasure she possessed" (458). Before returning home, Jo, with "a silent kiss," "dedicated herself soul and body to Beth" (462), and later in a poem she asks Beth to "Give me that unselfish nature" (512). Gradually, Jo begins to feel "that

I don't lose you; that you'll be more to me than ever, and death can't part us." Beth promises, "I shall be your Beth, still" and urges Jo to take her place, assuring her, "you'll be happier in doing that, than writing splendid books, or seeing all the world." In response, "then and there Jo renounced her old ambition" and "pledged herself to a new and better one" (513).

Just as Germain's death (and in *Moods* Warwick's death) symbolized the internalization of the values he represents, so Beth's indicates that Jo has internalized the values of little womanhood.[20] After Beth dies, Jo assumes her role: she takes shelter in her mother's arms, sits in Beth's little chair close beside her father, and assumes Beth's housekeeping duties with her implements. Turning to Meg for comfort, Jo is urged to consider marriage and domesticity as a means of bringing out "the tender, womanly half" of her nature (533). Marmee, realizing it is now safe to do so, encourages Jo to "write something for us, and never mind the rest of the world" (535). After she has done so, her father mails the piece to a popular magazine, where it is accepted and much acclaimed. Jo wonders, "what *can* there be in a simple little story like that, to make people praise it so?" Her father tells her, "you have found your style at last"; but Jo demurs: "If there *is* anything good or true in what I write, it isn't mine; I owe it all to you and mother, and to Beth" (535). Jo's stories now, rather than letting "the passions have a holiday" (330), are "little stories," "humble wanderers," received by a "charitable world" and sending back "comfortable tokens to their mother, like dutiful children" (535–36). The image of the female artist as mother, her works as dutiful children, and their reception as charitable suggests Jo's withdrawal into the domestic and dependent sphere from which she had sought escape. As we have seen, illness or death of a sister affects the art of Diana in "A Modern Cinderella" and Psyche in "Psyche's Art." But Diana, in a burst of penitence, only *says* that she will modify her aspirations; Psyche, despite the commemorative nature of her bust of May, does not, like Jo, disavow her own role in creating it and, further, renews her dedication to art. Jo, in contrast, alters both her present practice and future plans, for love and approval now mean more to her than anything else in the world.[21]

More subversive than Jo, and potentially the more successful artist, is Amy, for she is not afraid to assert herself, take risks, and appear selfish or foolish. As the pampered baby of the family, she does not feel Jo's need to earn its love or avoid its disapproval. Therefore, from the beginning of the book, she is the least willing to engage in self-sacrifice. When her sisters decide to spend their Christmas dollars on presents for Marmee, Amy resolves to spend but a part of hers. (She later weakens but only for the purpose of making the most impressive display!) The most worldly of the sisters, she is also the most eager to venture out into the world or, something the others never try to do, bridge the gap between world and home. Thus Amy attends school while Beth stays home, teases to accompany the older girls on their grown-up outings, and braves their ridicule by planning a luncheon for her wealthy classmates. The only one to invite outsiders (apart from the Laurences) into the family circle, Amy is removed from that circle in times of crisis. When Beth is ill, Amy stays with Aunt March; when Beth is dying, Amy remains in Europe, where she, not Jo, satisfies a lifelong ambition to study art abroad. Even Amy's marriage to Laurie takes place there rather than in the bosom of the family as Meg's does. Perhaps most significant, in the family tableaux that end both parts of *Little Women,* Amy is a figure somewhat apart, and it is she, not Jo, who is portrayed as the artist, engaged herself in portraying the family. At the end of part 1, a scene in which everyone else is paired, "Amy was drawing the lovers" (289); at the end of part 2, Amy, albeit "with a beautiful motherly expression in her face, sketched the various groups" (598). It is as though Amy's comparative detachment from the family and its self-denying ethos frees her to record it.

Amy's subversiveness, like that of *Little Women* itself, is easy to overlook because, as in Jo's play, she appears the conventional heroine, Jo the hero. Always ladylike, Amy shrewdly defines Jo's version of independence as a desire to "go through the world with your elbows out and your nose in the air" (321). Jo's unconventionality, while genuine, is, as Amy implies, a matter of appearance and manners; she is only independent of those for whom she cares nothing. Amy, on the other hand, moderates her behavior so as to please those who can help her, but she is truly independent of her family's judgment, as when she plans her luncheon party. While Jo would flaunt her unconventionality, Amy conceals hers in order to preserve and foster her genuine independence and what would appear to be the rudiments of a feminist consciousness. Like Jean Muir, Amy recognizes women's vulnerability. As she tells Jo in preparing to pay some social calls, "Women should learn to be agreeable, particularly poor ones; for they have no other way of repaying the kindnesses they receive" (366). Not only does Amy recognize that poor women are dependent solely upon their power of pleasing; she depreciates the power so often attributed to them—the power of moral influence. Whereas Jo would show her disapproval of fast young men in an attempt to curb them, Amy denies that it would have "a particle of effect" (366). She later tells Laurie, "You men tell us we are angels, and say we can make you what we will; but the instant we honestly try to do you good, you laugh at us, and won't listen, which proves how much your flattery is worth" (502). Amy's willingness to forgo asserting her independence and to practice the art of pleasing pays dividends for her art. During a call on Aunt March and Aunt Carrol, Jo blurts out, "I don't like favors; they oppress and make me feel like a slave; I'd rather do everything for myself, and be perfectly independent" (368). Amy, by accepting patronage "when it is well meant," earns the trip to Europe that Jo has coveted.

Amy's early "artistic attempts" are treated mockingly, but even these suggest her artistic independence. For example, Amy casts her own foot and has to have it dug out of the plaster by Jo, who "was so overcome with laughter while she excavated, that her knife went too far" and "cut the poor foot" (317). The image implies that Amy puts herself into her work and that Jo, in an attempt to extricate life from art, does injury to both. Further, at the end of a long passage that seems to disparage Amy's art, the narrator adds that Amy "persevered in spite of all obstacles, failures, and discouragements, firmly believing that in time she should do something worthy to be called 'high art'" (317). Unlike Jo, Amy does not give up or modify her art in response to male criticism. By the time she again meets Laurie, who is impressed with her artistic progress, Amy has independently discovered that "talent isn't genius." As she tells him, "Rome took all the vanity out of me" (498). While Jo subjects her work to Professor Bhaer's "moral spectacles," Amy uses the gauge of superior work, in this case the greatest masterpieces. Perhaps a still more independent female artist might have questioned the appropriateness of the gauge, for its use recalls Bhaer's advice to Jo—that she learn from Shakespeare how to develop her characters. Nonetheless, Amy does not allow external authority or fear of impropriety to determine the course of her career. Even after surrendering her ambitions, Amy continues working for her own pleasure; she does not need parental encouragement—or permission—to resume a proscribed activity.[22]

Amy's courtship and marriage reflect her greater independence but also point up its limitations. During courtship, she is assertive: when driving with Laurie, she holds the reins, and, unlike her sisters, who marry their tutors, she plays Mentor to Laurie's Telemachus as well as the Prince to his Sleeping Beauty. While Laurie is still languishing for Jo, looking like "the effigy of a young knight asleep on his tomb" (497), Amy wakes him up as he had thought only Jo could do. As Laurie later tells Jo, Amy's lecture was "a deal worse than any of your scoldings" (549). It is Amy, then, who makes a man of Laurie, whereas Jo would keep him "her boy." As Amy says, "I know you'll wake up, and be a man in spite of that hardhearted girl" (505). Laurie's manhood seems achieved and traditional gender roles restored when, just prior to his proposal, he rows while Amy rests. But the proposal itself is prompted when Amy relieves him of an oar, and the two pull smoothly together through the water. And the letter they send home to announce their engagement is described as a "duet." Theirs is the one joyous, seemingly egalitarian marriage in the book. Thus Amy playfully allows herself to regress upon their return home. Once there Laurie calls her "little woman," Jo buttons her cloak as though she were a child, and Marmee holds her on her lap "as if being made 'the baby' again" (559–60). Yet when we think of Meg "enthroned" on John's knee, then laid on the shelf, and when we think of Jo in "Beth's little chair close beside" her father (not to mention the regressions of Sylvia Yule both after marriage and after separation from her husband), we have to wonder whether Amy has truly succeeded where Jo failed.

The very qualities that exempt Amy from the most painful restrictions of little womanhood—unwillingness to suffer and adaptability to circumstances—prevent her from escaping them altogether. Or to put it another way, Amy, like Jean Muir, is only clever enough to transform the liabilities of her condition into assets. Just as the sacrifice of her Christmas dollar becomes an occasion for display, so Amy consistently converts female suffering into aesthetic pleasure. During Beth's first illness, Amy, with the help of Aunt March's Catholic maid, fits up a closet as a little shrine in which she thinks "good thoughts" and prays for Beth's recovery. At the same time, however, she delights in the careful disposition of her few treasures, and her "beauty-loving eyes were never tired of looking up" at "a very valuable copy of one of the famous pictures of the world" (239–40). Similarly, after Beth dies, Amy's gentle melancholy, especially when compared with Jo's raw grief, takes on an aesthetic quality. When Laurie finds Amy mourning in a château garden, "Everything about her mutely suggested love and sorrow; the blotted letters in her lap, the black ribbon that tied up her hair, the womanly pain and patience in her face; even the little ebony cross at her throat seemed pathetic to Laurie, for he had given it to her, and she wore it as her only ornament" (524).

Amy's greatest art, we begin to suspect, is not her painting or sculpture but rather the graceful way in which she, like Jean, exploits her little womanhood. The incident in which Amy tries to cast her own foot is again instructive: Amy gives herself to art by becoming an art object. Unlike Cecil Stein, Amy molds herself, but she nonetheless conforms to a male model of femininity. In a passage that allies Amy with the sensation heroines Sybil, Cecil, and Jean, Alcott describes Amy awaiting Laurie. Like Sybil awaiting Guy, Amy "once arranged herself under the chandelier, which had a good effect upon her hair." Unlike Sybil, Amy thinks better of her ploy, but she removes herself from under the chandelier only to place her "slender, white figure against the red curtains," where Laurie finds her "as effective as a well-placed statue" (470). On this occasion, Amy's simple dress is covered "with a cloud of fresh illusion" (469), and Laurie's play on the word further suggests that Amy, like Jean, is a mistress of effects. Combining the plasticity of the actress with the immobility of the statue, Amy has in one sense lost, in another retained, the stiffness that prevented her from being a convincing heroine in Jo's play. Amy can now *play* the role to perfection, but in her conscious playing of it and in her inability to break out of it, she is both more than a conventional heroine and less than a true hero.

Jo, in the dark chapter "All Alone," bitterly compares herself to Amy: "Some people seemed to get all sunshine, and some all shadow; it was not fair, for she tried more than Amy to be good, but never got any reward,—only disappointment, trouble, and hard work" (530). Amy, as Jo dimly recognizes, manipulates the forms of little womanhood but rejects their self-sacrificial essence; thus she avoids the painful sacrifices incumbent upon most women. Jo resents the forms but, having long accepted their underlying principle, is unable to escape them. Later in this chapter, the narrator denies that Jo becomes "the heroine of a moral storybook": "if she had been . . . she ought at this period of her life to have become quite saintly, renounced the world, and gone about doing good in a mortified bonnet, with tracts in her pocket. But you see Jo wasn't a heroine; she was only a struggling human girl, like hundreds of others" (534). But this denial, while ostensibly distinguishing Jo's—and normal women's—behavior from that of morbid martyrs and ridiculous fanatics, serves rather to confound them. The narrator goes on to vindicate

Jo's self-immolation or to show how she vindicates herself: "She had often said she wanted to do something splendid, no matter how hard; and now she had her wish,— for what could be more beautiful than to devote her life to father and mother, trying to make home as happy to them as they had to her? And, if difficulties were necessary to increase the splendor of the effort, what could be harder for a restless, ambitious girl, than to give up her own hopes, plans and desires, and cheerfully live for others?" (534). The narrator's first question implies that nothing could be more splendid than for Jo to repay her parents, but, if their teachings have brought her to this pass, for what is she repaying them? And even if she does owe them a debt of gratitude, could she not repay them better by making something of herself? If they have devoted themselves to her happiness, can they be happy in her sacrifice? The narrator's second question implies that "nothing" could be harder, but, if so, then why should this hardship be imposed? The narrator's rhetorical questions thus provoke real questions, questions that the book as a whole seems designed to raise.

According to the narrator, self-immolation prepares a woman for marriage: "Grief is the best opener for some hearts, and Jo's was nearly ready for the bag; a little more sunshine to ripen the nut, then, not a boy's impatient shake, but a man's hand reached up to pick it gently from the burr, and find the kernel sound and sweet. If she had suspected this, she would have shut up tight, and been more prickly than ever; fortunately she wasn't thinking about herself, so, when the time came, down she dropped" (533). Jo's self-oblivion, reflected in her newly selfless writing, brings Professor Bhaer to her. At the end of the chapter "All Alone," Jo, having just heard of Amy and Laurie's engagement, wanders up to the garret where genius used to burn. There she peruses "four little wooden chests in a row, each marked with its owner's name, and each filled with relics of the childhood and girlhood ended now for all" (538). This burial ground of all the sisters' hopes and aspirations prompts a poem that recapitulates (just as Marmee's sermon anticipated) the movement of *Little Women*. As described by Jo, the lids of the "four little chests" bear the stamp of their owners' personalities: Meg's is "smooth and fair," Jo's "scratched and worn," Beth's "always swept," and Amy's "polished." The stanza Jo devotes to herself, her epitaph, as it were, alludes to "Dreams of a future never found" and "Half-writ poems, stories wild." The lines "Diaries of a wilful child, / Hints of a woman early old" compress into a few words the fate of "wilful" female children in a patriarchal society. The lines that draw the Professor are doubtless the next ones: "A woman in a lonely home, / Hearing like a sad refrain,— / 'Be worthy love, and love will come'" (586). While to him the lines may suggest ripening, to some readers (and perhaps to Jo, who hastily destroys his copy of the poem) they suggest the culture's insistence on marriage as a woman's only alternative to confinement in a lonely home. And the context of the lines is suggestive not of ripening but of decay.

Self-immolation prepares a woman for marriage in part because it unfits her for a satisfying life outside marriage. Spinsterhood, as the unmarried Alcott well knew, provided no sure escape from unremunerated domestic service. In fact, the prospect of spinsterhood is so forbidding that it can hasten ripening and "harvest time," as the final chapter is called. As Jo approaches her twenty-fifth birthday, she anticipates life as a "literary spinster, with a pen for a spouse, a family of stories for children, and twenty years hence a morsel of fame, perhaps" (540). As though to correct Jo's bleak vision, the narrator supplies a lengthy passage to the effect that spinsters can lead "useful, happy" lives (542). But spinsters, as described by the narrator, sound like superannuated Beths. Girls are urged to appreciate their "many silent sacrifices of youth, health, ambition, love itself," and boys are exhorted to chivalrous regard for "the good aunts who have not only lectured and fussed, but nursed and petted, too often without thanks" (541). The word *old* recurs throughout the passage, and the narrator ends by tacitly admitting the ineffectuality of her argument: "Jo must have fallen asleep (as I dare say my reader has during this little homily)" (542). At this point, Laurie breaks in, to enliven Jo temporarily but also to remind her of what she has lost—her youthful exuberance and spontaneity. As she tells him, "You may be a little older in years, but I'm ever so much older in feeling, Teddy. Women always are; and this last year has been such a hard one, that I feel forty" (547). Little wonder, then, that Jo, so ripened, drops at once into the matrimonial bag extended by Professor Bhaer. Breaking into the newly re-formed family circle, Bhaer immediately creates a masculine circle around him. The "burial customs of the ancients, to which the conversation had strayed" (555), spells the death of our hopes for Jo.

Because Professor Bhaer represents the patriarchal values around which the March circle ultimately revolves, his seeming disruption of that circle serves rather to perpetuate it and to preserve Jo's place in it. Jo, by establishing with her husband a school for boys at Plumfield, the estate that she inherits from her Aunt March, remains what Beth was—a retainer—only on a much larger scale. As Jo predicts, a strict division of labor by gender will obtain at Plumfield: "Fritz [Bhaer] can train and teach in his own way, and father will help him. I [like the maiden aunts?] can feed, and nurse, and pet, and scold them; and mother will be my stand-by" (593). Among Bhaer's trainees is Jo herself, much as Marmee was her husband's: "Jo made queer mistakes; but the wise Professor steered her safely into calmer waters" (595) just as he earlier rescued her from "the frothy sea of sensational literature." But Jo now finds "the applause of her boys more satisfying than any praise of the world,—for now she told no stories except to her flock of enthusiastic believers and admirers" (597). Comparing the end of part 1 with the end of part 2, we can appreciate Jo's reluctance to look into the future for fear of seeing "something sad" (289). Not only is her literary silence sad; so too are the gender-segregated groups of the final family tableau. Although Marmee, stretching out her arms to embrace the scene, can wish no "greater happiness" for her "girls," Alcott has allowed us to question whether it be happiness at all. Alcott's contemporary readers were disappointed by her refusal to marry Jo to Laurie; modern readers are disappointed that Alcott, supposedly succumbing to the demands that Jo marry someone, married her to Professor Bhaer. But just this sense of disappointment, even outrage, this reluctance to accept the traditional happy ending as a happy one, attests to the subversive power of Alcott's design.

In "A Whisper in the Dark" and *Behind a Mask,* Alcott's madwoman and bad woman expose, however cryptically, women's wrongs and wounds. In *Moods* and *A Marble Woman,* the death of a male character signifies that, with the death of patriarchy, such wrongs could be rectified, such wounds healed, divided selves made whole, and unmated pairs well matched. In *Little Women* the androgynous natures of Jo and Laurie, and their mutually sustaining friendship, suggest the realization of that possibility. But for all its sprightly tone, *Little Women* is among the most pessimistic of these early fictions. The imagery of death surrounding Jo's rejection of Laurie and acceptance of Professor Bhaer conveys a tragic loss of opportunity. In *Moods* and *A Marble Woman,* Warwick and Germain die; in *Little Women* Beth dies but is reborn, not only in Jo but as Amy's daughter of that name, the "shadow over Amy's sunshine" and the "cross" for both parents (601). In the earlier and seemingly more somber works, Alcott predicts, at least symbolically, a new order; in *Little Women* she documents the persistence and pernicious effects of the old. In "Psyche's Art" Alcott warned of the dangers of "duty" or domesticity for the female artist but also celebrated its legitimate place in art. She further hinted at spinsterhood as a desirable alternative to marriage for women artists, allowing them to draw on their experiences as sisters and daughters but to escape the demands on wives and mothers. But in *Little Women,* as we have seen, the domestic exploitation and entrapment of even single women is unsparingly presented. Even were Jo to escape from family obligations, her hunger for "all kinds" of love, as she confides to Marmee, would go unsatisfied. However much we may deplore Jo's "absolute surrender" to conventional marriage, we would regret an equivalent "sacrifice of her nature" to her art.

Jo, in the last chapter of *Little Women,* exclaims in a burst of enthusiasm, "I do think that families are the most beautiful things in all the world!" (595) And *Little Women* has long been taken as an argument, more or less convincing, for that assertion. But Jo "was in an unusually uplifted frame of mind, just then" (595). Even Jean Muir is capable of writing to her friend Hortense, "Something in the atmosphere of this happy home has made me wish I was anything but what I am." The next moment she declares, "Bah! how I hate sentiment!" (99). Jean's sense of exclusion and estrangement from an institution that she knows to be far other than its sentimentalized image nonetheless has power to threaten her identity. Rather than surrender that identity, however, Jean resolves to humble "an intensely proud family" by first creating, then dispelling, the idyllic family scenes that exist only in the sentimental imagination. Alcott, in her preface to *Little Women,* instructs her "little Book" to "show to all / That entertain, and bid thee welcome shall, / What thou dost keep close shut up in thy breast." What we find there are cozy scenes, theatrical performances, and many "a sweet sermon upon self-sacrifice" (*Mask* 68) such as Jean delivers. But we also find what Jean discloses when she bares *her* breast—the self-inflicted wounds that are a woman's price for her well-nigh obligatory membership in the patriarchal family. Thus Alcott, in her guise of mentor to girl readers, replicates Jean's lessons to Bella Coventry: that behind the charming model of little womanhood lurks a figure "early old" but with the power to detonate that model.[23]

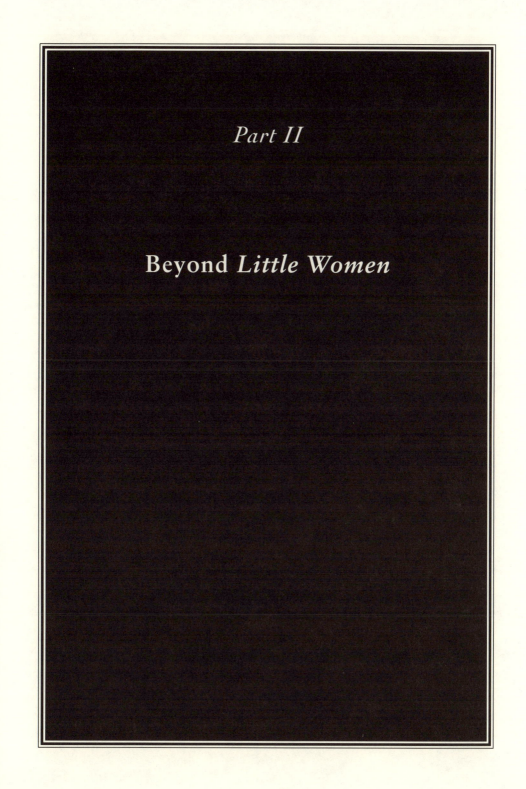

Part II

Beyond *Little Women*

CHAPTER 6

"The Anxiety of Influence":
Little Men

Cinderella is deliberately and systematically excluded from meaningful achieve-ments. . . . The paradox of this acceptance of a condition of worthlessness in the self, along with a conviction of the ultimate worthiness and heroism of one's role, is part of the terrible appeal of the fairy tale.

Madonna Kolbenschlag,
Kiss Sleeping Beauty Good-bye (63–64)

In seeking political power, are we abdicating that social throne where they tell us our influence is unbounded? No, No! . . . A direct power over one's own person and property, an individual opinion to be counted, on all questions of public interest, are better than indirect influence, be that ever so far reaching.

Elizabeth Cady Stanton,
Eighty Years and More (376)

In the works that immediately follow *Little Women,* Alcott becomes more overtly concerned with contemporary feminist issues: Becky in *An Old-Fashioned Girl* (1870) produces a statue of "the coming woman" and places a ballot box at her feet; Nan, Jo's protégée in *Little Men* (1871), is described as a "rampant reformer" and aspires to be a doctor; Chow-chow and her mother in "Cupid and Chow-Chow" (1874) agitate for women's "puckerage," or suffrage; and Christie, the heroine of *Work* (1873), becomes a women's rights advocate. Yet despite her more openly avowed feminism in the 1870s, Alcott often seems to support, and has been interpreted as supporting, women's indirect influence rather than their direct political power, their immobilizing pedestal rather than their mobilizing platform.[1] The eponymous heroine of *An Old-Fashioned Girl,* when urged to work for the less fortunate of her sex, fears to be thought "strong-minded" and instead wields her influence to reform—then marry—her cousin Tom; Nan is tamed, at least temporarily, by the combined influence of Jo, Daisy Brooke, and Amy's daughter, Bess; Chow-chow and her mother are not only tamed but humiliated; and even Christie, who worships male heroes, ends up advising a wealthy woman to use her social position to create a "purer atmosphere." Were Alcott's feminism represented solely or even primarily by her radical or reforming characters, each of whom is compromised, we would be justified in seeing it as tepid or confused, like the "needle, pen, palette, and broom" lying, together with the ballot box, at the "coming woman's" feet. Instead, her characters' susceptibility to influence—the ease with which they are swayed by or tempted to sway others—conveys their need for other sources of power. Alcott's moderately progressive program, then, is a kind of smoke screen as well as a conductor of more incendiary ideas.

In *Little Men* Alcott returns to the heroine of *Little Women,* Jo March, who with her husband, Fritz Bhaer, has established Plumfield, a school for boys. At the beginning of the story Nat Blake, the orphaned son of a street musician, joins twelve other male inmates, including the Bhaers' young sons, Rob and Teddy, as well as Meg's son, Demi. He is soon followed by his friend Dan, a tough, somewhat older boy. The cast of characters is complete when Jo persuades her husband to accept tomboy Nan as a companion for Daisy, Demi's twin and the school's lone girl. Frequent visitors at the school are Laurie, who has contributed financial support, and Bess, affectionately referred to as Princess Goldilocks. The novel has no real plot but concentrates on the gradual adjustment of the three newcomers over the course of a year. Just as in *Little Women* Alcott used the March girls' amusements and pastimes to cast doubt on Marmee's "preachments" and practice, so in *Little Men* she uses the children's "pranks and plays" to expose the ambiguous nature of Aunt Jo's educational experiment. And as she did in *Little Women* and its predecessors, Alcott in *Little Men* uses a theatrical performance to reveal her heroine's inner conflict. But whereas in the earlier works the heroine herself played conflicting roles—villain and hero, Lady Macbeth and Juliet, Judith and Roundhead maiden, in *Little Men* the Plumfield children enact the various roles—Cinderella, Stepmother, and Fairy Godmother—that Jo tries vainly to reconcile.

Critics who value *Little Men* and its sequel, *Jo's Boys,* tend to view Plumfield as a feminist utopia, a revision of Bronson Alcott's similarly named but less successful utopian experiment, Fruitlands.[2] Such a view seems to be supported by Nat's first impression of the school as "a sort of heaven" or "cozy dream" (16). When Jo tucks Nat into his dormitory bed at the end of his first day, he bursts into tears of gratitude because everyone is "so kind—and it's so beautiful" (14). But even these opening chapters, narrated largely from Nat's point of view, afford a different perspective on Plumfield. For example, Jo, in her role of Fairy Godmother to Nat's Cinderella, notices his wet shoes and insists that he change into Tommy's slippers: "They are too big; but that's all the better; you can't run away from us so far as if they fitted" (7). Jo's pleasantry not only suggests that Plumfield might be a place from which one would want to escape but also prefigures the episodes in which Nan and Dan do run away. But why would one wish to escape Plumfield with its "jovial games," its "freedom and fun" (8)? One reason, we are led to suspect, is that the doctrine of freedom is part of a larger policy of containment. Plumfield pillow fights, for example, are actually a means of maintaining control. As Jo explains to Nat, "I was to allow a fifteen-minute pillow fight every Saturday night; and they promised to go properly to bed every other night" (17). Life at Plumfield, as it turns out, is strictly regulated. Even Demi, the model boy, who had been "early taught the secret of self-control" (21), must moderate his appetite for fiction. After reproving a gluttonous boy, nicknamed Stuffy, Professor Bhaer warns Demi, "You are greedy also, my son, and you like to stuff your little mind full of fairy tales and fancies." He admonishes Stuffy to "eat but three times a day" and Demi to "read but one storybook a week" (47).

Aunt Jo has also had to forgo her taste for fiction—but for the writing of it rather than the reading of it. However, she has not entirely abandoned writing, and in fact it has become a major instrument for social control at Plumfield. As Nat and later his friend Dan learn, Aunt Jo keeps a "conscience book" (32), a record of each boy's progress. At the end of the week she shows the boy what she has written, and he is either gratified by a favorable report or shamed by an unfavorable one. Thus

Jo's book functions like Patty's patchwork quilt: both record moral and psycho-logical growth. But whereas the quilt enables Patty to express herself, Jo's book records only *her* version of the child's experience. It is, then, not the equivalent of the quilt so much as Aunt Pen's commentary *on* the quilt. Although reading and writing fiction are discouraged at Plumfield, story telling is still another form of moral training. The Sunday after Nat arrives, Professor Bhaer tells the story of a garden, containing twelve little plots. These plots, of course, correspond to the twelve Plumfield boys, and Professor Bhaer's description of each plot—the care it has received or the neglect it has suffered—serves the same purpose as Jo's con-science book and suggests the way in which these small allegorical plots have supplanted her more ambitious literary ones. Equally significant, the image of the twelve plots neatly laid out implies that Plumfield is less interested in nature than in culture, less interested in encouraging spontaneity than in imposing order, less interested in breaking down barriers than in preserving traditional boundaries, including those between the sexes.

The notion of Plumfield as a feminist utopia perhaps derives from Jo's concep-tion of her school or "family as a small world" (369) and her belief in "bringing up little men and women together" (112). Yet, as we learn at the end of *Little Women,* a strict division of labor by gender obtains at Plumfield. Jo's school is no different from her sister Meg's household, in which Demi's "mother had cherished an innocent and loving heart in him; his father had watched over the physical growth of his boy . . . while Grandpa March cultivated the little mind" (20). In his letter on behalf of Nat, Laurie writes to Jo: "You cure his overtasked body, Fritz help his neglected mind" (11). In regard to Franz, Bhaer's nephew, we learn that "His uncle was fitting him for college, and his aunt for a happy home of his own hereafter" (19). We also learn that some of the boys "were readier to open their hearts to him [Bhaer] than to a woman, especially the older ones, who liked to talk over their hopes and plans, man to man. When sick or in trouble they instinctively turned to Mrs. Jo, while the little ones made her their mother confessor on all occasions" (42). If Plumfield is Alcott's model for society, then she envisioned one in which women still nurse the body and nurture the emotions while men stimulate the mind and foster, as well as pursue, careers.

Despite her rebellion in *Little Women* against gender-role stereotyping, Jo in *Little Men* seems to acquiesce in and even encourage it. When Daisy is excluded from the boys' rough-and-tumble games, Jo compensates by giving her a miniature stove. Daisy's new "play" then becomes an early means of exercising feminine influence: "We will make your little messes rewards for the good boys. . . . If little men are like big ones, good cooking will touch their hearts and soothe their tempers delightfully" (82). But Jo neglects a much better opportunity for the sexes to influence each other by refusing to let the boys cook. In an echo of Meg and Amy's objections to Laurie's membership in the Pickwick Club, Jo tells them, "This is for Daisy, and Bess, and me, so we don't want you" (70–71). She goes so far as to enact a "law that no boy should touch, use, or even approach the sacred stove without a special permit from the owner thereof" (83) and declares the kitchen off-limits even to Professor Bhaer. Although Jo hopes in doing so to give Daisy, at that time the school's sole girl, a sense of self-worth, she only intensifies her isolation and fussy femininity. Daisy's "little raptures" over her "sweet rolling pin," "darling dishtub," and "cunning pepper-pot" (74) parody the pride that women are urged to take in relegation to a separate sphere.

Not only in their "plays" but in their studies are Daisy and, later, Nan deliberately segregated. Jo believes in teaching them needlework as well as cooking, and when Professor Bhaer objects that "needlework is not a fashionable accomplishment," Jo retorts, "My girls shall learn all I can teach them about it, even if they give up the Latin, algebra, and half a dozen ologies it is considered necessary for girls to muddle their poor brains over nowadays" (224). When the boys, encouraged by Laurie, transform a barn into a science museum, "the ladies were invited to behold the institution" only after the transformation is completed (185). At no time is the division of labor between the sexes more marked than in the final chapters depicting the preparation of Thanksgiving dinner. "For days beforehand, the little girls helped Asia and Mrs. Jo in storeroom and kitchen. . . . The boys hovered on the outskirts of the forbidden ground" (353). "When at last the day came, the boys went off for a long walk, that they might have good appetites for dinner. . . . The girls remained at home to help set the table, and give last touches to various affairs which filled their busy little souls with anxiety" (354–55). Alcott's mock-heroic treatment of little womanly activities, as indicated by such terms as "forbidden ground" and earlier "sacred stove," serves to deflate their importance and to dispel the mystique with which they have been enshrouded. Similarly, the nicknames that Jo gives the girls—Mrs. Shakespeare Smith and Mrs. Giddygaddy—

remind us how, for women, higher aspirations are subordinated to commonplace drudgery, petty cares, and insignificant busyness that are nonetheless productive of anxiety.

Meanwhile the boys, especially Demi, are introduced to the serious business of life. When John Brooke, Demi's father, dies suddenly, he is held up to the boys as a model, not only because of his integrity—his refusal to participate in sharp business dealings—but also for the frugality that enabled him to leave his wife, Meg, "independent" for life. Professor Bhaer, never missing an opportunity for an exemplum, tells his solemn audience of little boys: "when we looked among his papers, all was in order, not a debt remained; and safely put away was enough to keep Meg comfortable and independent. Then we knew why he had lived so plainly, denied himself so many pleasures, except that of charity, and worked so hard that I fear he shortened his good life" (324). His son, Demi, takes the lesson in responsibility to heart and longs to know about "figures and things, else I can't have nice, neat ledgers like his." He asks how he can make money, for "father told me to take care of mother and the little girls" (326). When he earns a few dollars, he begs his mother to buy something "for herself and the women-children, who he felt were left to his care" (327). From John Brooke's example both men- and women-children learn that female "independence" is dependent upon the activity of an enterprising and responsible male.[3]

Demi is also quick to learn the privilege that goes with male responsibility— that of tyrannizing a little over Daisy, his female dependent. Although Daisy "regarded her brother as authority on all subjects" (5) and "the best boy in the world," she admits, when Demi is accused of bullying her, "You do hurt me sometimes, but you don't mean to" (118). One such time involves the "Naughty Kitty-mouse," an invention of Demi's that Jo nervously dismisses as "a silly game." While playing it, Demi, through his spokesman the Kitty-mouse, causes Daisy "maternal woe" (128) by demanding that she "sackerryfice" her paper dolls. "A most whimsical and tyrannical imp was the Naughty Kitty-mouse, and Daisy found a fearful pleasure in its service, blindly obeying its most absurd demands, which were usually proclaimed from the lips of Demi." So fearful is her pleasure, so pleasurable her fear, that Daisy "never thought of denying the unseen tyrant anything it demanded." Rob and Teddy, the two young Bhaers, also participate, "although they did not understand half that went on" (126). These "rites," based on Professor Bhaer's lessons about the ancient Greeks, culminate in the burning of a lifelike female doll, whose writhings terrify the younger children. The dark side of male sacrifice, as practiced by John Brooke and extolled by Professor Bhaer, is female immolation, as performed, albeit unconsciously, by their sons. Demi's reference to the Kitty-mouse as "she" ("She must have every one, quick or she will scratch us!" [128]) suggests that such "rites" are an attempt to propitiate and suppress female power.[4]

Jo hopes that Daisy's gentleness will help make gentlemen of the boys, but, as in the Kitty-mouse episode, it seems merely to bring out their aggressiveness. More effective for Jo's purpose, at least superficially, is Daisy's cousin Bess. If Meg's Daisy is the little woman who submits, Amy's Bess is the little woman who charms. Bess, or Goldilocks,[5] is dainty and fastidious; she will allow no one to touch her and will only touch others as a mark of her special favor. When Bess visits Plumfield, the "lads crowded round the pretty child, admiring her long golden hair, dainty dress, and lofty ways." She responds to this adulation by "smiling down upon them, and graciously patting their heads with her little white hands" (176). We are told that her "natural refinement . . . had a good effect upon the careless lads about her" (219). When Bess leaves, each boy "dimly felt that he was better for having known a creature so lovely, delicate, and sweet; for little Bess appealed to the chivalrous instinct in them as something to love, admire, and protect with a tender sort of reverence" (227–28). It is hard to imagine Demi or any of the boys tyrannizing over Bess as they do over Daisy, but the lesson for little women seems to be that, in order to avoid such treatment, they must retire from the rough-and-tumble world of little men and take refuge in an unreal fairy-tale world. The lesson for little men—an exaggerated regard for the "Princess," the little woman who keeps to her pedestal—is no more genuinely edifying.

Bess's visit is described as a "peaceful episode," whereas the Naughty Kitty-mouse is a violent one, but both image a patriarchal society. In the game Bess inspires, that of a princess surrounded by her court, the boys hold positions of power—chancellor of the exchequer, prime minister, philosopher, and standing army. Daisy "took the humble post of chief cook, while Nan was first maid of honor" (222). Jo and her husband approve "the pretty play in which the young folk unconsciously imitated their elders, without adding the tragedy that is so apt to spoil the dramas acted on the larger stage" (222). But the Naughty Kitty-mouse was also a "childish imitation" of adult drama, perhaps inspired as much by immediate examples of domestic tyranny as by the ancient Greeks. The imitations of male dominance and feminine influence are complementary, and both prepare the stage for adult tragedy. In fact, Bess's "play" stands in relation to Plumfield as does Plumfield to the larger society. Both Bess's court and Plumfield are comparatively peaceful, orderly communities where feminine influence—that of Bess or Mrs. Jo—appears to govern but where males hold positions of power and privilege.

Alcott uses two newcomers, "Naughty Nan" and "firebrand" Dan, to expose the price that must be paid for such peace as exists at Plumfield. Jo, in urging Professor Bhaer to admit Nan to the school, offers somewhat contradictory reasons. Although she describes Nan as "running wild at home," she argues that having another girl at Plumfield will help the boys "learn gentle ways" (113). And although she tells him Daisy is "getting prim and Bettyish, and needs stirring up" (114), she assures him that Nan "only needs to be taught what to do . . . to be as nice a little girl as Daisy" (113). After presenting these reasons, Jo implores her husband (that she needs to do so is in itself revealing), "Then I may have Nan, may I?"[6]—because, as she implies, Nan is a kindred spirit, a reminder of what she once was herself: "I feel a great sympathy for Nan, because I was such a naughty child myself that I know all about it. . . . I know how to manage her, for I remember how my blessed mother managed me" (113). Yet Jo, both by subjecting Nan to the gentling influence of Plumfield and by making her an agent of influence herself, endangers the very quality that so attracts her, the quality that the combined influence of Marmee, Beth, and Professor Bhaer has considerably chastened but not utterly destroyed in Jo.

Whereas the boys exploit Daisy and idolize Bess, they respect Nan. For one thing, they soon learn that whatever they "dared her to do she instantly attempted, no matter how dangerous." Further, in the classroom, "Nan showed them that girls could do most things as well as boys, and some things better" (123). Unlike Daisy, who "knew nothing about woman's rights" and "did not undertake what she could not carry out," Nan "attempted all sorts of things, undaunted by direful failures, and clamored fiercely to be allowed to do everything that the boys did" (255). Daisy dreams of keeping house for her brother when she grows up; Nan dreams instead of having a doctor's office. As though to demonstrate her commitment to medicine and her indifference to the housewife's role, Nan tears up a doll's skirt to make "a neat little bandage" for Emil's injured thumb. Jo, perhaps thinking of her own thwarted ambition, intervenes with Professor Bhaer, arguing that Nan "will be one of the sharp, strong, discontented women" if she does not have "something to live for." She proposes that they give her "the work she likes, and by and by persuade her father to let her study medicine" (256). But Jo's admirable efforts to "manage" Professor Bhaer and Nan's father are offset by the influence, both direct and indirect, that she brings to bear upon Nan.

Despite Nan's forceful personality, Jo is able to use both Daisy and Bess to modify it. As Jo reports to Laurie, "Daisy's example has its effect upon her, and I'm quite sure that a few months will work wonders" (183). From Daisy, Nan learns herself to substitute feminine influence for direct action. Excluded from the boys' club, Nan initially "caused great excitement and division among the gentlemen by presenting endless petitions, both written and spoken, disturbing their solemnities by insulting them through the keyhole, performing vigorous solos on the door, and writing derisive remarks on walls and fences" (137). Nan's behavior is moderated when Jo persuades her and Daisy to start "an institution of their own, which they called the Cozy Club" (137). This club, far from serving their own enjoyment, exists for the purpose of enticing, then edifying, the boys. As Daisy confides to Nan: "Aunt Jo likes to have the boys play with us, if they are not rough; so we must make them like our balls, then they will do them good" (140). Princess Bess's example is still more potent than Daisy's: "Nan was especially benefitted by a week in the society of a well-bred lady. . . . for, seeing how everyone loved the little princess for her small graces and virtues, she began to imitate her, because Nan wanted much love, and tried hard to win it" (220–21). Nan, then, gradually begins to conform to what is expected of a little woman for the same reason that Jo did in *Little Women*—her overpowering need for love and approval.

Nan, on her arrival at Plumfield, is, like Nat, jocularly warned against running away (121), and when she inadvertently does so, we witness a striking example both of Jo's (and Marmee's) "management" and of Nan's need for approval. Nan, "thirsting for adventures," leads Jo's son Rob away from their huckleberrying party, and the two become lost for several hours.[7] After their rescue, Jo, to impress upon Nan the seriousness of her escapade, ties her to the sofa, just as Marmee once tied Jo. Nan soon manages to get free, but she hastily reties herself upon overhearing Jo say that "she is an honorable little girl, and knows that I do it to help her" (213). Nan's desire to merit Jo's praise condemns her to "a long afternoon attached to the sofa. Mrs. Bhaer lengthened her bonds so that she could look out of the window; and there she stood watching the boys play" (215). By tying Nan so loosely to begin with and then lengthening her bonds, Jo reveals her sympathy with the girl's desire for freedom. But by enabling Nan to view the boys from the window, Jo exposes an unconscious purpose behind her program for Nan—to keep her a spectator of the male-dominated world rather than a participant in it. The episode ends on a humorous note, with Nan admonishing a bee: "If you have run away, you'd better go right home and tell your mother you are sorry, and never do so any more" (216). By becoming a "manager" herself, however, Nan points up the underlying pathos of *Little Men*—how Jo attempts to tame those who are only acting out her own innermost impulses and, more generally, how each generation of women is co-opted into socializing the next.[8]

In her attempts to influence the "firebrand" Dan, Jo is equally caught between a desire to express her own need for freedom and a sense that she must control it. Jo identifies with Dan as much as or more than she does with Nan. As she tells her husband, "He won't bear sternness nor much restraint, but a soft word and infinite patience will lead him as it used to lead me" (161). When Dan begins to chafe against the restrictions of Plumfield, Jo tells him, "I used to feel just so, and once I really did think for a minute that I would bolt" (276). She goes on to tell him, much as she told Nan, that only her mother's love kept her at home, and in Dan's case, rather than literally tying him, she relies on the strength of his emotional attachment: "leave him free, and the mere sense of liberty would content him, joined to the knowledge that his presence was dear to those whom he loved best" (277). Such lenient treatment of Dan, who deliberately runs away from the farm to which he is sent by the Bhaers, compared with the severe treatment of Nan, who gets lost in her quest for adventure, suggests that Jo's relationship with Dan serves even more complex psychological needs. By associating his "wildness" with "manliness," Jo can consciously dissociate herself from it and more safely indulge her unconscious longing for it. And in setting herself the task of taming him through love, she can recapture, at least temporarily, the kind of feeling she once had for Laurie but relinquished in order to marry Professor Bhaer.

Between Dan and the Professor there exists from the first a subtle antagonism. Something about Bhaer elicits Dan's worst qualities—his sullenness and swaggering toughness. Bhaer, for his part, believes Dan a "harm to others." Jo sees no connection between their antagonism and her attitude toward Dan, even though,

with him, she becomes the irrepressible girl of *Little Women*. When Dan helps her
clamber up a tree, she confesses, "I haven't climbed a tree since I was married. I
used to be very fond of it when I was a girl" (268). When Dan is exonerated of a
crime, Jo gives way to youthful exuberance, "waving her dish towel and looking
as if she wanted to dance a jig for joy, as she used to do when a girl." At "the sight
of Mrs. Jo's delight," Dan "suddenly bolted across the hall into the parlor, whither
she instantly followed, and neither was seen for half an hour" (251). Especially in
the episode in which Rob and Nan are lost, Jo depends on Dan rather than on
Rob's father. As they search, "the steady look in his eyes . . . made her feel as if,
boy though he was, she had someone to depend on" (205). After they have been
found, Jo "put her arm on Dan's broad shoulder" "with a look that made him
color up with pride and pleasure." Jo then promises, "'You shall be my oldest son,'"
and she sealed her promise with a kiss that made Dan hers entirely" (210). In the
language of this episode, and the virtual absence of Professor Bhaer from it, Alcott
effectively conveys both the ground of Jo's attraction to Dan and her husband's
dislike of the boy who, we are told, possesses "the manly virtues which we most
admire and love" (246).

In encouraging Dan, as she encourages Nan, to repress or at least sublimate
the craving for "entire liberty," Jo often intensifies his conflict. Just as she holds
the more conventional Daisy up to Nan as a model, so she encourages Dan to
emulate Daisy's twin, Demi, even though Dan protests that Demi is "so kind of
precious, and so good, and I'm such a bad lot" (268–69). To convince Dan that
he is not a "bad lot," Jo entrusts him with the care of her son Teddy, the first person
at Plumfield to respond to Dan and break through his reserve. Although "no more
powerful restraint could have been imposed on him" (270), Jo, by making Dan a
surrogate parent for her child, unconsciously makes him a surrogate partner for
herself. A short time later Jo sees Dan running as though "possessed by some
strange desire to run himself into a fever or break his neck" (275). When Dan
confesses that "the devil gets into me sometimes, and then I do want to bolt," Jo
tries to soothe him with the reminder that he has a mother in her, but Dan, dimly
recognizing that Jo, for all her good intentions, is a source of his "badness," replies,
"it isn't just the same is it?" Dan, having been promoted to the role of surrogate
parent for Jo's son Teddy, is no longer content with his previous role as Jo's "oldest
son." He promises to stay at Plumfield only after Jo, taking "the big, brown hand

a minute," assures him that "I want you very much" (277). More beneficial to Dan than Jo's solicitude is the task he assigns himself—that of taming a spirited colt. In pitting his strength and intelligence against the colt's, and at the same time rewarding it with his affection, Dan succeeds in both exercising and exorcising his demon, or at least in bringing it under his control. In the same way Jo, by engaging in a loving struggle for Dan's loyalty and commitment, not only finds an outlet for her own passionate nature but reinforces her sense of mastery over it. But ironically, in attempting to curb Dan, she spurs his impulse to run away.

Whereas Professor Bhaer rejects the notion that Jo was ever like the "rascal" Dan (161), Laurie, as "the first boy Mrs. Jo had ever had to take care of" (181), sees the resemblance and identifies with Dan himself. Given their former bond and continuing closeness, one would expect to find the Professor jealous of Laurie, for even the children remark on their "way of sending messages to one another, without any words" (177). Laurie is constantly thinking of Jo's comfort and happiness, and both recall their adolescent friendship with great nostalgia. Jo becomes a girl again with Laurie, as she does with Dan. When he arrives at Plumfield for a visit, "Mrs. Bhaer . . . stood smiling and clapping her hands like a girl" (175) and soon becomes "very like the lively Jo of old times" (181). The feeling between them ranges from a playful camaraderie to an almost painful tenderness, as when "Mrs. Jo stroked the curly black head at her knee as affectionately as ever, for, in spite of everything, Teddy was her boy still" (181). But it is just Laurie's perpetual boyishness, as opposed to Dan's growing manliness, that distinguishes the two and safeguards Laurie from the Professor's suspicions. As the narrator indicates, Jo continues to think of Laurie as "Teddy," her former nickname for him but also the name of her younger, and Dan's surrogate, son. The strong feeling that Jo has had for Laurie persists in this novel, but it is now complemented by her equally strong feeling for Dan. The difference between the two relationships is that the former is now a sentimental attachment whereas the latter is, at least covertly, an erotic one.

Despite the festive ending that characterizes all the March novels, *Little Men* leaves the reader with a sense of sadness and loss. When Laurie attempts to compliment Jo on the progress of her boys, she tries to give the credit to Professor Bhaer and her girls—Nan, Daisy, and Laurie's daughter, Bess. They, she argues, have all contributed to the boys' development:

Daisy is the domestic element, and they all feel the charm of her quiet, womanly ways. Nan is the restless, energetic, strong-minded one; they admire her courage, and give her a fair chance to work out her will, seeing that she has sympathy as well as strength, and the power to do much in their small world. Your Bess is the lady, full of natural refinement, grace, and beauty. She polishes them unconsciously, and fills her place as any lovely woman may, using her gentle influence to lift and hold them above the course, rough things of life, and keep them gentlemen in the best sense of the fine old word.

As though he recognizes Jo's wistful envy of the "lady" or "lovely woman" as represented not only by Bess but by Bess's mother, Amy, Laurie protests, "It is not always the ladies who do that best, Jo. It is sometimes the strong brave woman who stirs up the boy and makes a man of him." But Jo remains firm: "No; I think the graceful woman, whom the boy you allude to married, has done more for him than the wild Nan of his youth; or, better still, the wise, motherly woman who watched over him, as Daisy watches over Demi" (369). Laurie, catching Jo's allusion to her mother and knowing her veneration for Marmee, gallantly concedes, "All three did much for him, and I can understand how well these little girls will help your lads" (370).

While Jo's reluctance to take credit for Laurie's supposed maturation pays tribute to the traditional woman and her edifying influence, it at the same time casts doubt on the reality of that achievement and points to her own failure to be the "strong brave woman" Laurie so much admires. Jo's notion, on which she has modeled her life, that a woman's most exalted task is to mold and elevate the character of men, or, in her case, that of "little men," and that two kinds of woman—the wise and motherly (like Marmee, Meg, and Daisy) and the ladylike and graceful (like Amy and Bess)—are best equipped to do it, dooms her to a life of unresolved conflict. Incapable of playing the role of ladylike woman, Jo strives to become the motherly one; as she tells Laurie, "I only loved them and let them see it. Fritz did the rest." But the strong-minded one (like Nan)—the woman who resembles the manly Dan and the boyish Laurie, and who is incomprehensible to the staid Professor Bhaer—cannot be repressed without great sacrifice; as Laurie observes, "you look as if 'only loving' had been rather hard work sometimes"

(368). As we have seen, Jo's attempts in *Little Women* to ignore Laurie's passion and play mother to "her boy" arrest his development as well as her own; her present attempts to treat Dan, despite his already awakened sexuality, as her eldest son create for him guilt and conflict; and her preference, as a once strong-minded woman herself, for the motherly or ladylike one, places Nan in a double bind. Ironically, then, Jo's view of woman, including herself, as moral influence restricts the full range of her potential influence at Plumfield and even adversely influences those she loves.

At the end of Plumfield's Thanksgiving celebration, and the end of the book, we see Nan confront the difficult choices that Jo's influence has presented her. After Jo's boys have displayed their athletic and academic prowess, her girls, significantly, enact the drama of Cinderella. In this production Nan, like Jo in "The Witch's Curse," plays two roles. First, as Fairy Godmother, Nan transforms the rags of Bess, the play's heroine, into a "splendid dress, because you are good" (363). One might interpret this action as Nan's acquiescence in the general view that Bess's charm, or splendid dress, signifies her worth and deserves male adoration. But one might also infer Nan's contempt for the "rags" of charm until empowered and made "splendid" by a "rampant reformer" such as she. Later in the play Nan assumes the role of stepsister and "performed that operation [of cutting off her toe in order to fit the slipper] so well that the herald was alarmed" (365). In Alcott's novel, as in the Grimms' version of the tale as well as Anne Sexton's parody,ʼ this grisly episode hints at the self-mutilation women, such as Jean Muir, are willing to undergo in order to win male approval. But the word *operation,* by reminding us of Nan's chosen profession, suggests that it is the skillful operation itself, not the "fitting" operation of finding a husband, that will ultimately absorb her, as we in fact discover on reading *Jo's Boys.*

Nan, in playing both the Fairy Godmother and the evil stepsister who performs her "operation" at the bidding of Cinderella's stepmother, reenacts Jo's dual role in regard to her. As Louise Bernikow writes of the Grimms' version of "Cinderella," "Not only do we have a good and bad mother, but two different ways of seeing connections between women, particularly between mothers and daughters. The first mother—the 'real' one or the 'good' one—embodies matriarchal values. . . . The patriarchal mother or the mother in a patriarchal world is herself degraded, robbed of her power. Like the stepmother in this story, her energies are directed to patriarchal institutions, to becoming skillful at manipulating within them" (29–30). Jo tries to be a "real" or "matriarchal" mother—a fairy godmother—to her girls, as well as to her boys. But in the patriarchal world that Plumfield mirrors, she inevitably becomes a "patriarchal" mother—or step-mother—and is "robbed of her power." Just as Nan as Fairy Godmother helps Bess as Cinderella into a pumpkin coach she finds "a rather tight fit" (364), so Jo, for all her good intentions, helps her girls accommodate themselves to constricting gender roles rather than escape them. Bess's response to Nan's gift of "a pair of silver paper slippers"—"'My dlass ones, ain't they pitty?'" (363)—seems innocent enough, but, in the context of the larger story, it confirms the pitiful nature of Jo's efforts to play Fairy Godmother.

In begging Laurie not to "pitty" the "faded old woman" she has become (368), Jo seems dimly aware of her transformation—ostensibly into a fairy god-mother but actually into an attenuated "Modern Cinderella." Earlier the narrator tells us that "Mrs. Jo sat smiling over her book as she built castles in the air, just as she used to do when a girl, only then they were for herself and now they were for other people, which is the reason, perhaps, that some of them came to pass in reality—for charity is an excellent foundation to build anything upon" (166). Tied to the Plumfield hearth, deprived of the literary work that in *Little Women* constituted her "castle in the air," she now builds castles for others, just as Cinderella helped her stepsisters dress for the ball. While apparently approving Jo's substitution of others' castles—Dan's as a naturalist, Nat's as a musician—for her own, Alcott implies that women's dreams for others, especially for men, have a far greater chance of being realized than do women's dreams for themselves. *Little Men* concludes with "Father and Mother Bhaer" surrounded by a merry flock of Plumfielders: "the circle narrowed till the good professor and his wife were taken prisoner by many arms, and half hidden by the bouquet of laughing young faces which surrounded them" (372). But the image is one of constriction and suffocation as well as merriment. Jo, by choosing the hearth as her base of operations, "only loving" as a career, and charity as a foundation on which to build castles in the air, does not transcend the limitations of woman's traditional sphere but becomes entrapped within it.

CHAPTER 7

"The Quest for Identity":
Work: A Story of Experience

Not only is a woman's quest for identity deflected from engagement with the outside world . . . and "doomed to that inward search" called narcissism, but that inward quest seems doomed itself to frustration, if not failure.

Ellen Cronan Rose, "Through the Looking Glass:

When Women Tell Fairy Tales" (210)

"Do you really think . . . that the charm of inspiring, as you call it, is what any reasonable creature would prefer to be doing? To make somebody else a hero rather than be a hero yourself? Women would need to be disinterested indeed if they like that best."

Margaret Oliphant, *Hester* (331)

Little Men concludes with Jo imprisoned in a narrow circle of childish arms; *Work*, a novel for adults published two years later, concludes with its heroine, Christie Devon, clasping hands with "a loving league of sisters, old and young, black and white, rich and poor" (442).[1] The similarities and differences between these two endings point to a complex relationship between the two books, indeed between *Work* and Alcott's entire personal history and literary career prior to 1873. As its subtitle, *A Story of Experience,* suggests, *Work* incorporates much of its author's previous nonliterary experience: her fierce desire as an adolescent for financial independence, her fascination with the stage, her work at a series of unsatisfactory jobs, her suicidal despair, her friendships with Thoreau and Theodore Parker, and her service as a Civil War nurse.[2] Begun in the early 1860s when Alcott was revising *Moods, Work* also bears the mark of the fiction that intervened between its inception and its publication over a decade later. Representing an even longer period in its heroine's life, *Work* portrays Christie's uneven progress from youth to middle age. At twenty-one Christie resembles the restless, rebellious adolescents Sylvia Yule and Jo March. As a professional actress and then as a governess who falls under the spell of *Jane Eyre,* Christie shares some traits with Jean Muir. Her next stage, one of self-abnegation and despair, followed by resignation, again recalls Sylvia and Jo. But Christie finally emerges from her long apprenticeship more like Faith Dane than Aunt Jo or Mother Bhaer, for from her androgynous male mentors as well as from her "league of loving sisters" she relearns the lesson that both she and Jo, in common with most young women, unlearn: the need to engage directly with the outside world and to render her own account of that engagement.

Like most of Alcott's domestic fiction, *Work* is an episodic novel, and like *Little Women,* part 2, its episodes fall into three phases: youthful ambition and adventure, disillusionment and despair, and recovery facilitated by courtship and marriage. As several critics have observed, *Work* begins like a male bildungsroman, with Christie declaring her independence of her Uncle Enos and leaving his farm to find work in the city.[3] But her successive occupations—domestic servant, actress, governess, companion, and seamstress—are among the few open to working- and middle-class women. Initially high-spirited, Christie enjoys listening to the tales of her fellow servant, the escaped slave Hepsey, as well as mimicking her fashionable employer, Mrs. Stuart, until a fire she starts while reading in bed leads to her dismissal. Undaunted, Christie accepts a minor part in a chorus line and gradually earns a reputation for herself as a character actress. But an injury sustained while trying to protect a jealous rival from a falling stage prop leads her to see that she has been jeopardizing her womanhood. After leaving the stage, Christie takes a job as governess and, under the influence of *Jane Eyre,* is tempted to marry the children's uncle, Philip Fletcher. When he condescends to her as a former actress, however, she summarily rejects him. Christie is next employed as a companion to the invalid Helen Carrol, only to find that her charge is suffering from intermittent hereditary madness. After Helen's suicide, Christie finds employment as a seamstress but resigns in sympathetic protest when her friend Rachel is exposed as a "fallen woman." Having lost both Helen and Rachel, who insists they must part, Christie falls into a deep despair. Like Jo after the loss of Beth, she tries to find salvation in living for others but only succeeds in bringing herself to the verge of suicide. Saved by Rachel, who providentially intervenes, Christie makes a temporary home with the laundress Cynthy Wilkins and begins the long process of recovery.

Like Jo after the frustration of her ambitions, Christie becomes, for a time at least, a more conventional heroine.[4] In fact, her quest now seems to be less for some heroic action to perform than for someone to hero-worship. Through Cynthy, Christie meets one candidate, the liberal minister Mr. Power, who introduces her to another, David Sterling. Employed to help David with his nursery business, Christie learns that he is suffering from a secret sorrow, begins to find him a romantic figure, and gradually falls in love. Mistakenly believing that her love is unrequited, she reluctantly leaves the Sterling household to become a kind of secretary to Mr. Power. At one of his social evenings, she reencounters Philip Fletcher, who promptly renews his suit. Touched by his continued devotion, Christie is tempted to accept his offer but is deterred by her love for David. Not long after, her patience is rewarded. David, elated to have found his long-lost sister, Letty, who turns out to be none other than Christie's friend Rachel, declares his love and the two marry. But the story does not end there. As Jo had longed to do in *Little Women,* Christie participates in the Civil War; when David enlists, Christie, as Alcott did herself, volunteers as a nurse. After David's death she supports his mother, sister, and their daughter by continuing his nursery business. On receiving a legacy from her uncle, she furthers David's rescue work with unfortunate women. Finally, at forty, Christie discovers her own work, that of an advocate for women's rights. It is only in this final section of the book, in which Christie comes to terms with the meaning of David's life and death, that she moves beyond her role as conventional heroine and hero-worshiper, and becomes the true hero she—and Jo—at first promised to be.

Christie's heroic aspirations are apparent from the outset, but her early experiences reshape the fairy-tale hero into the sensational heroine.[5] In the book's first sentence, Christie proclaims to her Aunt Betsey, "there's going to be a new Declaration of Independence"; she then proposes "like the people in fairy tales [to] travel away into the world and seek [her] fortune" (1–2) and boasts in response to her aunt's skepticism of the "yeast put into [her] composition" (3). But Aunt Betsey's "interlarded" retort—"You be better riz than me; though . . . too much emptins makes bread poor stuff, like baker's trash" (3)—suggests that a woman's quest is not so simple. Ironically, Christie leaves Aunt Betsey's kitchen not for the world but for another kitchen, where the escaped slave Hepsey counsels the outraged new servant to black her master's boots as she is told. From Hepsey, who plans to steal her mother out of slavery, Christie learns what many women and slaves have long known—how to perform the duties of a faithful servant while harboring a rebellious spirit, how to exploit a role that is foisted on one, and how to preserve a sense of identity even when that identity is continually denied. "Mrs. Stuart never dreamed that her quiet, respectful Jane [as she insists on calling Christie] kept a sharp eye on all her movements, smiled covertly at her affectations, envied her accomplishments, and practiced certain little elegancies that struck her fancy" (26). By turning the role to which she has been reduced into an actor's part, Christie, like Jean Muir, avoids being marginalized, but, like Jean, she is finally found out. Ostensibly dismissed for being "too fond of books," Christie's real crime, exposed to Mrs. Stuart by her reading, is her possession of a life beyond her servant's role, a life independent of her mistress's will. The night of the fire Christie dares to laugh at Mrs. Stuart's consternation, thus obliterating the distinction between mistress and maid that she had only affected to observe.

Something in the very nature of acting, of regarding a role as an actor's part, seems to create irony and foster subversion. But, as in the case of Jean as Judith or Jo as swaggering villain, acting, on-stage at least, can express as well as camouflage female rebellion. Christie, "resolving not to be a slave to anybody" (34) after her experience at the Stuarts', becomes a chorus girl in a spirit of defiance. Uncle Enos's view of "'play-actin' as the sum of all iniquity . . . rather strengthened her purpose, for a delicious sense of freedom pervaded her soul, and the old defiant spirit seemed to rise up within her at the memory of her uncle's grim prophecies and narrow views" (37). Christie's first role, as an Amazon queen, is admirably suited to her frame of mind. On opening night she sees reflected "a warlike figure with glittering helmet, shield and lance, streaming hair and savage cloak. She liked the picture, for there was much of the heroic spirit in the girl" (41). Just as Jo, as hero, relished rescuing the heroine, so Christie revels in the "'grand tableau' of the martial queen standing in a bower of lances, the rescued princess gracefully fainting in her arms, and the vanquished demon scowling fiercely under her foot" (43). Alcott, by having the narrator compare Christie and Christie compare herself to such women as Boadicea, Joan of Arc, Zenobia, and Britomart, suggests that onstage women can wield a kind of power that offstage few possess.

Alcott's allusions remind us of female heroism—the legacy of it as well as the potential for it—but they also function ironically. As early as her initial interview, Christie must quell "the old defiant spirit" and subject herself to the demeaning scrutiny of the manager, Mr. Sharp. After he puts her through her paces as though she were a horse and renders his verdict ("Good tread; capital figure; fine eye"), a "strong desire to make off seized the girl; but, remembering that she had presented herself for inspection, she controlled the impulse, and returned to him with no demonstration of displeasure" (38). At her first rehearsal Christie further learns that the stage, rather than revolutionizing patriarchal society, merely replicates it, for she discovers her Amazons to be a "most forlorn band of warriors . . . huddled together . . . looking as if afraid to speak, lest they should infringe some rule" (39).[6] Christie quickly finds the chorus line every bit as tedious as the kitchen, and more degrading. Long before the play's run has ended, Christie has learned the lesson of Becky, the feminist sculptor in *An Old-Fashioned Girl:* "women have been called queens a long time, but the kingdom given them isn't worth ruling" (258). But Christie's highly compressed statement, made years later to David Sterling— "I'd rather *be* a woman than *act* a queen" (267)—does more than recognize, like Becky's, the factitious nature of the power men grant to women; it also expresses her realization that, insofar as the acting profession does confer real power on women, it is a power at odds with their traditional strengths. Just as the Amazons were said to have removed their breasts the better to aim their weapons, so Christie, in her increasingly successful career, begins to sacrifice traits essential to her womanhood.

As Christie moves from chorus girl to character actress, she begins to enjoy the economic and psychological benefits that men have long derived from work outside the home, especially "a never-failing excitement in her attempts to reach the standard of perfection she had set up for herself" (48). At the same time, however, she finds herself in the classic double bind that continues to hamper ambitious women—the forced choice between self-fulfilling achievement and affiliation with others: "She had no thought now beyond her art, no desire beyond the commendation of those whose opinion was serviceable, no care for any one but herself" (49). In articulating her dilemma, Christie sounds much like Jo March on giving up sensation fiction: "If three years of this life have made me this, what shall I be in ten? A fine actress perhaps, but how good a woman?" (51). But whereas Jo succumbed to the judgment of Professor Bhaer, Christie realizes that the stage, no less than domestic servitude, deprives her of an identity. Just as she became "Jane" at the Stuarts', so in the theater she is known as "Miss Douglas." And just as the fashionable household erected barriers between mistress and maid, so the theater divides successful from less successful actress. By the night of Christie's benefit performance, in which she plays the Irish actress Peg Woffington in Charles Reade's *Masks and Faces,* she and her former friend, Lucy, "might have played the Rival Queens with great effect" (52). The plot of Reade's novel *Peg Woffington,* on which his play is based, turns on Peg's impersonation of her own portrait, which ends only when she leaves its frame. Christie, while playing Peg, comes to realize Lucy's love for the actor whom she, Christie, is playing opposite, "and when Peg left the frame, her face expressed the genuine pity that she felt" (54). Christie, in expressing genuine pity rather than feigning it and in coming to the rescue of her fellow actress, steps outside the male framework within which she has achieved a measure of success. Her resulting injury and retirement from the stage suggest that women do so at their professional peril, but, like Peg Woffington in stepping from *her* frame, Christie does recover her identity.

Acting continues, however, to play a paradoxical role in Christie's career, as it does throughout Alcott's fiction. As we have seen, women's comparative powerlessness predisposes them to acting, which both protects by disguising their true identity and enables them to express it in another guise. Through acting women can vicariously—and sometimes actually—experience power, but they can also, as Christie often comes close to doing, lose all sense of self. In her next incarnation, as a governess, Christie is tempted to play Jane Eyre to Philip Fletcher's Rochester. Although she does not initially intend, like Jean Muir, to seduce the master of the house, her resolve to be "very quiet and reserved, as became a meek and lowly governess" (75) does nothing to discourage Fletcher's attentions. As if preparing a script, she begins reading *Jane Eyre,* and though she tells Fletcher that she "never can forgive" Jane for "marrying that man, as I haven't much faith in the saints such sinners make" (80), she comes perilously close herself to accepting a new if luxurious servitude. Only when Fletcher reminds her of the sacrifice he is making in marrying a former actress does she rebuke him, at which point the penchant for acting that has endangered her comes to her aid. The narrator *says* that Christie "was no actress off the stage, and wanted to be very true just then" (86), but the truth is more compelling for "her old dramatic fervor in voice and gesture" (87). Fletcher pays homage to her power even as he tries to disempower her: "Very well done! . . . I am disappointed in the woman, but I make my compliment to the actress" (88). Fletcher's implied charge—that her air of authority and command of language expose a lack of femininity—exemplifies how men, by creating a disjunction between woman and actress, have attempted to keep women in their place. But in this scene Christie's power as an actress, rather than being at odds with her womanhood, derives from the very delicacy that Fletcher accuses her of lacking. Finally, the same ability that threatened loss of self in role enables Christie, at the end of this episode, to view her present role with a saving objectivity: "now a short scene with my lady and then exit governess" (89).[7]

In the next episode of *Work,* Alcott shifts her focus from Christie, whose acting has empowered as well as endangered her, to Helen Carrol, who has become entrapped in, even literally imprisoned by, traditional roles. In relating Christie's involvement with Helen, the victim of hereditary madness, Alcott reverts more obviously to her sensational mode and, as in "A Whisper in the Dark," presents a paradigm for the wrongs of woman.[8] Helen first appears like a fairy-tale heroine, "so beautiful and pale and still, that for an instant Christie thought her dead or sleeping" (95). But despite the reserve of both Helen and her mother, Christie soon learns the truth—that just as she had earlier found herself playing Jane Eyre, so mother and daughter together reenact the history of Jane's alter ego, Bertha Mason. Mrs. Carrol married for money, knowing the strain of madness in her husband's family; Helen, when the truth was revealed to prevent her own engagement, succumbed to insanity. Both believe Helen to be the victim of her mother's worldly ambition; in fact, both are victims of a system that keeps women economically dependent and limits their ambitions to the marriage market. This is the true family or patriarchal curse that Mrs. Carrol has perpetuated and Helen, like Sybil, inherited. By making the curse in Helen's family patrilineal rather than matrilineal as in Sybil's (and Bertha's), Alcott directly associates female madness with patriarchy.

Helen Carrol, then, is not so much an aberration as a type of Victorian female passivity and her madness the rage that seethes beneath the passive surface. Significantly, Helen is attracted to Christie when she learns that her companion has been an actress. Helen too had wanted to act, for "it would have given me something to do, and, however hard it is, it couldn't be worse than this" (99). Helen's longing for the stage, and her family's opposition, suggest once more that acting is for a woman a form of power and as such threatens those who wish to keep women passive within their sphere. Helen's conservatory is described as "a little world where perpetual summer reigned" (100), and her brother Harry regards her room as "a safe refuge from the temptations that beset one of his thoughtless and impetuous nature" (103). But Helen's room, like the Victorian home, is not an Eden, to which men can return and recover their lost innocence, but an artificial and confining construct. In Helen's conservatory "birds carolled in half-hidden prisons" (100), and she later reveals to Christie another room, with "barred windows, guarded fire, muffled walls, and other sights to chill your blood" (110), in which she spent a year. Like Jean Muir's, Helen's bosom bears a scar, but in her case that of a genuine suicide attempt. Her rage, which she is impotent to vent upon the world, has, like Jean's, turned inward, transforming her, like Sylvia Yule or Cecil Stein, into a "marble woman." We last see Helen "ready for her grave," surrounded, as was Snow White in her casket, by awed admirers.

What Helen calls "the old tragedy of our house," the house of patriarchy, is not only rage and repression but also isolation from and, as in the case of Snow White and other fairy-tale heroines, enmity toward other women. After Helen has told her story, Christie "put both arms about her, and held her close with a strong but silent tenderness better than any bonds" (113). The lack of tenderness—the substitution of constraining for sustaining bonds—has exacerbated Helen's misery. Physically separated from the rest of the household, especially from her younger sister, Bella, she is further separated by a gulf of guilt and recrimination from her mother. The irreparable harm Mrs. Carrol has done her daughter is indicated when her gift of a fleecy white robe, meant as a peace offering, becomes Helen's shroud. Later in *Work*, David's mother gives Christie a white shawl "like a pile of snow flakes" for her birthday (257), indicating that Christie has been able to create the bonds that Helen was so tragically denied.

Christie, by becoming a supporting actor in as well as an audience for the Carrols' tragedy, helps prevent its recurrence. First, she recounts her "whole history in the most expansive manner" (99). This power to make a narrative of her life, a power shared by the escaped slave Hepsey and later by Cynthy Wilkins, laundress, is a power denied Helen and Rachel, the "fallen woman" whom Christie next befriends. Helen must conceal her madness (or feminine rage) and Rachel her crime (of female sexual experience). But Christie persuades first Helen, then her mother, to break the silence imposed by the family curse. On hearing their stories, Bella rejects her lover, who, she later learns, was interested only in her money. Thus by refusing to perpetuate the curse of madness, Bella averts another and more pervasive one—that of male tyranny and female oppression. We later learn that Bella, by remaining single and devoting herself to her brother, manages to preserve his sanity as well as her own. While Bella's devotion to her brother appears still another instance of feminine influence and self-denial, she demonstrates that women, by sharing the truth of their oppression with daughters and sisters, can also save their sons and brothers. *Work* ends with the reappearance of Bella, who, having launched Harry on his career, now seeks an occupation of her own. In the final tableau she joins hands with Christie, Hepsey, Cynthy, Rachel, and Christie's daughter, Ruth—a sisterhood in place of the sister whom she lost, and never really knew.

Lack of such female solidarity casts Christie first as martyr, then as victim, a role that threatens to become her last. Sobered by her experience with the Carrols, Christie is horrified by her next employers, Miss Cotton and Mrs. King, whose names connect their cruelty with that of the male-ruled textile industry. After resigning in protest of their treatment of Rachel, Christie attempts to reconcile herself to loneliness and poverty by living for others. When life still seems dull and meaningless, she seeks refuge in religion but finds a faith of "machinery," "fear," and "strife" rather than "the tender trust of little children in their mother's love" (147). Threatened with eviction by her landlady, Mrs. Flint, and turned from the door of a woman for whom she sews, Christie is mocked by her glimpse of a bride surrounded by her sisters and receiving her mother's "last, loving touch to her array" (156). Having wandered to the river, Christie begins to "wonder how a human body would look floating through the night" and suffers a near-fatal loss of self in role: "It was an awesome fancy . . . for she seemed to see the phantom she had conjured up, and it wore the likeness of herself. . . . So plainly did she see it, so peaceful was the white face, so full of rest the folded hands, so strangely like, and yet unlike, herself, that she seemed to lose her identity, and wondered which was the real and which the imaginary Christie" (158). The supposed corpse, resembling Helen's and many another set piece of Victorian art and fiction, suggests that Christie no longer views herself as actor in her own drama but as a passive participant in a conventional script. As the allusion to Narcissus implies, Christie, in attempting to starve rather than satisfy the cravings of self, has not become unselfish but instead—like Sylvia Yule, Cecil Stein, and Beth March—has abdicated from responsibility. Christie's rescue by Rachel, who "tenderly laid the poor, white face upon her breast, and wrapped her shawl about the trembling figure clinging to her with such passionate delight" (160), reveals a need as desperate as Helen's for a woman's love. It also indicates that the selflessness enjoined on Victorian women can involve them in an almost infantile regression.

Christie's task in the next decade of her life, and in the remainder of the book, is twofold: she must learn once more to direct the drama of her life rather than become entrapped in prescribed roles, and she must regain faith in and reestablish bonds with other women. Christie begins both tasks when Rachel takes her to stay with the laundress Cynthy Wilkins. At first Christie is content to be the passive object of Cynthy's care. She allows Cynthy to tuck her into bed and awakens with the sense "that a skillful hand had taken the rudder" (170). As she tells Cynthy the next morning, "I slept like a baby, and feel like a new creature" (172). In many ways Christie finds herself back before the beginning of her adventures, in an atmosphere of domestic warmth and abundance (most of her conversations with Cynthy take place in the latter's kitchen) with a motherly woman, given, like Aunt Betsey, to homely metaphoric speech. But before long Christie realizes that she must resume her own life and, turning to Cynthy for advice, receives instead a story, the "cure for despair" of the chapter's title. Neither the moral of the story nor its substance—how Cynthy resolved an early marital conflict—is as important as the mere telling of it, for like Hepsey, who could give Christie "a comedy and tragedy surpassing anything she found" in books, and like Christie herself, who told Helen "her whole story in the most expansive manner," Cynthy possesses one key to women's power—the capacity to see and present their lives as drama or story. To Christie, who has lost this capacity, Cynthy indeed provides an antidote for despair. As Christie, still laughing, runs upstairs, she wonders "if she could be the same forlorn creature who had crept so wearily up only the night before" (195).

Cynthy Wilkins provides Christie with a temporary haven in which she can satisfy her craving for unconditional maternal warmth and affection. And she prepares her to relinquish it by renewing her sense of life's drama and the role that women can play in it. In order to play "a braver part . . . on a wider stage," however, Christie needs to combine what she has learned from Hepsey and Cynthy of female narrative—its metaphoric truth in humble detail—with the more vigorous, organized discourse of Mr. Power, the social reformer who is Cynthy's minister. Although Power is described as an "indomitable man" (208) and at first impresses Christie as a "stern judge" (213), he eventually becomes both model and mentor. Christie, on attending his church for the first time, finds much of what she sought in vain during her spiritual crisis. Struck by the preponderance of women in Power's congregation—"delicate girls," "sad-eyed women," and "anxious mothers" (205), Christie is also impressed by its spontaneity. As people join "at their own sweet will" in a hymn, she thinks that "the natural praise of each individual soul was perhaps more grateful to the ear of God than masses by great masters" (206). Power's prayer too is different from any she has ever heard, more of "a quiet talk with God," whom he addresses as the "dear father and mother of souls" (207). Power, in lessening the distance between himself and his congregation on the one hand and between himself and an androgynous rather than a patriarchal god on the other, undermines the hierarchical divisions and dualities upon which patriarchal institutions depend.[9]

Before Christie can join Mr. Power on "a wider stage" than that of the private home, she must, as the chapter title "Beginning Again" indicates, undergo a lengthy convalescence and apprenticeship. In some ways the gentle Quaker Mrs. Sterling continues the maternal care provided by Cynthy Wilkins. If Christie was reborn at the Wilkinses' and felt at first like an infant, she feels herself a child in the Sterling home. Here too it is the kitchen where Christie comes to know her hostess—or, in this case, employer. But the Sterling kitchen is in sharp contrast with the Wilkinses': "tidy with the immaculate order of which Shakers and Quakers alone seem to possess the secret," it is a kitchen where "Nothing burned or boiled over" and where "there was no litter or hurry" (221–22). Whereas the cheerful clutter and confusion of Cynthy's kitchen enabled Christie to forgo vain attempts rigidly to control her life, the order and serenity of Mrs. Sterling's kitchen help her to reorganize her self and reorder her priorities. And as she works side by side with Mrs. Sterling, Christie is reminded of Aunt Betsey's kitchen and "the good old-fashioned arts" she learned there (222). Christie's return to the kitchen—first Cynthy's, then Mrs. Sterling's—represents a return to past sources of strength, the solidarity she shared in Aunt Betsey's and Hepsey's kitchens but found threatened, compromised, or destroyed by the patriarchal home, the male workplace, and the female workplace organized on a male model and governed by male notions of propriety. Christie's primary responsibility, however, is not to the kitchen, and her primary companion is not Mrs. Sterling. Between the domestic and wider economic spheres, between nature and culture, lies the neutral territory of David's greenhouse. Unlike Helen Carrol's hothouse conservatory, a symbol of women's enforced idleness, David's greenhouse, though at times an idyllic place, combines features of workroom, laboratory, and sales gallery. Here Christie finds meaningful work and a puzzle, which she does not finally solve until after David's death.

Even before meeting David, Christie finds, in cleaning his bedroom, a welter of signs that mislead her. Rooms, as the narrator comments, "usually betray something of the character and tastes of their occupants" (223), and Christie is first struck by the volumes of Plato, Shakespeare, Milton, and Montaigne such as she "remembered . . . in her father's library," "books in unknown tongues" (224), and busts of Goethe, Schiller, and Linnaeus. Significantly, however, "Faust was full of ferns," "Andersen's lovely 'Märchen' fluttered its pictured leaves in the middle of an open Plato," and "In the middle of this fine society, slender and transparent as the spirit of a shape, stood a little vase holding one half-opened rose" (224). The fern, fairy tales, and half-opened rose mark, interrupt, and comment on the weighty male texts. Christie, blinded by "a feminine interest" and by her previous discovery of a woman's fan, letters, and needlework, can only wonder "if the dear, dead, or false woman had been fond of roses" (224), and she interprets the busts—broken, cracked, and covered with dust—as idols. In other words, she sees David as a man dwelling in both a personal and a patriarchal past. But the condition of the busts as well as David's pictures—of a monk, Martin Luther, and Mr. Power looking as if about "to shake hands in spite of time and space"—suggest that he has grown beyond both outworn idols and the "idle strife," so typical of patriarchal institutions, which had interfered with Christie's ability to worship. Most significant of all is the "sunny recess" filled with "bags and boxes of seed, bunches of herbs, and shelves full of those tiny pots in which baby plants are born and nursed till they can grow alone" (223). David's room implies an attempt to reconcile many opposites; chief among these, as signified by his books and baby plants, are masculine culture and feminine nature/nurture.

Having misread the signs of David's room, Christie proceeds to cast him in the role of brooding, melancholy, masterful hero. Reverting to her Jane Eyre role, but without her previous ironic detachment, Christie dons a silk apron before entering the conservatory. At David's suggestion she somewhat sheepishly exchanges it for a sturdy pinafore but is less willing to revise her romantic expectations, even when he is "paternal" as opposed to "masterful" and refuses to order her about (236). On becoming better acquainted with David, Christie comes to appreciate the strength behind his unassertive manner, but her appreciation gives rise to further dissatisfaction. As she complains to Mr. Power, "he *won't* be ambitious. . . . isn't it natural for a young man to have some personal aim or ambition to live for?" (251–52). Mr. Power, as though to contest the traditional view of manliness, upbraids Christie for wanting David to be "what the world calls great" as well as good and accuses her of hero worship (he later as a joke presents her with a copy of Carlyle's *Heroes and Hero-worship*). But Christie is not content until she discovers in David the counterpart of her restless longing. When he confesses that "I am sad, dissatisfied, bad, and selfish" and that "I often tire of this quiet life, hate my work, and long to break away, and follow my own wild and wilful impulses," she "could no more help regarding David as a martyr and admiring him for it" (276–77, 285). In this mood of hero worship she becomes convinced "that home was woman's sphere after all" and domestic perfection "an end worth living for, if masculine commendation rewarded the labor" (288 -89).

Ironically, Christie's efforts to worship David and abase herself run counter to his aspirations, which, like Mr. Power's, involve empowering the weak rather than exalting the powerful. Just as Mr. Power's "heart was truly an orphan asylum," so David's cottage is literally a "beneficent, unostentatious asylum," where women "could rest and recover themselves after the wrongs, defeats, and weariness that come to such in the battle of life" (247). And David's conservatory, like his room, subtly suggests the new order that he and Mr. Power envision. In the conservatory the "damp, sweet air made summer. . . . All manner of beautiful and curious plants were there; and Christie walked among them, as happy as a child who finds its playmates again" (229). Very different is this Eden from Rappaccini's garden or Bazil Yorke's marble one. Although distinctions between the sexes are not wholly erased—David acknowledges that some tasks are "better fitted for a woman's fingers" (230) and that "women have a tender way of doing such things that we can never learn" (235), he clearly values, envies, and tries to emulate women's gifts. When Christie explains the significance that she attaches to each bouquet, David wistfully admits, "I can grow the flowers, but not read them" (233). Nonetheless, David's discourse on flowers reveals a sensitivity that we associate with women. In answering Christie's questions he gives "not dry botanical names and facts, but all the delicate traits, curious habits, and poetical romances of the sweet things, as if [he] knew and loved them as friends, not merely valued them as merchandise" (236). As he and Christie work side by side in the conservatory, first preparing flowers for a dance, then for a child's funeral, they represent a model of mutuality and cooperation. Christie begins a song and David completes it; David prepares a bouquet, and Christie, by gathering flowers from outside the conservatory, gives it the final touch, the fresh perspective women can bring to male enterprise. Significantly, "that little task performed together seemed to have made them friends" (235). The merging of spheres temporarily replaces hero worship with mutual respect.

Alcott uses a discussion of double carnations to indicate how, between them, David Sterling and Mr. Power encourage Christie to accept David's androgynous nature and reclaim her own. Christie initiates this discussion by lamenting to Mr. Power that David "won't seem to care for any thing but watching over his mother, reading his old books, and making flowers bloom double when they ought to be single" (252). When David joins them, Christie continues to express her dissatisfaction but does so indirectly by repudiating the flower itself. Objecting that "double-carnations are so untidy, all bursting out of the calyx as if the petals had quarreled and could not live together," she denies the masculine in her nature and protests the feminine in David's. But to persist in such denial will produce, as David argues, a flower "poor and incomplete with little scent or beauty." The single carnation is tellingly described as "a poor pale solitary maiden" in contrast to "the great crimson and white carnations near by, filling the air with spicy odor"

(255). Mr. Power's reflection that he might "be the gardener to mix the colors of the two human plants before him" (255) obviously anticipates the union of Christie and David, but his, as well as David's, preference for double flowers, together with the narrator's description, indicates the author's preference for rich and complex individuals. Both David and Mr. Power are gardeners, one literal, the other metaphoric, and both are bent on doubling the strength as well as beauty of the human plant by grafting the best qualities of one sex onto those of the other.[10]

As though to help Christie recover the fire and ambition that she would prefer to project onto David, Mr. Power encourages her to play increasingly demanding roles. After David expresses a desire to see her act and she performs some comic characters from Dickens, Mr. Power requests "a touch of tragedy." Christie at first demurs, then compromises by consenting to "give you Miss St. Clair as Juliet." In doing so Christie both reenacts her own life prior to her arrival at the Sterlings' and again illustrates the functions of acting for Alcott's heroines. Intending to "burlesque the poison scene . . . she soon forgot St. Clair in poor Juliet, and did it as she had often longed to do it, with all the power and passion she possessed" (271). In impersonating and burlesquing St. Clair as Juliet, Christie reenacts her role as the servant Jane, her impersonation of the actress Miss Douglas, and her brief masquerade as Jane Eyre; as often before, she protects herself, here from possible failure in a demanding part before people she values, by regarding her role as simply that and by distancing herself from it. By forgetting St. Clair in Juliet, on the other hand, Christie, as she had as Amazon, Peg Woffington, and finally Jane Eyre, merges self with role and expresses rather than conceals emotion. As Mr. Power perhaps anticipated, Christie is "inspired by her superb success," and David "much impressed by the dramatic ability which Christie's usual quietude had most effectually hidden" (272–73). But though Christie's performance as Juliet releases emotion and rekindles ambition, it also recalls the danger of losing self in role. Having completely identified with Juliet, Christie in her excitement swallows the vinegar that serves as poison just as earlier, having identified with female victims, she narrowly escaped a victim's death.

In a further effort to rouse Christie from the "quietude" that has really troubled her more than David's, Mr. Power asks her to play Shakespeare's Portia. It is little wonder that the androgynous Portia, who dared to leave home for courtroom in the guise of a male, is "a favorite character" of his. Just as Power can "thunder" against injustice yet "whisper consolation like a mother" (248), so Portia refuses to "wrest once the law to [her] authority" for fear that "error . . . will rush into the state," yet insists that "mercy is above this sceptered sway" (IV.i). Portia at the beginning of the play is the fairy-tale heroine, rendered passive by patriarchy: "I may neither choose who I would, nor refuse whom I dislike; so is the will of a living daughter curb'd by the will of a dead father" (I.ii). But her story does not end, as do fairy tales, when the hero solves the riddle of the caskets. Instead Portia must venture forth to save her husband's friend, who is equally bound by a tyrannous male will. Thus Portia's career reverses that of Christie, who early assumed the hero's role only to play increasingly passive female parts. As she tells Power when he asks her to play Portia's role: "I used to study it, but . . . gave it up" (273). And the speech from *The Merchant of Venice* that she finally consents to give—the one in which Portia's "willing spirit / Commits itself . . . to be directed, / As from her lord, her governor, her king" (274)—honors the letter, not the spirit, of Power's request. Not only does she continue to cast Power in the role of hero; she eschews all personal ambition ("though, for myself alone, / I would not be ambitious in my wish") and assumes the familiar role of "little woman"—"an unlesson'd girl, unschool'd, unpractis'd."

Although her performance as Juliet and Lady Macbeth, passionate and ambitious women, displays a range of emotion concealed beneath her "usual quietude" and thus forces David to "unmask" himself (282), Christie's decision to play the self-abnegating, feminine rather than the self-assertive, androgynous Portia indicates that her "cure for despair" is not complete. In fact, it anticipates a resumption of the martyr role that plunged her into despair. Perversely assuming that her love for David is not returned, Christie, the morning of her departure from the Sterling household, "fell to slicing bread with an energetic rapidity which resulted in a cut finger" (304). When Christie rubs her pale cheeks to restore their color, David comments, "How well you women know how to conceal your wounds." Christie's response—"It is a valuable accomplishment for us sometimes: you forget that I have been an actress" (307)—suggests once more how women immolate themselves for men and then conceal the self-inflicted injury. Christie persists in her role as wounded woman even when, as Mr. Power's assistant, she is called upon to act in the real world. In a passage similar to the one in *Little Women* that begins "if she [Jo] had been the heroine of a moral story book," the narrator informs us that if Christie "had been a regular novel heroine at this crisis, she would have grown gray in a single night, had a dangerous illness, gone mad, or at least taken to pervading the house at unseasonable hours with her back hair down and much wringing of the hands. Being only a commonplace woman she did nothing so romantic" (310). True, Christie is not driven to opium like Cecil, to madness like Sybil, or to sleepwalking like Sylvia, but she does, like her fictional as well as real-life sisters, become a kind of martyr, "enamoured of self-sacrifice" (324).

So enamored, Christie is blind to the opportunities that she will later embrace. Although exposed to "eager women just beginning their protest against the wrongs that had wrecked their peace; subdued women who had been worsted in the unequal conflict and given it up; resolute women with 'No surrender' written all over their strong-minded countenances," Christie finds "only one face worth looking at till David came, and that was Mr. Power's" (313). The reappearance of Philip Fletcher offers temporary diversion: Christie yields "to the fascination of the hour ... half unconsciously assuming something of the 'dash and daring' which Mr. Fletcher had once confessed to finding so captivating in the demure governess. He evidently thought so still, and played his part with spirit" (317–18). But the theatricality of their meeting suggests a larger unreality. Christie, in the days that follow, begins to suspect that her new sense of power, like most women's during courtship, is the prelude to a lifetime of subjection: "she could not conquer a suspicion that, however much Mr. Fletcher might love his wife, he would be something of a tyrant, and she was very sure she never would make a good slave" (324). Advised by Cynthy Wilkins that "ef any one wants to go a sacrificin' herself for the good of others there's a better way of doin' it" (327), Christie laments, "Nobody else wants her!" (329). In response, Cynthy gives not just the conventional wisdom, "I know there's a mate for her somewheres, so she'd better wait a spell and trust in Providence," but advice that flies in the face of convention: "for the Lord knows there's a sight of good works sufferin' to be done, and single women has the best chance at 'em" (329).

Ironically, David Sterling has all along been attempting to redress the societal wrongs that Christie, in her inward quest, ignores. Before meeting David, Christie is intrigued and puzzled by Mr. Power's remark that David "pities and protects womankind as the only retaliation for the life-long grief one woman brought upon him" (217). Only after David's reunion with his sister Letty, the Rachel whom Christie earlier befriended, do we learn that his "retaliation" is actually reparation. As David tells Christie, he responded to his sister's seduction in true patri-archal fashion: "Letty had brought a stain upon our honest name that time could never wash away. . . . I could *not* forgive; wrath burned hot within me, and the desire for retribution would not be appeased" (344–45). After hearing of Letty's supposed death, David attempted to atone "for that harshness to one woman by years of devotion to many" (346). To do so, as we have seen, David eschewed traditional male traits like ambition and refused the role of hero that Christie would cast him in. While David labored with and for women in home and garden, Letty, who had "hated dependence, even on a brother who would have worked his soul out for her" (343), learned to make her way in the world. Only when the two are reunited, only when David is symbolically healed and made whole, can he commit himself to Christie in marriage. Christie, after accepting David's proposal, admits to Mr. Power that "'double flowers' *are* loveliest and best" (354). David, by reclaiming his sister and the sister in him, enables Christie to preserve her female bonds and to renew her quest for a fuller identity.[11]

Since David seems to represent the androgynous hero that such figures as Moor/Warwick and Yorke/Germain merely anticipated, one may wonder, with Christie, why he has to die. One answer, according to Mr. Power, is that "the seeming incompleteness of his life was beautifully rounded by the act that caused his death" (410–11). Even before that act, David's participation in the Civil War is of a piece with his civilian life. The narrator tells us that David "though he had tended his flowers like a woman . . . now proved that he could also do his duty and keep his honor stainless as a soldier" (387). But David does not simply exchange his nurturing qualities for martial ones. Military prowess, as reflected in rank and decoration, means nothing to David. He "might have risen rapidly, but was con-tent to remain as captain of his company; for his men loved him, and he was prouder of his influence over them than of any decoration he could win" (386–87). We are told that a "noble nature soon takes its proper rank and exerts its purifying influence" (387), but few men are content with such intangible "rank," and few women have the opportunity to exert a "purifying influence" outside the home. Appropriately, David dies not in battle with the rebels but in helping a woman slave to escape. Christie, at his deathbed, protests, "it is not just that you should suffer this for a creature whose whole life is not worth a day of your brave, useful, precious one! Why did you pay such a price for that girl's liberty?" David answers,

"Because I owed it;—she suffered more than this seeing her baby die" (405). He goes on to tell Christie, "You will do my part, and do it better than I could" (406). David realizes the long-accumulated debt white males owe women as well as oppressed races—a debt that must be paid no matter what the cost. He also recognizes that the rationale for white male privilege—that their lives are worth more because they contribute more to humanity—is specious; far from being irreplaceable in any given role, men can be replaced, and perhaps surpassed, by women.

Despite the egalitarian nature of their marriage, symbolized by their wedding in uniform, Christie continues to idolize David. On her wedding day, she proclaims, "I've found my hero at last" (365), and when David is fatally wounded, she finds it almost easier to accept his death than the lack of glory surrounding it. David, as we have seen, was content to exert influence over his men and repay the debt he owed to women. For this, Mr. Power assures Christie, he "received a better reward than any human hand could give him, in the gratitude of many women, the respect of many men" (410). But Christie "could not be content with this invisible, intangible recompense for her hero" (411). Understanding and acceptance come only when Christie, in her grief, takes refuge in David's room. There, by "reading his books, thinking of his love and life, listening to 'David's voice'"—the wind in his old flute—she comes at last to read that room aright (412–13). When, in the final chapter, Christie is presented with "a quaint and lovely picture of Mr. Greatheart, leading the fugitives from the City of Destruction" (440), she is able, like Hepsey, who "considered David worthy of a place with old John Brown and Colonel Shaw" (441), to recognize the resemblance to her husband and to understand the true nature of his heroism.

As though to symbolize the new order that David dies for, Alcott has Christie give birth to a daughter, Ruth, and transform the Sterling home into a model community. First, she "took garden and green-house into her own hands" (415), sharing the proceeds with Letty and Mrs. Sterling.[12] When Uncle Enos, to whom she has been reconciled, argues, "That ain't a fair bargain," Christie answers tartly, "we don't make bargains, sir: we work for one another and share every thing together" (419). Ironically, Uncle Enos is helpless to dispose of the profits he has hoarded for years and leaves them to Christie. This legacy enables her to continue David's work, which she does by employing several young girls to help with the nursery business. Most important, though, Christie at forty finds work of her own, work that takes her, like Portia, out of the private and into the public sphere. As advocate for working-class women and as mediator between them and their middle-class sisters, Christie can fulfill herself both as actress and as woman.

In "At Forty," the final chapter of *Work,* Christie discovers "the task my life has been fitting me for" (430), a task she shares with her forty-year-old creator. At a women's meeting, Christie is struck by the contrast between two types of speech—the personal anecdotes of the working women and the impersonal addresses of their educated sisters, who, in imitation of male models, offer utopian visions, revolutionary polemics, and statistical surveys. Christie, feeling "a strong desire to bring the helpers and the helped into truer relations with each other" (427), makes "her first speech in public since she left the stage" (428). This speech, and the manner of its delivery, bridges the gap not only between working- and middle-class women but between female private and male public performance. First, Christie, when invited to the platform, insists on remaining among her audience, for like Mr. Power she would lessen the distance between instructor and instructed, leader and led. As a result, her audience "saw and felt that a genuine woman stood down there among them like a sister, ready with head, heart, and hand to help them help themselves" (429). The speech itself, as when Christie first refused Philip Fletcher, combines the art of the actress with the feeling of a woman: "That early training stood her in good stead now, giving her self-possession, power of voice, and ease of gesture; while the purpose of her heart lent her the sort of simple eloquence that touches, persuades, and convinces better than logic, flattery, or oratory." Further, she combines the best features of her mentors' styles—the "unconscious eloquence" of a Hepsey or Cynthy with the "wise counsel" of Mr. Power: "words came faster than she could utter them, thoughts pressed upon her, and all the lessons of her life rose vividly before her to give weight to her arguments, value to her counsel, and the force of truth to every sentence she uttered" (428).

Many have commented on the parallels between Christie Devon and Louisa May Alcott: their early work experience, their love of the stage, their depression and contemplated suicide, their service as nurses during the Civil War. It is also tempting to see Christie's aborted theatrical career, like Jo's aborted literary one, as Alcott's denial of her real talent and to see Christie's period of self-sacrifice and self-abnegation, her assumption of the domestic, little woman role, as Alcott's career as a children's writer. Christie's performance at the women's meeting, then, would be analogous to *Work* itself, or at least its final chapter—a performance in which Alcott could, like Christie, claim to be "'strong-minded,' a radical, and a reformer" (437). But whereas we are led to believe that Christie's speech is the beginning of a new career, *Work*, most critics would argue, remains an anomaly in a well-established one. Yet Christie's various performances, both on- and off-stage—as Jane, Amazon, Peg Woffington, Jane Eyre, Juliet, Portia, and reformer—can all be interpreted as representing aspects of Alcott's art. Like Christie, Alcott can assume a demure, domestic posture, preserving an ironic distance between herself and her persona. As Christie uses a dramatic context, so Alcott uses a literary text—and the dramatic contexts she creates within it—to both conceal and reveal, often simultaneously. But the danger of women's acting, that of losing themselves, as Christie occasionally does, in culturally prescribed roles, is one that Alcott, despite appearances to the contrary, assiduously avoids.

Christie's last performance, as speaker before an audience of working-class women, bears the same relation to her early stage career as Alcott's domestic fiction bears to her sensation stories. Christie, as we remember, adopted a stage name just as Alcott published her sensation tales anonymously or pseudonymously. Christie felt that her profession alienated her from both other women and, by its competitive nature, her own womanhood; Alcott's sensation fiction, while doubtless read by many women, did not succeed in unifying as diverse a female audience as did her domestic fiction. Finally, Christie's speech, like Alcott's domestic fiction, uses her own experience and the familiar details of domestic life to create an art that appears artless but has persuasive power. Thus it seems compatible with womanhood—even the Cult of True Womanhood—but in fact presents a powerful plea for the "new emancipation" that Christie envisions. Christie, after a long struggle, finds the best use for her dramatic and self-dramatizing talents in a public role consistent with, in fact dependent for its success upon, her womanhood. Alcott, in dramatizing Christie's moment of self-discovery, conveys her own sense of vocation. *Work*, according to its subtitle, is "a story of experience," and it ultimately proves, like so many of Alcott's fictions, to be the story of her artistic experience. When asked to contribute to Elizabeth Cady Stanton's *Revolution*, Alcott wrote to her family, "I think I'd rather keep to my own work and lecture the public in a story, than hold forth...in the papers" (144). Like Christie, Alcott chose to "make folks laugh and cry with a few plain words" (442), thus "quietly insinuating a better state of things" (437), for, like Cynthy Wilkins, she realized that women would "need a sight of boostin'" if they were ever to stand alone (442).

CHAPTER 8

"An Identity 'Other' Than Their Own":
A Modern Mephistopheles

Women have long searched, and continue to search, for an identity "other" than their own. Caught in the conventions of their sex, they have sought an escape from gender. A woman author who was not content to expound the titillations of romance, or to live out Freud's family romance, had two means of escape. One was to hide her identity as an author within the shelter of anonymity, the safety of secrecy, to write while protecting the quotidian self leading her appropriate life. The other was to create in her writings women characters, and sometimes male characters, who might openly enact the dangerous adventures of a woman's life, unconstrained by female propriety. Some, like Charlotte Brontë, did both.

Carolyn Heilbrun,
Writing a Woman's Life (111–12)

When romances do really teach anything, or produce any effective operation, it is usually through a far more subtle process than the ostensible one.

Nathaniel Hawthorne, Preface to
The House of the Seven Gables (352)

In creating the heroines Jean Muir, Jo March Bhaer, and Christie Devon, Alcott not only portrayed the roles that women were forced to assume or strategically adopt; she suggested the external forces and internal conflicts that she, like most women artists, had to confront, circumvent, or resolve. This preoccupation with the woman artist continued through the 1870s and 1880s—in her last sensation fiction, *A Modern Mephistopheles,* in the uncompleted novella *Diana and Persis,* and in her last March novel, *Jo's Boys.* But in turning from *Work* to the earliest of these, *A Modern Mephistopheles,* one is apt to be disappointed. For while *Work* ends with a mature heroine successfully combining her art with political action, *A Modern Mephistopheles* ends with the death of its still-childlike heroine. In fact, Gladys combines traits of Sylvia Yule, Cecil Stein, and Beth March, and, more than theirs, her little womanhood and its obligatory martyrdom seems glorified. Alcott's epigraph, the last four lines of Goethe's *Faust,* appears to affirm the power of the female victim to confound evil and save man—or men.[1] However, Alcott's allusions throughout the text—to Goethe, to Tennyson, and especially to Hawthorne—do not indicate an allegory of female virtue purifying male vice. Instead, by appropriating and revising the tales of male authors, Alcott constructs an alternative identity for women—especially women artists.

When in 1876 Thomas Niles, Alcott's editor, first proposed that she contribute a novel to Roberts Brothers' No Name Series, a group of anonymous works by established writers, he expected her to revise an early tale, one that, according to a September 1866 journal entry, had been rejected as "too long & too sensational" (153). Early in 1877, however, Alcott went to the Bellevue Hotel and, in a burst of inspiration, wrote a novel that, except for its Faustian title and theme, bears little resemblance to the loose, episodic early manuscript.[2] One of the most tightly constructed of Alcott's novels, *A Modern Mephistopheles* consists of a succession of scenes, each involving two or more of what an early reviewer, Edward R. Burlingame, called her "psychological quadrilateral."[3] Chapters 1 through 7, which concentrate on the relationship between a wealthy, cultured invalid, Jasper Helwyze, and his protégé, the aspiring poet Felix Canaris, culminate in the latter's marriage, at the insistence of Helwyze, to Gladys, the ward of his former mistress, Olivia. The remaining eleven chapters focus on Helwyze's growing obsession with Gladys and on her efforts to disentangle herself and her husband from Helwyze and Olivia, who leads Felix into dissipation. All of the scenes, with the exception of the first, take place in one or the other of Helwyze's two homes, and, as we shall see, the ordering of interior space is especially significant. Motifs from earlier works abound: the Pygmalion and Psyche myths, the language of flowers, the reversal of gender roles. As suggested by the various webs of allusion and by the tableaux vivants in which Olivia and Gladys perform, Alcott overdetermines the symbolic significance of her characters as well as distributes the traits of a whole human being among them. Finally, in *A Modern Mephistopheles* Alcott exploits the circumstances of its publication not only to create a marvelously ironic text but to reflect and comment on the ironic nature of her entire career.

The early and final chapters of *A Modern Mephistopheles* establish its connections with Goethe's *Faust* and appear to emphasize the Faustian theme of male pride, ambition, and curiosity redeemed by female humility, patience, and purity. In the opening chapter, Felix Canaris, having had a manuscript rejected, is tempted, like Faust, to end his life but is prevented by a fateful knock on the door. After rescuing Felix, Helwyze employs him as a secretary, and by the end of a month the young poet has exchanged his liberty for "the success men covet and admire, suffer and strive for, and die content if they win it only for a little time" (17). Felix's volume of poems, when it appears, creates a sensation, and he is seemingly launched on a brilliant career. Amused for a while, Helwyze begins to tire of studying Felix for subtle signs of his corruption and turns his attention to Gladys. Observing the courtship of Felix and Gladys, Olivia calls them "Faust and Margaret, playing the old, old game," and Helwyze adds sardonically, "And Mephistopheles and Martha looking on" (36). Although Olivia is not flattered to be cast as Martha, she helps Helwyze to procure Gladys, ostensibly for Felix but in reality for himself. Having coerced Felix into marrying the girl, Helwyze proceeds to torture the young pair while tightening their bonds of obligation to him. Felix, though he reveres his wife, resents having been constrained to marry her and attempts to rebel against Helwyze—but actually plays into his hands—by leading a life of dissipation. Gladys is grieved by her wayward husband and disturbed by their benefactor's constant scrutiny. Olivia, who deserted Helwyze when he became ill (and, we infer, impotent) and who is now trying to regain his love, is bored by her dalliance with Felix and jealous of Helwyze's attentions to his wife.

Helwyze at first appears to revel in his Mephistophelean role but ends up suffering the most excruciating torment. As Gladys begins to reform her husband, and inspire his passion as well as his respect, she gently but effectually repels Helwyze. Finally, in an effort to plumb the depths of Gladys's soul, he gives her opium, but when, like Satan whispering at the ear of Eve, he tries to insinuate impure thoughts into her unconscious mind,[4] her response only tortures him the more. The climax comes when Gladys finally learns from Felix the secret of their bargain—that Helwyze is the author of the books upon which Felix's reputation rests. Although she forgives him, the shock sends her into premature labor, and both she and the child die. Helwyze, in reaction, suffers a stroke that leaves him paralyzed and completely helpless. At the end of the book, after Gladys's death and Felix's defiant departure to pursue a stage career, Helwyze meditates on the parallels between himself and his prototype. Thinking first of the end of *Faust,* part 1, he is struck by the contrast: "Goethe could make his Satan as he liked; but Fate was stronger than I, and so comes ignominious failure. Margaret dies, and Faust suffers, but Mephistopheles cannot go with him on his new wanderings" (288–89). But then, apparently thinking of the end of *Faust,* part 2, he concludes that the analogy between him and Mephistopheles holds after all: "In loving the angel I lose the soul I had nearly won; the roses turn to flakes of fire, and the poor devil is left lamenting" (289). Just as Mephistopheles, weakened by a fleeting desire for the male angels, allows them to rob him of Faust's soul, so Helwyze's love for Gladys produces the catastrophe that enables Felix to escape him. Helwyze believes that Gladys, like Margaret, will succeed in saving the man she loves, but he, like Mephistopheles, is doomed to Hell "because . . . *I* have no hope to follow and find her again" (290).[5]

Mephistopheles' attraction to the male angels points to a curious feature of *A Modern Mephistopheles,* for the relationship between Helwyze and Felix, like that between such Alcott heroes as Warwick and Moor, and especially Germain and Yorke, seems a complicated homosocial, if not a homosexual, one.[6] The scene describing their bargain abounds in allusions to Felix's classic beauty. His "luxuriant locks," "white throat," "large, dreamy eyes," and "voluptuous lips" are "redeem[ed] . . . from effeminacy" only by "an indescribable expression of fire and force" (14–15). Helwyze, after narrowly observing him from behind his volume of *Faust,* asks Felix to remain with him for a year, declining the offer of any service but his companionship. As he tells the youth, "It is not every one who can have antique beauty in flesh and blood as well as marble; I have a fancy to keep my handsome secretary as the one ornament my library lacked before" (16). Felix later professes gratitude to Helwyze, telling Gladys that "he asks nothing of me except such services as I love to render" (28), but in return for literary fame, Felix had promised to be "yours, body and soul" (17), and Helwyze boasts to Olivia that Felix, whose Greek ancestry is continually stressed, is his "Greek slave. . . . I bought my handsome Alcibiades, and an excellent bargain I find him" (37–38). As though sensing rejection, Felix is resentful when Helwyze first pressures him to court Gladys, and although he has no real desire for Olivia, he insists on his freedom to court her instead. After Olivia rejects him, as he half expects her to do, Helwyze taunts him with possessing "all the gifts which win women except wealth and ——" (86). In retrospect, the reader can supply for the missing word "character" or "integrity," but what the youth, described as "too beautiful for a man" (20), may also lack is a desire for women. As the narrator tells us, "A certain, almost brutal frankness characterized the intercourse of these men at times; for the tie between them was a peculiar one, and fretted both, though both clung to it with strange tenacity" (86).

Felix, however, functions not only as homoerotic object for Helwyze but as heterosexual agent. Although Felix possesses an almost feminine beauty and continually admires himself in mirrors and other polished surfaces, he is at times described as a model of passionate young manhood. In fact, it becomes increasingly clear that Helwyze, in buying Felix, is attempting to buy the youth, health, and manly vigor that he lacks. Helwyze, as Felix tells Gladys, once suffered "a terrible fall," which not only "tied him to a bed of torment for some years" (29–30) but prevented his marriage to Olivia. When Olivia now ironically suggests that Helwyze marry Gladys himself rather than marry her to Felix, Helwyze, "glancing at his wasted limbs," professes that his "passions are all dead, else life would be a hell, not the purgatory it is" (43). In contrast, Felix's "youth lent its vigor to the well-knit frame, every limb of which was so perfectly proportioned that strength and grace were most harmoniously blended" (14). Felix, then, serves as an extension of, a surrogate for, the impotent Helwyze in his relations with both Olivia and Gladys. As he tells Olivia, "I will give him to you, for I have fancied of late that you rather coveted him. . . . wait a little, and I will make a charming plaything for you" (38). In return, he asks that she help him procure her protégée, Gladys, for Felix, so that he can observe at close hand, as the voyeuristic

Mephistopheles observed Faust's seduction of Margaret, "how this young creature meets the trials and temptations life and love will bring her" (41). The sexual nature of his interest in both Olivia and Gladys is underscored by the flowers that he and Olivia handle and discuss. Olivia, to express her loyalty to Helwyze, plucks and offers him "a wine-dark rose" (43), which he idly strips petal by petal. When she would replace it with another, he requests instead her "spring flower," meaning Gladys, so that he can enjoy "the faint, vernal fragrance" of a nature "coyly hidden from common eye and touch" (45–46).

As suggested by their symbiotic relationship and literary collaboration, Helwyze and Felix represent the double-edged sword of patriarchal oppression. Gladys, after her marriage to Felix, begins to lead a "double life": "Heart and mind were divided between the two, who soon absorbed every feeling, every thought. To the younger man she was a teacher, to the elder a pupil; in the one world she ruled, in the other served" (122–23). Helwyze, whom Gladys calls her "master," is another version of the incestuous father or guardian, who seeks to mold and manipulate his child or ward. Felix, the young pagan, is vain and childish, dependent upon Gladys for moral guidance and instruction. Both men regard her as a childlike little woman or angel in the house and prefer her to the older, sexually mature Olivia. When Helwyze first asks Gladys to make his house a home for Felix, she defers to the older woman, but Helwyze insists, "Such women weary while they dazzle, the gentler sort win while they soothe" (74). Helwyze's description of "the gentler sort" aptly sums up the traditional view of women—their very powerlessness constitutes their power; by submitting to their exclusion from one world or sphere, they gain control in another. Different as Helwyze and Felix appear to be, together they represent two aspects of the masculine that most women have to contend with in one person. Further, Helwyze's mysterious "fall" and his ability to control both Felix and Olivia suggest the buried fear at the root of male tyranny and the way that tyranny, masquerading as authority, perpetuates itself by enlisting both younger men and older women in its cause.

Gladys's "double life," which far from being unique represents the life of everywoman, is reflected in the spatial division of Helwyze's home. This "home," in which the entire action of chapters 8 through 18 takes place, stands for the world, as suggested by the exotic treasures that fill it. Gladys, after her marriage, delights in "wandering alone through the great house . . . for Helwyze made this his world, and gathered about him every luxury which taste, caprice, or necessity demanded" (104). Within this world is the library, where Helwyze all but lives, and the "small, bare *cabinet de travail*," where Felix hopes to write his next book. From this room Gladys is, significantly, excluded. Felix tells her, "Mr. Helwyze is jailer, and only lets me out when I have done my stint." He warns Gladys that there is "No room . . . even for a little thing like you"; should she enter, she might "fare like Bluebeard's Fatima" (109). Felix's work ostensibly takes place within the home, but Gladys is nonetheless excluded from the workplace, forced patiently—or impatiently—to await Felix's emergence from it. With interest Helwyze watches Gladys "flit about the room, brushing up the hearth, brightening the lamps, and putting by the finished books, as if the day's duties were all done, the evening's rest and pleasure honestly earned, eagerly waited for. He well knew that this pleasure consisted in carrying Canaris away to her own domain" (123). Denied any employment except waiting on and studying with Helwyze, Gladys lives for the moment when Felix, who has been struggling all day to win honor and glory for her, reenters her sphere.

Yet even Gladys's domain, the supposedly private sphere, is compartmentalized so that only a tiny portion of it reflects her individuality and permits her to be herself. The outer chamber of the Canarises' apartment oppresses Gladys with its opulence and sensuality, for "deepest crimson glowed everywhere, making her feel as if she stood in the heart of a great rose whose silken petals curtained her round" (101–2). The inner chamber is in striking contrast, but the effect is such as to further the "double life" that Gladys is now called upon to lead. "White everywhere," with a "sheaf of lilies . . . on the low chimney-piece," this room, designed by Felix to be a replica of Gladys's "little room at home" (113), "seemed to shut out the world, securing the sweet privacy a happy woman loves" (102–3). In all the great house, only a curtained recess provides Gladys with a space reflective of her own nature rather than others' views of it, and even this is described as "a little woodland nook imprisoned between the glass-door and the deep window beyond" (103). Although containing "hardy vines," "rough arbutus leaves," "humble weeds," "damp fresh odors," and "sturdy grasses," this "veritable bit of the forest" (103–4) is tamed and marginalized, a tiny annex to the worlds of male exploration, conquest, and ambition and of female sexploitation, enclosure, and isolation.

Still another interior view, however, suggests that men as well as women are imprisoned in the house of patriarchy. Immediately after discovering the woodland nook, Gladys stumbles upon a series of such recesses. The first three, containing Eastern and classical treasures and well-worn volumes, seem to represent the masculine world of travel, art, and learning from which she is excluded, but the fourth indicates a spiritual isolation and emotional impoverishment greater than her own. The "least inviting of them all," it consists of "a single chair," placed "Behind the curtain of a window looking out upon the broad street." In "the worn spot in the carpet, the crumpled cushion on the window-ledge," Gladys finds "mute witnesses that Helwyze felt drawn towards his kin, and found some solace in watching the activity he could no longer share" (105–6). Felix imprisoned in his *cabinet de travail,* Gladys cloistered in an apartment half brothel, half nunnery, and Helwyze entrapped in a world of his own making are all equally the victims of patriarchy. In fact, Felix, in his role of household ornament and petted protégé, and Helwyze, with his impotence and immobility, are as much types of feminine powerlessness as they are of masculine power.

When Gladys, complaining of sleeplessness, is without her knowledge given opium by Helwyze, she, like so many Alcott heroines upon the stage, expresses truths about herself and her relationships with others.[7] Encouraged and aided by Olivia, who welcomes an opportunity to display herself before Helwyze and Felix, Gladys enacts four roles from Tennyson's *Idylls of the King.* In the first tableau, Gladys appears as "fair Enid, all in faded silk" (188) and sings the song of Fortune's wheel that Geraint, her tyrannical future husband, overhears before first meeting her. In another, Gladys appears as the "little novice" who sings "Too late" to Guinevere, played by Olivia. In the final tableau, Gladys sings Elaine's "Song of Love and Death" after Lancelot leaves her without a backward glance. But the most revealing of these performances is the one in which Gladys, to the astonishment of both Helwyze and Felix, plays Vivien to Olivia's Merlin and sings the temptress's song of seduction. To reinforce the disparity between Gladys's habitual modesty and Vivien's shamelessness, the narrator quotes the lines describing her as clothed in a "robe of samite without price, that more exprest / Than hid her" and "clung about her lissome limbs" (190), hastening to add that in "any other mood, Gladys would never have consented" to show "Shoulders and arms . . . rosy white under the veil of hair which swept to her knee" (191). Helwyze characteristically interprets this unwonted display as a tribute to her male viewers. But while Olivia, a "trifle *too* gorgeous, perhaps, for the repentant Guinevere" (193), may be playing to the male audience, Gladys in her opium trance seems to be acting out a truth of her own nature. Helwyze, watching the effect of the opium upon Gladys, is aware that "a double drama was passing on that little stage" (192) but not that Enid, Geraint, Elaine, Lancelot, Guinevere, Arthur, Vivien, and Merlin all have their counterparts within his own household.

For example, Gladys, in playing Enid, prepares to withstand Helwyze and reclaim Felix. The Enid idylls, one may recall, combine a tale of male bravado, possessiveness, and jealousy with a female quest for selfhood. Before their marriage, Geraint insists that Enid appear before Arthur's court in her "faded silk," for he believes that if she could "cast aside / A splendor dear to woman," he can "rest . . . Fixt on her faith" (348). Still fearful after marriage, he removes Enid from the court and finally out into the wilderness. Ironically, however, his efforts to establish and exercise his masculine prerogative drive "all his force . . . into mere effeminacy" (327) and expose Enid to the very threat of sexual violation that he is trying to avert. Enid, though at first she bears meekly with his irrational behavior, is more than a patient Griselda, who will suffer any amount of abuse without complaint; rather, she is a kind of Psyche figure, who liberates herself and Geraint from the cave of his uxoriousness and sensuality. Waking one night, she berates herself for being "no true wife" because she dares not reprove his degradation. Her reproof, like the tallow from Psyche's candle, is construed as betrayal, but it sets her on a journey that transforms her from passive victim into active agent. Time and again she saves Geraint from the dangers to which his foolhardiness has exposed him. And when his rashness places her at the mercy of an old suitor, she answers Limours "with such craft as women use, / Guilty or guiltless, to stave off a chance / That breaks upon them perilously" (359). Her courage and resourcefulness enable her to withstand and outwit her male adversaries and make a mockery of her "protector's" vaunted prowess. Felix, watching his wife play Enid, is a "little conscience-stricken by the look Gladys wore" (190). Although he is no jealous husband, his conceit masking insecurity, his lack of consideration, his recklessness and dissipation, and his propensity for violence are all mirrored in Geraint.

The little woman, who Enid at first appears to be, is rather Elaine, the lily maid, whom Gladys clearly resembles. Both are lovely, innocent, and associated with flowers that betoken purity and fragility. (Helwyze, in a scene immediately preceding the tableaux vivants, rudely ruffles the petals of a white cyclamen that Gladys regards as "the little symbol of herself" [178].) Further, both Elaine and Gladys are artists: Elaine fashions a case for Lancelot's shield (simulated in Gladys's performance by a "gay bit of tapestry") not unlike the "flowery wonders" that Gladys produces with her needle. Both Elaine and Gladys love men marred by guilty secrets who accept their favor or love without returning their devotion. As she sings Elaine's song, Gladys simultaneously pleads for her husband's love and anticipates her own death. On uttering Elaine's last line "with a shrill, despairing power and passion" (198), Gladys, overcome with opium and emotion, slips into unconsciousness, and Olivia, Helwyze, and Felix—like Guinevere, Arthur, and Lancelot—surround "the couch where lay 'the lily-maid,' looking as if already dead, and drifting down to Camelot" (199). Elaine, and Gladys at one level, represents the woman who prefers death to loss of or disillusionment with love and who never learns to value or find meaning in her own labor.[8] Significantly, Elaine, after Lancelot left her, was desolate, for "His very shield was gone; only the case, / Her own poor work, her empty labour, left" (450). Elaine on her barge, Gladys on her couch and later her deathbed, like Beth March and Helen Carrol as well as such fairy-tale heroines as Snow White and Sleeping Beauty, epitomize female powerlessness and passivity, and, to use Tennyson's words, their "supersensual sensual" appeal (398).

The Guinevere tableau, in which the vanquished queen is unwittingly reproached by the innocent novice, dramatizes the opposition between Olivia and Gladys, the sensual and the spiritual woman. In fact, Arthur's farewell to Guinevere in the idyll itself expresses the sentiments of Alcott's epigraph from Goethe: "I knew / Of no more subtle master under heaven / Than is the maiden passion for a maid, / Not only to keep down the base in man / But teach high thought . . . and all that makes a man" (542). But many readers have found Tennyson's Arthur, as did Guinevere, "cold / High, self-contained, and passionless" (540). His glorification of "supersensual sensual" love (which Vivien as well as Guinevere scorn) and his veneration for the virginal (which he shares with Helwyze) suggest that Guinevere, in betraying him, rejected a bloodless, limiting, unrealistic, and, in the case of his knights if not himself, hypocritical ideal of woman and the relationship between the sexes. Furthermore, Guinevere, until Arthur enters and shames her into self-abasement, consistently rebukes the "prattling novice." At one point she mutters,

"Will the child kill me with her foolish prate," then asks, "O little maid, shut in by nunnery walls, / What canst thou know of Kings and Tables Round" (536). The narrator, who calls the novice a "babbler," tells us that she "hurt / Whom she would soothe, and harmed where she would heal" (539). Later Gladys, unlike the novice she portrays, brings Olivia to repentance when, "with the only reproach much pain had wrung from her" (214), she reminds the older woman that she might have acted as a mother toward her rather than as a rival. And Olivia, in a reversal of the nun's refrain, protests, "It is not too late." But instead of privileging innocence over experience, novice (or little woman) over queen, the tableau and its aftermath imply that Gladys can only become a daughter, and as such a consolation for Olivia, by becoming a mother herself. Although still inhabiting her virginal room, her pregnancy proves that she is no longer "shut in by nunnery walls." Olivia, on entering, immediately notices "a new picture, an angel, with the Lily of Annunciation in its hand" (213). Having forsaken the roles of novice, angel, or lily maid, Gladys can announce her own generativity with their icon.[9]

Crucial to Gladys's transformation is her experience in the role of Vivien, "the evil genius of the Round Table." Seated upon the knee of Olivia as Merlin, Gladys proceeds to sing Vivien's siren song, by which she attempts to seduce the magician into surrendering the charm that will enable her to enslave him. Removed from its context, however, Vivien's song becomes Gladys's plea for Felix not to let "the little rift within the lover's lute" destroy their marriage. And when Gladys arrives at the final stanza, she, like other Alcott heroines, "seemed to forget her part," stretching "her arms towards her husband, as if in music she had found a tongue to plead her cause" (191). Gladys, in fact, appropriates and subverts Vivien's song, a cynical invitation to sexual license, by turning it into a meditation on the nature of wedded love. Yet the love that Gladys offers and that Felix comes to accept is not the "supersensual sensual bond" (398) that Arthur advocates and Vivien abhors but one that includes a frank recognition of female sexuality. Under the guise of seducing Merlin on-stage, Gladys prepares for lovemaking offstage. After her performance as Vivien, Felix, "excited by the discoveries he was making" (192), declares that "the woman suits me better than the angel" (193), and it is shortly after this fateful evening that Olivia discovers Gladys's pregnancy. But Gladys's subversion of Vivien's role is itself subverted. That her performance is more than a plea for wedded love is suggested by Felix's remark to Helwyze: "She said she could do '*anything*' tonight; and, upon my life, she looked as if she might even beguile you 'mighty master,' of your strongest spell" (190).

"Merlin and Vivien" can be read as the story of a woman's rage at having been denied access to power and her struggle to achieve it. Vivien's efforts to destroy Merlin, the architect of Camelot, are best justified by the nature of the charm that he withholds from her. According to Merlin, a king once offered a prize to whoever could provide a charm that would keep his wonderfully beautiful queen for him alone. The king was reported well satisfied, as Geraint doubtless would have been, when the queen "lay as dead, / And lost all use of life" (413). Earlier, when Vivien asserted that "Man dreams of Fame while woman wakes to love" (408), Merlin responded, "Rather use than fame" (409). Merlin's story reminds us that men, out of sexual fear and jealousy, have long deprived women not merely of fame but of what men like Merlin prize above fame—use. Merlin, after telling Vivien the story of the spell by which women are held subject, defends withholding it from her for the protection of Arthur's knights as well as himself. When she threatens to read his book in order to discover it, Merlin, "smiling as a master smiles at one / That is not of his school, nor any school / But that where blind and naked Ignorance / Delivers brawling judgments," taunts her with its inaccessibility: "Thou read the book, my pretty Vivien!" (413). He goes on to describe how "every margin [is] scribbled, crost, and crammed / With comment," so that "none can read the text, not even I" (414). In Merlin's book we find a powerful symbol of patriarchal learning, which in its exclusivity has become a source of mystification and obfuscation even to its supposed masters. Thus it seems but poetic justice, given the nature of Merlin's spell and his jealous hoarding of it, that Vivien condemn him to lie "as dead . . . lost to life and use and name and fame" (422).

As Felix suggests in hinting that Gladys might "beguile" Helwyze of his "strongest spell," the power struggle between Merlin and Vivien reflects that between Helwyze and Gladys. As Vivien, Gladys confounds the two men, who recognize an unsuspected part of Gladys in her role. But, ironically, Gladys, in playing Vivien, is acting under a powerful spell cast by Helwyze—that of the opium he has given her, and at the end of her performance as Elaine, she slips into an unconscious state "as if already dead." Then, not content with the success of one spell, Helwyze works a second. In another ironic twist on the Vivien and Merlin theme, it is the "master," the magician, who seeks access to the knowledge another would withhold: "Hasheesh had lulled the senses which guarded the treasure; now the magnetism of a potent will forced the reluctant lips to give up the key" (205). When, from the depths of Gladys's unconscious, comes the answer he seeks, it allies her with Vivien by declaring her his implacable enemy. First she tells him that her hope of freedom and happiness will be realized only when he dies, then that the thing she most dreads and fears is the knowledge of his love. Gladys dies after that dread knowledge becomes conscious but not before condemning Helwyze to share Merlin's fate. After the shock of Gladys's death, he awakens to find himself lying "in what seemed a grave, so cold, so dead he felt; so powerless and pent, in what he fancied was his coffin" (277). Like Merlin imprisoned in his hollow tree, Helwyze is "imprisoned in a helpless body" (280), and worse is the knowledge that "the brain will share [its] paralysis" (278). In one last stunning revision, this time of the tale Merlin tells Vivien, Olivia/Merlin benefits from the charm as had the king, for Helwyze's "affliction . . . made him more her own than ever" (282).

Tennyson, by creating a wide variety of female characters, celebrates the complexity of womankind; Alcott, by having her two female characters play a number of these, as well as an important male figure, reveals the complexity of individual women. Gladys as Enid and Elaine provides two versions of the mythic or fairy-tale heroine: the uncommon one who awakens to selfhood by performing labors and the all too common one who, having no labors to perform, succumbs to sleep, death, or, like the ancient queen described by Merlin, to death in life. Further, Gladys as Enid and Elaine points to the moral and emotional obtuseness of such heroes as Geraint, Gawain (Elaine's erstwhile suitor), and even Lancelot, along with their counterparts such as Felix. Olivia as Guinevere comments on the lack of true humanity or manliness in Helwyze, as in Arthur, that leads to their betrayals. And Olivia's surprising appearance as Merlin suggests women's inherent power, so long denied them, to construct their own Camelots and create their own texts as well as read and, like Alcott, revise male texts. Finally, Gladys's unexpected ability to play Vivien implies not only the repressed sexuality (as well as the erotic appeal) of the seeming nun or lily maid but also her longing for knowledge and use. The narrator tells us that Gladys, by the time of her final role, "was no longer quite herself. . . . Her identity was doubled; one Gladys moved and spoke as she was told . . . the other was alive in every fibre" (195–96). Acting in Alcott's fiction, like writing for Alcott herself, frees the woman who moves and speaks as she is told, who behaves so as to conform to the demands of patriarchal culture, to experience a fuller, more vibrant life, an "other" identity. Helwyze, briefly confronted with its existence, tries at once to deny it: "Fancy that modest creature on a stage for all the world to gape at. She was happiest in the nun's gown tonight, though simply ravishing as Vivien" (200).

Despite Helwyze's disclaimer, at least two scenes indicate that Gladys in her daily life is eager to exchange her "nun's gown" for the selfhood of an Enid or a Vivien. In one Helwyze tries to bribe her, as Mephistopheles and Faust do Margaret, with gifts from the press that he calls his "bazaar" (126). First, he throws over her head "a gauzy fabric, starred with silver," thus linking the "misty muslins" of Eastern bazaars, "into whose embroidery some dark-skinned woman's life was wrought" (127), with the silvery veil that Westervelt, Hawthorne's mesmerist in *The Blithedale Romance,* has his female subject wear. Gladys quickly rejects this symbol of women's economic and sexual oppression, both East and West, for Helwyze, in presenting it, quotes words that "suggested a sultan and his slave, and she did not like either the idea or the expression with which Helwyze regarded her" (128). Next Helwyze proffers a "pretty bracelet" on which are represented the nine Muses. But as he attempts to fasten it around her wrist, the clasp breaks and the "Nine Muses fell to the ground." Gladys, in remarking that "It is too heavy. I am not made to wear handcuffs of any sort" (129), rejects not only woman's traditional role as sexual slave but also her time-honored, equally enslaving role as muse. Finally, Helwyze tempts Gladys with what she finds most difficult to resist, an ivory "Kama, the Indian Cupid" (130). But this too Gladys reluctantly rejects, insisting that she will have no idol and implying her unwillingness to accept even Felix, whom the Cupid is said to resemble, from Helwyze's hands. In rejecting Cupid, Gladys unequivocally refuses love on any but her own terms, and, in declining all of Helwyze's gifts, indicates that the spoils of male experience cannot substitute for experiences of her own.

The second major scene in which Gladys triumphs over Helwyze derives significance from its resemblance to "Retsch's 'Game of Life.'" To Olivia, watching their chess match, "Canaris, flushed and eager, looked the young man to the life; Helwyze, calm but intent . . . pondering that last fateful move, was an excellent Satan; and behind them stood Gladys, wonderfully resembling the wistful angel" (183–84). But Gladys, rather than remaining a passive spectator like Retsch's angel, enters the game. As Olivia asks who wins, and Helwyze boasts, "I do, as usual," Gladys "touched a piece which Canaris . . . was about to overlook," enabling him to make "the one move that could save him" (184). While Olivia charges, "Not fair, the angel interfered," Gladys joins Felix in "exultant" laughter and declares, "I have won him; he is mine, and cannot be taken from me" (184). Thus once again Alcott appropriates and revises a male allegory to make several telling points—that women are regarded as angels and relegated to the sidelines of the game of life, that women have been conditioned to regard their exclusion as "fair" and their participation as "interference," that men, in excluding them, risk becoming checked or, like Merlin and Helwyze, immobilized, and that the woman who risks being charged with interference and dares to enter the game of life wins the so-called masculine side of herself.

Alcott, however, is most indebted to the allegory of *The Scarlet Letter,* which Helwyze and Gladys discuss in their final confrontation. Most obvious, of course, is the parallel between Helwyze and Chillingworth, whom Gladys convicts of "the unpardonable sin"—"the want of love and reverence for the human soul, which makes a man pry into its mysterious depths" (241). But as Helwyze points out, Chillingworth's sin is somewhat mitigated by his unrequited love for Hester, which has its analogue not only in Helwyze's passion for Gladys but in his earlier betrayal by Olivia. Felix, as Helwyze implies to Gladys, is a type of Dimmesdale, too cowardly to free himself from another's hold by confessing his guilty secret. Helwyze could also liken Gladys to the minister, for she too harbors a secret fear and loathing of her supposed benefactor, and Helwyze robs her of that secret much as Chillingworth bares the breast of the sleeping Dimmesdale. In fact, both Felix and Gladys, like the minister, are tortured by the man who, possessed of their secrets, longs for yet dreads the confessions that will destroy their chance of happiness but leave him desolate, without a purpose. Finally, Helwyze himself, despite his obvious resemblance to Chillingworth, is explicitly compared to Dimmesdale. The moment after his eyes reveal to Gladys *his* guilty secret, the love she dreaded to discover, "his usually colorless cheek burned with a fiery flush, and his hand went involuntarily to his breast, as if, like Dimmesdale, he carried an invisible scarlet letter branded there" (244–45).

Felix, masquerading as a brilliant representative of his profession; Gladys, secretly loathing her constant companion and benefactor whom she finally escapes in a saintly death; Helwyze, filled with adulterous longings—all are identified with aspects of Hawthorne's minister, hence represent aspects of each other. Helwyze and Felix are united in a symbiotic relationship by their differences; although of unequal power, each thinks the other can provide what he lacks. Felix, as Helwyze's creature, is in some ways Gladys's superior complement, but he is also, as their names suggest, her mirror image. Just as Helwyze clandestinely collaborates with Felix, so Gladys's ability to set what she takes to be his lyrics to music makes her seem "the embodied spirit of all that was most high and pure in his own wayward but aspiring nature" (22). From being mere collaborators, they become conspirators. Recognizing that they are virtual prisoners in Helwyze's household, they, at Gladys's instigation, refuse to let him conquer by dividing them but instead form a "domestic league" that "shut him out from their real life as inevitably as it drew them nearer to one another" (168). While together in their private quarters, he plies the pen, she the needle, in an effort to earn their economic independence. Felix, then, can be seen not simply as an emblem of one kind of masculine oppression, that inflicted by the egocentric and irresponsible boy-man, but also as the female self, torn between allegiance to the system of patriarchy, in which she finds herself entrapped, and the desire to preserve and develop her own identity. But because both Helwyze and Gladys are as multifaceted as Felix himself, his conflicting loyalties can also represent women's desire for masculine opportunities and achievements (Helwyze) and the need to venerate and be loved (Gladys).

Thomas Niles, on beginning to read the manuscript of *A Modern Mephistopheles* in January 1877, wrote jocosely to Alcott, "Canaris must be a 'No name' author." In so doing Niles revealed an unconscious understanding of the work that he professed to be baffled by ("The 'MM' is getting to be fearfully interesting—what the d——l is the devil up to?").[10] Just as Helwyze and Gladys are alter egos for Felix Canaris, so is he an alter ego for Alcott, whose other two creations stand for different aspects of her subversive art. When Gladys asks her husband why Helwyze wrote and allowed Felix to publish as his own a second book, he answers that Helwyze "cared nothing for the world's praise" but was pleased "to know that his powers were still unimpaired, and . . . to laugh in his sleeve at the deluded critics" (262). Similarly, when Olivia asks Helwyze why he allowed Felix to "deck himself out in your plumes" (270), he returns contemptuously, "What did *I* want with praise and honor? To be gaped and gossiped about would have driven me mad. It pleased that vain boy as much as fooling the public amused me" (271). Thus

Alcott, who regarded fame as "a new kind of slavery" (*Letters* 193), confesses her enjoyment of the No Name joke as well as her earlier anonymous and pseudonymous authorship. But if Helwyze, a demonic genius, is the secret author of Alcott's sensation fiction, he is no less the hidden inspiration behind the domestic. And while she did not as frankly express her pleasure in fooling the public as to the nature of those works, it must upon occasion have rivaled that of Helwyze.

The scene in which Helwyze reads aloud his own romance as Felix's, and thus successfully tempts him to appropriate it, can be viewed as rendering an experience that many authors have described—the experience of abandoning the conscious effort to complete a difficult or uncongenial writing task only to have the unconscious take over and brilliantly accomplish it. On hearing a superior version of the story over which he has agonized, Felix, though he can take no credit for it, feels "the irresistible conviction that it *was* good, strengthening every instant, till he felt only the fascination and excitement of the hour" (148–49). Later, recalling that hour, he confesses to Gladys, "I had resolved to deserve the love and honor you gave me; and again I tried, and again I failed, for my romance was a poor, pale thing to his. He had read it; and, taking the same plot, made it what you know, writing as only such a man could write, when a strong motive stimulated him to do his best" (262–63). Felix, as he describes himself to Gladys, is the writer who struggles within a *cabinet de travail* in order to meet a deadline, satisfy a publisher, or win the approval of his audience; Helwyze is the artist within some writers who, indifferent to external considerations, takes over and, stimulated by a strong internal motivation, writes with a power they do not recognize as their own. Rather than Felix appropriating Helwyze's work, Helwyze takes over Felix's by a process that Alcott and her writer heroine Jo March liken to getting "into a vortex." The difference between Helwyze, the artist responsible for Alcott's effortlessly written sensation stories and the subversive elements in her more inspired domestic fiction, and Felix, the methodical, formulaic writer who supposedly despised her own work, is reflected in a January 1879 journal entry: "At the Bellevue in my little room writing. Got two books well started but had too many interruptions to do much, & dared not get into a vortex for fear of a break down" (213).[11] Writing from the vortex was dangerous, Alcott knew, and not unlike the satanic bargain her hero makes.

If Helwyze is the demonic side of Felix's, and his creator's, art, Gladys, as her "domestic league" with Felix indicates, is the domestic, the little womanly artist that Jo March's father urges her to become and that Alcott has usually been taken to be. For one thing, Gladys professes to be wholly disinterested and attributes her own ingenuous nature to others. In her first conversation with Felix, she tells him that the thought of singing "for praise or money spoils the music to my ear" (25) and admires his first volume of poetry—most of it, ironically, composed by Helwyze—for having come "from your heart, without a thought of what the world would say" (24). According to Gladys, art should be artless. When asked where she found "the air that fits those words so well," she answers, "It came itself; as the song did, I think" (23). Further, Gladys feels that art should be morally uplifting. After hearing Helwyze read what she takes to be Felix's romance, she begs him to alter the ending lest "the moral point . . . be lost" (149). When Felix hesitates, she urges him to "Make it noble as well as beautiful, then people will love as well as praise you" (151).[12] As her power over Felix grows, she lures him from his *cabinet de travail,* where he struggles to create a masterpiece, to their private quarters, where Felix, the master of "half a dozen languages" practices the more humble craft of translation, the counterpart to Gladys's needlework: "The task now in hand was one that Canaris could do easily and well; and Gladys's example kept him at it when the charm of novelty was gone. . . . when he looked up, the glance of approval, the encouraging word, the tender smile, were always ready, and wonderfully inspiring" (168). Combining purity with practicality, Gladys, who boasts, "Oh, I am a thrifty wife, though such a little one!" (166), is the type of Victorian female artist, the "literary domestic," as a recent historian has called her.[13]

However, such a view, like that of Gladys as lily maid or nun, is oversimplified. Felix finds "glimpses of practical gifts and shrewd common sense in Gladys . . . very like the discovery of a rock under its veil of moss, or garland of airy columbines" (166), suggesting that Gladys's artistry is not so disinterested and artless as it appears. True, Gladys professes to be appalled at the thought of exploiting her musical talent for money, and she angrily denies Helwyze's insinuation that Felix writes with an eye toward profit, but her own needlework, like Felix's translations, is motivated by a desire to win their economic independence from Helwyze. More important, their collaboration succeeds in effecting their spiritual and psychological independence. In short, Gladys's scheme that they work together secretly, however humble the work itself, is tantamount to subversion. She proposes the plan with "a charmingly mutinous air," and Felix, though he fears Helwyze's wrath if he discovers it, feels a sense of "malicious satisfaction"·(166). Finally, the description of Gladys's needlework is itself suggestive: "Now a golden wheat-ear, a scarlet poppy, a blue violet; or the white embroidery, that made his eyes ache with following the tiny stitches, which seemed to sow seed-pearls along a hem, weave graceful ciphers, or make lace-work like a cobweb" (168–69). Like Hawthorne's rebellious Hester, whose elaborately embroidered scarlet *A* has been taken to stand for "artist," Gladys through her needlework simultaneously conforms to and defies the patriarchal authority that would define her. Thus Gladys's domestic and seemingly conventional art represents not only Alcott's domestic fiction as it has appeared to most readers but that fiction in all its subversive subtlety.[14]

On one level, then, Gladys and her art are at the service of Helwyze, as the symbol of patriarchal culture; on another, they challenge and work to undermine his rule. But on still another, she no less than Felix is inspired by Helwyze—the demonic, irrational, unconscious source of art that women have been discouraged from tapping. Gladys is not only songstress and seamstress but, under the direction of Helwyze, consummate actress. The night of the tableaux vivants it is both the opium and her long course of study with Helwyze that enable her to astound her audience, so that "in this brilliant, impassioned creature they did not recognize the Gladys they believed they knew so well" (192). Although later that evening Helwyze, in his attempt to penetrate her mystery, commits what critic Octavia Cowan has called spiritual rape, he has already engendered a more mature self.[15] In her penultimate confrontation with Helwyze, Gladys, wearing the passion-flowers that Felix has just given her, pays tribute to her patron even in defying him. Claiming that she now knows how to hold her husband—her "other" or "masculine" identity—she tells him: "I did not know my own power till you showed it to me; unintentionally, I believe, and unconsciously, I used it to such purpose that Felix felt pride in the wife whom he had thought a child before. I mean the night I sang and acted yonder, and did both well, thanks to you" (225). In an earlier conversation "the girl Gladys" had "found no language but her blushes; now the woman sat there steadfast and passion-pale, owning her love with the eloquence of fervent speech; both pleading and commanding, in the name of wifehood and motherhood, for the right to claim the man she had won at such cost" (227). In her treatment of Gladys, as in that of Felix,

Alcott pays tribute to the demonic source of her own artistic inspiration—the source of her domestic as well as her sensation fiction.[16] Like Gladys, Alcott's domestic fiction speaks "in the name of wifehood and motherhood" to demand for women the equivalent of manhood.

The death of Gladys and the life in death of Helwyze signify, like the deaths of Warwick and Germain in Alcott's earlier fiction, a hero's rejection of negative and internalization of positive aspects. Gladys as angel and Helwyze as master in the house of patriarchy lose their hold on Felix, who represents the androgynous female artist; Gladys as avenging angel and Helwyze as inspiring demon take possession. Evidence that Felix has internalized the positive values represented by Gladys and Helwyze can be found in the career he goes on to have. Shortly before the climax, in which he confesses Helwyze's authorship of his poems and romance, Felix discusses his plan for a new project, either a novel or a tragic play. Helwyze advises that Felix is better equipped to write the play but "could act one, better than imagine or write it": "you are dramatic by nature, and it is easier for you to express yourself in gesture and tone, than by written or spoken language. You were born for an actor, are fitted for it in every way, and I advise you to try it." The narrator tells us that "long afterward the conversation came back to him like an inspiration, and was the seed of a purpose which, through patient effort, bore fruit in a brilliant and successful career" (237). Helwyze may have given Felix a false start, but he also informs him of his true calling, one that is anticipated by Gladys's extraordinary example in enacting scenes from Tennyson. In fact, her appropriation of another's words, her use of such subtleties as "gesture and tone" to dramatize both her own plight and that of a society erected upon a flawed foundation, can be seen as a paradigm of the artist that we are led to believe Felix becomes and that Alcott actually became.

Without a doubt, *A Modern Mephistopheles* is Alcott's most elaborately disguised yet fullest disclosure of her artistic intents and purposes. By associating her artist hero, as well as his masculine and feminine alter egos, with Hawthorne's Dimmesdale, she confesses that she, like that pillar of the patriarchal community, is an accomplished actor. As we recall, Dimmesdale time and again confesses publicly to his sin only to be canonized as a saint for his confession. Even after he mounts the scaffold to acknowledge Hester and their daughter, Pearl, his loyal followers interpret the scene as a "parable," not an admission of guilt. Alcott, too, repeatedly confessed her commitment to radical reforms for women only to be revered as a defender of their traditional roles and values. Her decision, in 1887, to reprint *A Modern Mephistopheles* together with "A Whisper in the Dark" and acknowledge authorship of both seems motivated, like Felix's alteration of *his* title page, by a desire to convince her public that the author they admired—the author of the children's books—was someone other than they knew. But even as intelligent a contemporary and as close a friend as Ednah Cheney could not read the cryptic message of Alcott's posthumous volume any more than she could decipher the text of the novel when it first appeared. In her biography of Alcott, published the same year as the new edition of *A Modern Mephistopheles* and giving an account of it, Cheney could still write that the "realism which is delightful in the picture of little women and merry boys is painful when connected with passions so morbid and lives so far removed from joy and sanity. As in her early dramas and sensational stories, we do not find Louisa Alcott's own broad, generous, healthy life, or that which lay around her, in this book, but the reminiscences of her reading" (293). And the only significance that she can find in Alcott's belated acknowledgment of "A Whisper in the Dark" is that it serves "to show the quality of work which she condemned so severely" (395).

But if Alcott's contemporaries refused to see the hand of the sensation writer in the children's stories, her modern readers often see that hand as severely crippled. Ann Douglas, in her introduction to the modern reprint of Cheney's biography, chides her for failing to see that Alcott's "most interesting characters in the children's tales . . . are all imports into the world of domestic fiction from the earlier sensationalist writing" (xxii). But Douglas goes on to conclude that Alcott "settled for sprightly, careless, slangy children's versions of the domestic fiction of [Dinah] Mulock and [Charlotte] Yonge, but she devoted her best efforts to her gloomy, 'sensational' romances" (xxv). As these remarks of Cheney and Douglas imply, Alcott's popular success has depended, like Dimmesdale's, upon her audience's finding what it hoped and expected to find—a confirmation of its own values. But the real source of her power, as of the minister's, is the very oppression of spirit under which she labors, the burden which, if fully and openly shared, would relieve her heart but also relieve her of her office. Just as Dimmesdale's masterpiece, his election sermon—ostensibly the prophecy of "a high and glorious destiny for the newly gathered people," is pervaded by a "deep, sad undertone of pathos" (332–

33), so are Alcott's sprightly tales of little men and women, especially her master-piece—some would say utopian masterpiece—the March family trilogy. But here the parallels between her and Dimmesdale may end, for this strain of pathos need not be interpreted as the story of her guilt—either for having betrayed her feminist values or for elsewhere having flouted more conventional ones. Instead, as we shall see once more in *Jo's Boys,* the final work in this trilogy and the last novel Alcott completed, her burden is the culture's guilt and her fear that, despite apparent hopeful signs to the contrary, it will be perpetuated for generations to come.

CHAPTER 9

"Paradoxes of the Woman Artist":
Diana and Persis

Mary Cassatt exemplified the paradoxes of the woman artist. Cut off from the experiences that are considered the entitlement of her male counterpart, she has access to a private world a man can only guess at. She has, therefore, a kind of information he is necessarily deprived of. If she has almost impossible good fortune—means, self-confidence, heroic energy and dedication, the instinct to avoid the seductions of ordinary domestic life—she may pull off a miracle: she will combine the skill and surety that she has stolen from the world of men with the vision she brings from the world of women.

> Mary Gordon, "Mary Cassatt" (156)

I am the only faithful worshipper of Celibacy, and her service becomes more fascinating the longer I remain in it. Even if so inclined, an artist has no business to marry. For a man, it may be well enough, but for a woman, on whom matrimonial duties and cares weigh more heavily, it is a moral wrong, I think, for she must either neglect her profession or her family, becoming neither a good wife and mother nor a good artist. My ambition is to become the latter, so I wage eternal feud with the consolidating knot.

> Harriet Hosmer,
> Letter to Wayman Crow (quoted in Comini 21)

If *A Modern Mephistopheles* is Alcott's most oblique portrayal of the woman artist, *Diana and Persis* is the most direct. Composed exactly two years later, in the winter of 1878–79, the four-chapter novella—or novel fragment—seems to have been inspired both by Niles's renewed urging that she write "a full grown novel, *just like Moods*" and by May Alcott's experiment combining art with marriage.[1] Alcott's failure to complete and publish the work has been attributed to May's death later in 1879,[2] but it may have had more to do with Niles's reaction to the manuscript. Having read three chapters of a new work, presumably *Diana and Persis,* he reported in February, "I must be candid & say that the two opening chapters disappointed me—there seemed to be too much realism in them, the *motif* of the book seemed to be told too apparently & I don't think most readers want to know what the moral of a book is; it is something wh. should be so hidden that it requires reflection after reading to discover it." Such advice from Niles to Alcott seems ironic, but his strictures may well have echoed her own misgivings over making more explicit what elsewhere she had left implicit. So accustomed had she become to whispering her subversive messages that *Diana and Persis* perhaps seemed too obvious a statement; that very habit of muted utterance, however, ensured sufficient subtlety, and the tale is among her most suggestive and satisfying works.

In the opening chapter, Alcott immediately introduces the motif that Niles felt was too apparent—the conflict for women between creativity and domesticity. Percy, a young female painter, announces to her friend Diana, a sculptor, that she is departing for Europe, in part to escape the importunities of a suitor. Warm, charming, and impulsive, Percy is a more mature, self-directed version of Sylvia Yule, and the reader suspects that, despite her strong sense of artistic purpose, she will ultimately succumb, as did Sylvia, to her longing to love and be loved. Diana, on the other hand, is, as her name implies, cool, dispassionate, unswerving in her dedication to art and in her opposition to the "too costly . . . experiment" of marriage (386). The second chapter, which Niles could have criticized with some reason as too realistic, consists of Percy's letters to Diana, letters based in large part on May Alcott's to her family. These letters describe her carefree life as an art student in Paris—her casual domestic arrangements, her camaraderie with fellow artists, her temporary frustrations and setbacks, her steady progress and exhilarating breakthroughs.[3] But despite the recognition that Percy, like May, receives from her teachers and her success in having a still life, like May's, hung "on the line" at the Salon, we sense beneath both her gaiety and her earnestness a self-deprecating quality that bodes ill for her artistic career. Thus it is no surprise that chapter 3, entitled "At Home," describes Diana's visit to a now thoroughly domesticated Percy. Living near Paris in a charming apartment with her musician husband, August, and infant daughter, Diana, Percy is a picture of radiant, blooming womanhood, but her studio, as Diana quickly notes, is covered with dust.[4] Sensing Diana's skepticism, August argues that Percy will be the greater artist for having fulfilled herself as a woman, but Alcott's allusions suggest that Percy's aspirations will prove as ephemeral as "a midsummer night's dream." The fourth and final chapter of *Diana and Persis,* on the other hand, offers a more realistic solution to the female artist's dilemma and anticipates a future in which experiments such as Percy's might prove less costly. Diana, now in Rome and on the verge of greatness, begins to realize just how much she has had to sacrifice to her art. But her friendship with a small boy, Nino, and his father, Stafford, a widowed sculptor who respects her as an equal, promises to humanize her art and provide a mutually sustaining artistic collaboration as well as an outlet for her repressed emotions.[5]

The opening scene, in Diana's American studio, contrasts Percy's frank desire for intimacy and erotic experience with Diana's unacknowledged need for them. Percy, having forsaken love, vehemently protests having to choose between her "hungry heart" and her "ambitious spirit" (386). Not only must Percy wound a lover and refrain from doing "as other women do," something her beloved grandmother says she would be the happier for doing (386); "in escaping from the lovers who annoy me to the work I prefer I must also turn my back on the last of my kindred and my dearest friend" (384). Although Percy, at Diana's urging, prepares to sacrifice love, kinship, and friendship to art, both women tacitly acknowledge that, in doing so, she may jeopardize the very talent that she seeks to safeguard and foster. When Percy wishes for "a marble heart" to make her decision easier, Diana warns, "You would lose your greatest charm which is your tender and sympathetic nature. You could not paint as you do without it" (387), and Percy, after taking a vow of chastity, recalls that "love is the great teacher" (386). Alcott describes Percy as "a liberty-loving nature trying to divine and obey instincts as unerring as the flower's love of light, the bird's impulse to sing" (384–85), thus implying that Percy's capacity for love and her drive to create are interdependent and should, ideally, feed each other. Further, by naming her character Percy and making her a free spirit, Alcott reminds us that the male artist Shelley, while perhaps hampered by his commitment to Mary and their children, was not forced by his vocation to forgo love.

In the first chapter Percy's painting of a skylark symbolizes the plight of the woman artist and strengthens the ironic connection between her and Shelley. Diana praises unreservedly this painting, which consists of an expanse of sky, the "mere suggestion of a grassy field below . . . and midway between, a bird soaring and singing as if Heaven's gate was the goal of its desire" (387). But anticipating August's argument that Percy will be a better painter for her domestic experience, her grandmother had disturbed her by advising, "if you want that bird to be happy give her a comfortable nest full of little responsibilities, for the highest flyers need a home and that lark for all its twittering has got to drop sometime." Diana, "jealously covering with her slender hand the vague hint of a nest in the foreground," retorts, "My lark does not stoop to fill gaping beaks with worms while her own is full of music that delights all ears" (388) and exhorts Percy to "soar and sing and get above the clouds as soon as possible, and stay there as long as you can" (391). While Diana would dismiss the grandmother's remarks as "sickly sentiment," at least one of these—that "the same instinct that sent [the lark] up brings her down" (388)—corresponds to Diana's own perception that Percy's "tender and sympathetic nature," which makes her susceptible to love, also inspires her art. Yet, as Diana realizes, to surrender to love is all too often to surrender one's voice, to find it overwhelmed by a chorus of daily demands or to choke on repressed resentment at having to meet them. To sacrifice a song "that delights all ears" in order to "fill gaping beaks with worms" has traditionally been the woman artist's lot.[6]

But Alcott goes on to suggest that the rare woman who eschews that lot may nonetheless find herself imprisoned. Percy's name, her "ardent discontent," her impatience with "waiting for inspiration" at home rather than courting it abroad all ally her, like Christie Devon starting out to make her fortune, with masculine freedom and adventure. She boasts that "I leave all my finery behind me and go in light marching order" and claims that the "vastness and vagueness of the whole expedition is its charm. I feel like Columbus going to discover a new world, for when I went before, it was as a fine lady with all proper guards and guides; now I go alone with only my common sense and courage to protect me" (389). Diana listens "with both wonder and admiration at this energetic friend of hers who . . . was launching her little boat so bravely and blithely into the sea of experience and leaving so much behind her" (390). These metaphors of exploration and discovery, however, are undercut by others that suggest not freedom but confinement. In order to compensate for her lack of "proper guards and guides," Percy vows that on "the continent I will veil myself like a vestal virgin" (385). When Percy expresses her resolve "to live like a hermit and toil like a slave," "the idea of this impulsive, attractive creature trying to live alone oppressed [Diana] as if she saw a child about to be shut into a prison cell" (389). Although "No nun in her cell ever led a more austere and secluded life than this fine creature intent upon her self-appointed task" (391), Diana shrinks from the idea of Percy leading such a life. And while a nun's cell is perhaps preferable to a prisoner's, neither affords so much as a view of the longed-for "sea of experience."

Diana's heart is less hungry than Percy's only because, prior to Percy's departure, its appetite has been partially satisfied. In a succinct statement of the woman artist's predicament, the narrator says of Diana and Persis, "The same aim was theirs, success and happiness; but with Diana success came first, with Percy happiness; both being conscious at times of that secret warfare of thwarted instincts and imperious ambitions, the demands of temperament as well as of talent" (392).[7] Diana's "secret warfare," her hidden hunger, is apparent in the "sudden kindling of the absorbed face" when Percy enters (383); Percy's "noble discontent" wakes "longings in her own ambitious soul" (386), and "the approaching separation" from Percy "melted . . . the native coldness that lay like a light frost upon her youth and beauty" (384). The "demands of temperament" are especially obvious in Diana's jealous fears, as when Percy mentions a walk on Wimbledon Common with a male friend. In fact, Alcott suggests that Diana's love for Percy, so much more possessive than Percy's affection for her, is *her* way of trying to satisfy the natural craving for intimacy without "spoiling [her] life by any commonplace romance" (386). Diana can subordinate happiness to success, can claim that "Success is impossible, unless the passion for art overcomes all desultory passions" (393), largely because her relationship with Percy, by providing sufficient happiness, has hitherto freed her from a preoccupation with obtaining it: "One friendship was the only luxury she allowed herself and in this she found not only the solace but the stimulant she needed" (392). Even after Diana loses Percy—first to

Paris, then more irrevocably to August—their friendship provides Diana with the "motive" for art that Percy complains she lacks and never really finds. Diana's monumental Saul, the masterpiece she produces after her separation from Percy, is a projection of her "secret warfare," an inner conflict not unlike Saul's own. Although Diana does not suffer Saul's madness, she comes to understand the various denials that produced it, including the submerged eroticism of his love for David. Like Saul, who sacrifices a healing intimacy out of a misguided ambition and lust for power, Diana is tempted to reject feeling and her feminine side, to embrace male values and succeed in a masculine role. But her Saul, rather than manifesting such choices, serves as a warning against them and, by representing the plight of the woman artist, attests to her essential womanliness.

In chapter 2 Alcott skillfully adapts her sister's letters so as to emphasize the constraints—psychological as much as material—on the woman artist. True, Percy finds it exhilarating to draw from live models, including male nudes; the household she shares with two female artists is free from domestic drudgery; and her circle of young artists of both sexes seems an egalitarian, cooperative community (although Percy's reference to the "little homes we women naturally make for ourselves" providing solace for male artists, "often homesick and lonely, longing for society after the day's work is done" [401], suggests the persistence of traditional roles). Especially at the studio of an older woman artist, Miss Cassal (based on Mary Cassatt), Percy finds a virtual utopia—one in which men and women befriend rather than compete with, patronize, or denigrate each other. Little wonder, then, that Percy urges Diana to join her and "find yourself a new world" (405). But while Miss Cassal's "maternal sympathy and generosity" (401) encourage reciprocity between the sexes, recognition of her own genius is denied on the basis of gender; because her "pictures are handled in a masterly way and with a strength one seldom finds in a woman's fingers . . . men are jealous of her, and her 'Joel' was refused at the last Salon merely because of its boldness and power" (400). The tyranny of the male art establishment is reflected in the press, according to which "women . . . unsex themselves" by integrating the all-male life classes and prove their lack of talent by "getting no medals at the Salon" (the very institution that rejects bold and powerful women's art). Percy responds indignantly to these charges: to the first she argues, "That little band of dignified and earnest women so far from unsexing themselves . . . made by their mere presence a purer atmosphere about them"; to the second she asks, "How can we when hitherto we were not allowed to study at the life schools yet expected to do as well in a third of the time and with half the help men have?" (399).

But though Percy is sensitive to the most blatant forms of gender bias, she is blind to the more subtle forms of sexism within her own studio and to the way in which these affect her aspirations. On the surface the studio, one in which women students have access to live models and expert instruction, would seem to provide a benign atmosphere. Yet Percy's letters betray frustration, intimidation, and an inability to take her own work seriously. Her frustration initially stems from a self-imposed restriction: "My eye for color is a gift that blinds me as well as others to my bad drawing, so I am going to sit on the low seats and learn" (386). Her confinement to "drawing in black and white," however, actually interferes with her ability to see. As she writes of one model, "His rich coloring distracts me because I can not paint it . . . and I try vainly to get a good copy" (396); and of another, "If I could have put the fine dark face and red drapery into color I should have been happy, but as it was only drawing I did not get on very well" (403). On the one hand, Percy's talent for and dependence on color suggest the emotional capacities and needs that will distract her from a single-minded devotion to her art. On the other hand, the color that she feels she must deny herself represents the female artist's way of comprehending experience, a way that must be subjected to male scrutiny and sacrificed if it fails to satisfy male standards of artistic quality.

Initially, Percy attracts the attention of her "masters" when she follows her natural bent, but her need for their validation and her absolute reliance on it expose a lack of real artistic independence.[8] Percy is first distinguished from her classmates for a head in oils: "The great M, our most dreaded critic . . . gave me a look, a nod said, 'This flesh is luminous' . . . No more, but I was much elated" (399). Percy's second triumph, a drawing of a black male model, owes its success not to her natural talent as a colorist but to her female heritage of resistance and rebellion. Indignant at the bigotry of her Southern classmates, Percy delivers "an anti-slavery lecture which would have delighted Grandma, who longs for the stirring times when she and her stout-hearted contemporaries sat out many a mob knitting with majestic composure" (403). Caught up in her enthusiasm, Percy becomes oblivious to the daunting presence of "the great M" and dashes off a vigorous sketch that meets with his approval. Percy attributes her success to female inspiration rather than to male instruction—"Tell Grandma I owe this success to her, for the principles she taught me inspired my pencil and so brought me to honor" (404), but it is M's praise that causes her to "vaingloriously exalt" herself (403). Percy is also praised for "good strong work" when, dissatisfied with an uninteresting face that the class is asked to draw, she draws instead the model's more expressive boots: "I booked them, to the great amusement of the class, for they were done *con amore,* with big brushes and lots of paint, and do look as if they would get up and walk out of the canvas" (405). But once again it is not the experience of painting female fashion from the heart but male praise that makes her "begin to feel as if I had the *right* to be here" (405).

Percy's judgment of her own work is initially confirmed by M, but her greatest triumph ironically serves not only to shake that judgment but to convey how the woman artist—or writer—is encouraged to modify or abandon her ambitions. Despite the praise of Anna, a fellow artist, Percy is convinced that her still life is "a stupid little affair" until, to her astonishment, M approves it: "Send it to the Salon and I shall be proud to call you my *élève.* . . . Take that into the class and show those ladies what painting simply what you see without trying to *make a picture* will do for one. . . . you cannot do better than to go on in this way" (405–6). One reason for Percy's astonishment is her contempt for still life, a reaction to the male notion that "flowers or still life" were "the only things . . . delicate and proper [enough] for a lady's brush" (399). As she explains to Diana, it was only her rage over the failure of an ambitious portrait that led her to stoop to the "onions and copper kettle style" (405). Percy's condescending attitude toward still life, including her own, together with M's approval and the example he would make of her, suggest how women artists are encouraged to work and praised for their success in "minor" genres and forms even as they learn to devalue them. No wonder that Percy is confused, for M seems to be granting her admission to his sacred circle of protégés even as he discourages her from "trying to make a picture." Although Percy does not consciously interpret them, his words imply that he will allow her this triumph if, unlike the ambitious, self-directed Miss Cassal, she and her peers are willing to settle for similar small, nonthreatening successes in the future.

Percy's ambivalence toward her accomplishment continues, for she cannot believe that what she has produced—women's art, domestic art—is really worthy to be called art at all. As she writes incredulously to Diana, "I am actually going to send that insignificant study to the Salon. I shall never believe it is good till I see it there, for in spite of all my master says I feel that if I ever do win fame it will be in painting heads and not pots and pans" (406). On Varnishing Day, Percy does see it there, looking "like a postage stamp, surrounded by the immense pictures whose gilded frames seemed to make a sort of glory, to my eyes at least, about this unpretending child of mine. I looked at it with new respect and saw that it *was* good, vigorous work; simple in subject and unaffectedly treated. I fancy this very simplicity is the secret of its success" (408). Although Percy's satisfaction, even audacity, would seem in evidence—she indirectly compares herself to God and to the mother of God, she can only approve her work, see that it is good, when it is assigned a place in and by the male establishment ("after reading my name in the fat catalogue with a nice little notice after it, I went on to view thirty more rooms full of pictures, feeling that I too was an artist" [409]). By her own admission, her work possesses no glory, no glamour, no divinity of its own, only that conferred by its surroundings.[9] Percy concludes from her experience what men have long endeavored to teach women—that "we too often attempt more than we are equal to, and so fail. It is a good lesson to me and teaches me both humility and a proper regard for patient thoroughness" (408–9). On one level Alcott uses her sister's description of her own experience to suggest that art by women, including women's (domestic, modest, small-scale) art, has its place in the firmament of artists and that, if looked at from a woman's perspective, can be seen as occupying a central place. On another level, however, Percy's reaction to her success reveals how women are persuaded to subdue their ambitions, to see just how small and insignificant their talents are.

The enormous canvases that dwarf and imprison Percy's still life—even that term suggests how her artistic voice has been silenced, her career stalled—imply that the sentence Percy imposed upon herself in jest has become a reality. Still another work of art—a portrait not by Percy but of her—reminds us that the woman artist's life can be as constraining as a more conventional one.[10] Anna's portrait of Percy "in peacock blue with all [her] curls out on holy day and a muff and a hat, which turn the studious grub into a gay butterfly" (406–7) indicates that the artist's model, unlike the artist, is free to express her feminine nature; she need not pose as vestal virgin or honorary male. But despite Percy's greater freedom in sitting for her portrait, her identification with it is ominous. In describing the unloading of her still life and Anna's portrait at the Palais de l'Industrie, Percy writes, "out I came with my little study in its ten franc frame behind me" (407). After the portrait is accepted at the Salon, she imagines "a certain lady in blue sitting in state to be surveyed by admiring nations" (408). At the moment of her greatest triumph, when she has supposedly escaped the "fine lady" role, she is happy to be enshrined as an icon of genteel womanhood. Thus Anna's portrait not only comments ironically on Percy's painting—an exemplar of the modest, ladylike art that she has been persuaded, against her previous judgment, to practice—but anticipates her metamorphosis from an artist of "pots and pans" into the wife who must scrub them.

In chapter 3 Percy seems to be taking an indefinite "holy day" both from art and from responsibility for her own life. More disturbing than "the dust upon the easel and the dried-up paint upon the palette" (412–13) is her new passivity. After the first excitement of Diana's visit has worn off, Percy is content to remain "very quiet through dinner" (421), and while August and Diana discuss Ruskin, she puts the baby to bed. Later, on an evening walk, Percy listens complacently while Diana and August debate whether "women cannot have all, and must decide between love and fame." August eloquently asserts that "a woman can and ought to have both if she has the power to win them. . . . why is not a woman's life to be as full and free as [a man's]? . . . Love alone is not enough for any large and hungry soul," a term that seems to comprehend both Percy's "hungry heart" and her "ambitious soul" and to deny an irresolvable conflict between them. But Percy's reaction to these stirring words—"You see, I have someone to fight my battles for me now"— casts doubt not upon their sincerity and truth but upon their relevance to *her.* Marriage to a strong man—and motherhood—have already relegated Percy to the sidelines of her own life. After this discussion, August "wrapped Percy in her shawl and took her home with a gentle sort of authority which she seemed to like, while Di secretly resented it" (424). In fact, Percy seems to have surrendered her agency and become an object of desire for and contention between Diana and August. Significantly, the point of view in this chapter is never Percy's; it is always either the unmarried woman's or the married man's.

Access to August's point of view enables us to see the discrepancy between his spirited defense of women, so much like Adam Warwick's, and his inner conflict in regard to Percy, who resembles Sylvia. Prior to lapsing into passivity, Percy had "listened to Diana's plans with a growing ardor in her face, an unconscious tone of regret now and then in her eager voice, an entire absorption in the subject which for the first time in her married life made her forgetful of his presence." Then August views Diana as "the fair serpent who was beguiling his impetuous Eve":

> The generous desire that Percy should have all the happiness life could give her, even if he were not the donor, struggled with a fear that, by this rousing of the old ambitions, something of the old unrest and discontent might mar the beautiful repose which had possessed her for a year. He knew by sad experience how hard the effort is to bind a passionate desire and hold it captive at the feet of duty, yet he also knew what rich compensations such sacrifices sometimes bring. . . . He was more ambitious for this young wife of his, both as woman and artist, than she was herself, but manlike he loved the woman best, and yearned to keep her for a little longer all his own. (419–20)

Later he finds Percy wearing her "'painting frenzy' look" as she and Diana sketch his naked, squirming daughter "in the costume of Cupid." The jest with which he covers his displeasure—"Unnatural mother! Would you sacrifice your child at the altar of your insatiable art?" (421)—exposes his very real fear that Percy's ambition is "unnatural" and "insatiable" and will eventually drive her to sacrifice not her "passionate desire" for art but "the peace of home" (419).[11] Thus Alcott enables us to infer why Percy has become quiet and docile: she instinctively knows that it is safer to accede to her husband's unspoken wishes than to act upon his more enlightened pronouncements.

Percy insists that "I have done a good deal of work this last year—how could I help it with August to inspire and criticize and rejoice over me" (415), yet it becomes increasingly clear that Percy has relinquished the role of artist to her husband. At the end of the day it is August who plays the violin while Percy lies "obediently" upon the sofa, planning the next day's meals. Not only is August said to resemble Shelley, but his skylark succeeds where Percy's failed.[12] Although Percy portrayed her skylark, the emblem of herself, aspiring to the goal of "Heaven's gate," she confessed to Diana that she could "only twitter up a little way and tumble down again all out of breath" (391). In contrast, when August plays, "the fine clear echo of the climbing harmony melted into silence with no fall to mar the strain that seemed to lift and leave the listener at Heaven's gate." Ironically, Diana, on hearing him play, becomes convinced that he "is worthy of her, and will work the miracle if man can" (425). But while August may effect a miraculous triumph over gravity with his own art, he seems ill equipped, however good his intentions, to help launch, let alone sustain, Percy's artistic flight. Later in Rome Diana ruefully thinks of Percy "in the nest that filled so fast the mother bird had little time for friendship" (428) or, we can infer, for art.

The romantic aura Alcott creates in chapter 3 further serves to predict Percy's artistic frustration as well as Diana's personal fulfillment.[13] As she approaches Percy's home, Diana "felt as if passing out of the small, dull world of reality into the enchanting regions of romance, and gave herself up to the new charm with the wondering delight of a child turning for the first time the pages of a fairy story" (411). At lunch with Percy and August, the "sense of having stepped into a romance grew upon Diana . . . and she kept saying to herself, 'I shall wake presently in the old studio at home.' But she had no wish to wake, for she heartily enjoyed this glimpse of the sweet old story forever being told" (419). Finally, after watching the sun set over an old château, Diana is lulled into a reverie as August "gave them some exquisite things from the Midsummer Night's Dream, with the fitting accompaniment of wandering wind, soft dusk and the rustle of leaves eager for the coming of elves" (425). So enchanted is Diana by the music and the moonlight that she begins "wondering if she could be happy with a musical husband in a home like this" (426). Yet the dreamlike atmosphere to which Diana finds herself susceptible reinforces the image of a fragile Eden. Diana herself earlier warned Percy, "don't expect it to be midsummer always," suggesting that Percy and August, like the lovers in Shakespeare's play, will at length awaken from their dream of love. Percy is undisturbed by Diana's warning—"I knew you'd say that, and take immense comfort in pitying my delusion"—but the narrator's equivocal comment on this exchange indicates that both Percy and Diana have much to learn: "Diana regarded her with the affectionate compassion which the uninitiated usually shows for those whom love's glamor blinds to the possibility of there ever being a rough side to life" (414).

Diana's initiation in chapter 4 is anticipated throughout chapter 3. Like Percy, who needed to take a "holy day" from art, Diana now feels "like one released from the quiet solitude of a prison cell" (410), and August's music, especially, has the power to "set wide the doors of her heart to let a new emotion in" (411). Despite her sense of rivalry with "this unknown August who had usurped her place in Percy's life" (417), she is perhaps more influenced by him than by either Percy or their daughter, whom she embraces with a warmth that surprises her. Because August has a fresh as well as a masculine perspective, he can observe what Percy, blinded by familiarity as well as by her domestic preoccupations, fails to see—that Diana "is not all the artist but a woman to be loved as well as admired" (425), and he subtly communicates that discovery to Diana. For example, in thanking her for relinquishing Percy to him, he "threw up a great red rose which lit on Diana's breast and seemed to warm the cool grey of her dress as pleasantly as these new interests gave color to her life" (418). Significantly, Diana in chapter 4 is described as "a slender yet stately figure in pale grey with no touch of color but the knot of crimson carnations in her bosom" (432), thus recalling Hester Prynne and her susceptibility to passion. In still another small but telling incident, Diana pockets her gloves in emulation of Percy, who predicts, "you will come to it in time and enjoy the freedom as I do" (422).[14] While the unsuspecting Percy may find herself confined again—or repeatedly, as the later allusion to her rapidly filling nest implies—she has in some ways tasted a kind of freedom for which Diana now hungers.

In the "midsummer night's dream" of chapter 3, August seems to have cast a spell upon Percy and to be guarding her jealously from those who might break it; in chapter 4, as its title "Puck" implies, the theme of enchantment continues, but Diana is as one awakening from a trance, freed from a prohibition. The chapter opens with Diana, now established as a sculptor in Rome, enjoying another sunset and the "delicate life of awakening Nature." In a "tender mood . . . full of . . . voiceless longings, and vague expectations"(427), she is accosted by a small boy, whom she impulsively embraces. Just as Diana, whom "children did not usually interest" (412) and whose eyes "looked straight forward above the level of the little heads of children" (432), was startled by her strong response to Percy's daughter, so she is astonished by her reaction to the child Nino: "That innocent kiss had been like the stroke upon the rock, and all the pent-up tenderness of her nature seemed to gush out, sprinkling the dust of what for a moment at least looked like a desert path along which she was following a mirage. She was amazed to feel how thirstily she drank of the sweet water so unexpectedly brought to her dry lips and laughed at herself even while she prolonged the draught."[15] Further metaphors and allusions—"The touch of that rosy mouth seemed to have unsealed the closely folded lips" and "the last clasp of childish arms had warmed the fair statue into still fairer flesh and blood" (432)—combine to suggest that the seemingly enchanted life of the successful female artist may be no better than a prison.

Alcott's portrayal of Nino's father, Stafford, "a well-known sculptor whose fame was already made," reinforces the idea that ambition cannot compensate for lack of love and that such a lack can render one powerless to gratify ambition, if indeed it survives.[16] In Stafford's case, the death of his young wife a few years earlier has "paralyzed the cunning hand and chilled the ambitious spirit just when both were ready to achieve their best" (431), and when he alludes to his grief, Diana "felt as if her Saul had spoken" (439). Like the Saul and his creator, Stafford is under a spell, and his inability to work, let alone find consolation in it for his grief, recalls how Percy, on rejecting love, lacked a motive for her art. Thus Alcott, by using one of her characteristic gender-role reversals—at one point Stafford says to Nino, "You make a woman of me" (435)—exposes as unrealistic society's expectation that the woman artist, in order to achieve, will sacrifice what the man is unable to do without. And in addition to demonstrating that success and happiness should be interdependent, not mutually exclusive, goals for women as they are for men, Stafford represents the sort of man who can help them attain these goals.

Stafford, as both mentor and potential mate for Diana, contrasts with both Percy's condescending "M" and her uxorious husband. Like Percy, Diana eagerly, even nervously, awaits the male artist's appraisal of her work. Having met Stafford with "the glad humility of a pupil saluting a much honored master" (434), Diana "pined to learn his opinion of her statue, for if *he* praised it she would be satisfied" (436). Yet the relationship between Stafford and Diana differs from Percy's with her master as well as from the master-pupil relationships that, as we have seen, exist between so many Alcott heroines and the men they come to love. For one thing, Diana has been laboring independently for at least four years and has developed considerable confidence in her work. Rather than craving reassurance, she demands praise as her due: "The masculine fibre in her nature demanded recognition as it does in all strong natures" (436). Percy found it hard to accept even M's valuation of her still life; not until she saw it hung "on the line" at the Salon could she admit that it was good. To Diana, on the other hand, "the honest opinion of such a man was more to her than any medal she might hereafter win" (438). Perhaps more important, despite Diana's high regard for Stafford's opinion, their relationship is, from the first, one of mutual respect and equality—if not of experience and reputation, at least of talent and dedication. On their first meeting "a mutual interest made the strangers friends by the free masonry of their craft" (434). M, on praising Percy's still life, welcomed her as his "élève"; Stafford, after viewing the Saul, gives Diana's hand "the cordial grasp one man gives another when he says heartily, 'Comrade, well done!'" (438).

Stafford, of course, appraises the woman as well as the artist, but whereas August was relieved to find her softer and more feminine than he had expected, Stafford is surprised and delighted by her strength. Like August, Stafford appreciates Diana's beauty and latent sensuality—on their first meeting he observes her slender, ungloved hands, but he is equally pleased with the "virile force" of her Saul. Throughout the scene in her studio, sexual attraction is enhanced rather than lessened for Stafford by his respect for Diana as a fellow artist. His offer to cast her Saul in marble is, as Diana realizes, prompted by more than chivalry or even gratitude for her having befriended Nino: "he not only thanked her as a woman but greeted her as an artist worthy of the name. . . . such recognition was very precious to her sensitive pride, her love of justice, and the independence she cherished as she did her life" (439). In trying to account to himself for the feeling Diana arouses, Stafford concludes that he is attracted by both likeness and difference: "he saw curiously blended an image of his own ambitious youth and a faint likeness to the wife he mourned" (440). Stafford's appreciation of Diana reflects his own androgynous nature and suggests that, unlike August, he will not, "manlike," love the woman better than the artist.

Chapter 4 closes as did chapter 3 with a male's observation of and meditation on Diana. However, where August admires her silent and smiling, "proud head leaned like a drowsy flower" (425), Stafford finds "something piquant in listening to the boldest opinions from this handsome creature's lips, uttered with a certain calm conviction and unsparing truthfulness which contrasted curiously with the patient care with which she put one sweet morsel after another into the rosy mouth

[Nino] held up so persistently." Alcott's metaphors of hunger and thirst culminate when Diana produces "her little store of sugar biscuits and dates hanging like great amber drops from the stem they grew upon, and fed the child, who leaned against her knee, contentedly smearing his lip with honey and scattering crumbs over the purple lap that held his plate" (441). The lush description, both regal and erotic, suggests that Diana, in feeding Nino, is nourishing herself and, unlike Percy trapped in a maternal snare, freeing herself for a fuller, more abundant life. Stafford's reflection, as he watches, differs markedly from August's conclusion that "she is not all artist but a woman to be loved as well as admired" (ironic, as at the moment she is contemplating "the land of promise for such as she," meaning the artist [425]). Instead, Stafford "feels as if there was a fine man and a fine woman working there together, and one scarcely knows which to admire most" (441). If, as its editors have concluded, *Diana and Persis* is indeed unfinished, "one scarcely knows" how Alcott could have contrived a more felicitous ending.

But perhaps the most satisfying symbol of a possible union between Diana and Stafford, between the feminine and masculine in both women and men, and between love and art, is their collaboration on Diana's head of Nino. When, during Stafford's visit to her studio, he alludes to his grief and reminds her of her Saul, she hears Nino's voice and observes how "the music of this little David soothed the troubled soul of the man." Hoping to divert him further, Diana unwraps the head she has been molding, and, in doing so, becomes herself a type of David: "If Diana had sought for comfort suited to his mood, she could have found nothing better than this, for both man and sculptor felt the tender tact with which she touched the one happy note that made music for him." As he watches her begin to work, he again feels the harmony rather than the conflict between woman and artist: "It was as if he saw a woman giving the motherless boy the gentle caress he needed, for she used no tool, but with her own deft fingers twined the little curls back from the brow" (440). Only one touch is needed to make the head a perfect likeness of Nino, and this Stafford himself supplies: "making one effective dent in the round chin which gave Nino's dimple to the life . . . he smiled as if his fingers felt the charm of their old mastery" (440–41). In collaborating with Diana on her project, which, as he recognizes, is not only a work of art but an act of love, Stafford breaks the spell that has been holding him a prisoner. The last sentence of *Diana and Persis* tells us that Diana, after Stafford's departure, "added a pair of winged shoulders and called [the statue] Puck" (441). This addition gives the incident still greater resonance, especially if we recall Cecil's infant Cupid in *A Marble Woman*. By having Diana give wings to *her* cherub rather than destroy him, Alcott turns the warning of the early story—that psychic wholeness and successful art cannot be achieved by repression—into a positive statement.[17]

In addition to revising her own earlier story, Alcott in *Diana and Persis* again revises *The Scarlet Letter*. Diana, who Stafford observes "passing through the streets like a grey nun unfolded [*sic*] in her own sweet thoughts and high purposes as in a veil that shut out the admiration of man's eyes" (433), and who appears to him at the Pincio as "a slender yet stately figure in pale grey with no color but the knot of crimson carnations in her bosom" (432), represents, like Hester, the sexual repression enjoined on women and the spiritual isolation of those who, like Diana, entertain the "boldest opinions" or, like Hester, possess an "estranged point of view" (290). In both cases their secret rebellion is acted out by a capricious "elf-child," who, deprived of one parent and overindulged by the other, signifies the way in which women have been denied the full range of human experience. But whereas Pearl insists that Hester, after removing the scarlet letter, replace it, Nino "snatched . . . from Diana's bosom" the crimson flowers that represent her repressed passion. Outwardly and even inwardly, Hester acquiesces in society's judgment, for she "recognized the impossibility that any mission of divine and mysterious truth should be confided to a woman stained with sin. . . . The angel and apostle of the coming revelation must be a woman, indeed, but lofty, pure and beautiful; and wise, moreover, not through dusky grief, but the ethereal medium of joy" (344–45). Diana, by embracing Nino and by sharing her "virile force," her "boldest opinions," with his father, reclaims her instinctual life and reveals an intellectual one. Hester predicts that "at some brighter period, when the world should have grown ripe for it . . . a new truth would be revealed, in order to establish the whole relation between man and woman on a surer ground of mutual happiness" (344). Alcott, in *Diana and Persis*, for once allowed herself to declare that such a revelation was at hand.

Diana and Persis, while more realistic than *A Modern Mephistopheles*, is also, as its allusions to *The Scarlet Letter* suggest, an allegory—of the woman artist, past, passing, and to come. Although Diana has been identified with Alcott and her contemporaries, Percy with May and a younger, more liberated generation, it is Diana who represents the future. Both Diana and Percy seem to move in the apparent direction of Psyche, Alcott's earlier artist heroine, from the conflicted ambition represented by their skylarks, Sauls, and, in Psyche's case, Venuses, to the domestic tranquillity represented by their sketches and busts of children. Or, to use a symbol common to both stories, each passes through a stage as "studious grub," emerges from an artistic "chrysalis," to become a true or little woman, "rich in the art which made life happy to herself and others." Percy's study and eventual recognition in Paris anticipates Diana's in Rome, Percy's happy marriage to August prepares us for Diana's romance with Stafford, and Percy's delight in her infant daughter forecasts Diana's in Nino. But though each woman seems to win a measure of success only to find it hollow compared with the joy afforded by a more traditional role, their careers are actually as different as the two endings of Psyche's story. Diana, like Percy, Psyche, and the March sisters, appears to adopt a more domestic art, but she is joined in it by her male colleague, and, like Psyche's bust of her sister May—"the figure of a child looking upward as if watching the airy flight of some butterfly"—her Puck signifies release, not containment, of the creative spirit.

In *Diana and Persis,* as in *A Modern Mephistopheles,* Alcott presents not only an allegory of the woman artist but the portrait of a particular one. Like the texts, textiles, and theatricals of other Alcott heroines, the various works of art described in the novella, including those actually produced by May Alcott, provide paradigms—both misleading and revealing—of the author's career. Some would doubtless see its trajectory in Percy's skylark and still life—the one representing her early ambition, the other her ambivalence toward her success as a purveyor of "sentimental tales" and "middle class domestic virtues" (Kaledin 251–53). Percy's abandonment of portraiture, her acceptance of M's advice to paint "simply what you see without trying to *make a picture*," does sound like Alcott's abandonment of adult fiction for children's books based on immediate experience.[18] But Diana's artistic development, as represented by her Saul and Puck, constitutes a truer paradigm. Diana's Saul, like Alcott's Jean Muir and Jasper Helwyze, signifies "a woman's power" and the demonic element in women's art; he also, like Helwyze and Jean's male adversaries, embodies the self-defeating nature of patriarchy. In turning from Saul to Puck, Diana approximates Alcott's move from the sensational to the domestic. Diana begins molding Nino's head much as Percy begins her still life and Alcott began *Little Women*—"more because she found it impossible to settle to any other task than because she hoped for any great success" (436),[19] but, like Alcott's, her conception changes. With the assistance of Stafford (or her alter ego), she comes to realize Nino's "naughty smile," his elfin nature, gives him wings, and calls him Puck. Thus the horror and madness of her early work is succeeded not by innocuous blandness or by cloying sentiment but by "a midsummer night's dream" in which appearances are deceiving, convictions shaken and subverted. In *Jo's Boys*, the last of Alcott's domestic novels, that dream becomes a nightmare.

CHAPTER 10

A Voice of One's Own:
Jo's Boys

For all artists the problem is one of finding one's own authenticity, of speaking in a language or imagery that is essentially one's own, but if one's self-image is dictated by one's relation to others and all one's activities are other-directed, it is simply not possible to find one's own voice.

> Germaine Greer,
> *The Obstacle Race* (325)

We ourselves, by maintaining this artificial diversity between the sexes, have constantly kept before us the enigma which we found so hard to solve, and have preserved in our own characters the confusion and contradiction which is our greatest difficulty in life.

> Charlotte Perkins Gilman,
> *Women and Economics* (331)

In the preface to *Jo's Boys* (1886), her last novel, Alcott attempts to "account for the seeming neglect of AMY": "since the original of that character died, it has been impossible for me to write of her as when she was here to suggest, criticize, and laugh over her namesake." The influence of May Alcott, however, is by no means absent from the book that lets "the curtain fall forever on the March family" (338). Amy's role, while subordinate, is significant, and her daughter, Bess, Princess

Goldilocks in *Little Men,* has become an aspiring sculptor, who, like her mother, Psyche, and Persis, seems based on Alcott's artist sister. By alluding to May in her preface, then modeling two characters on her in the text itself, Alcott invites us to scrutinize them carefully and thereby discover links with *Diana and Persis.* But, as we have seen, the novella, written for an adult audience, envisions a bright future for the female artist; the novel, addressed to the author's "patient little friends," presents the obstacles that continue to obstruct her path. Whereas allusions to *A Midsummer Night's Dream* transform *Diana and Persis* into a romantic comedy, references to *Othello* in *Jo's Boys* hint at tragedy. Like its predecessors *Little Women* and *Little Men,* with their sprightly surface and underlying pathos, *Jo's Boys* confronts us with a paradox—that Alcott distilled into bromides for children her most bitter cultural medicine, *not* to be confused with Aunt Jo's "moral pap for the young."[1]

At first, however, Alcott would seem to be attributing to Jo the views she expressed in an 1874 letter to Maria Porter. In congratulating Porter on her election to the Melrose school committee, Alcott wrote:

I believe in the same pay for the same good work. Don't you? In future let woman do whatever she can do; let men place no impediments in the way; above all things let's have fair play,—let *simple justice* be done, I say. Let us hear no more of "woman's sphere" either from our wise (?) legislators beneath the State House dome, or from our clergymen in their pulpits. I am tired, year after year, of hearing such twaddle about sturdy oaks and clinging vines and man's chivalric protection of woman. Let woman find out her own limitations, and if, as is so confidently asserted, nature has defined her sphere, she will be guided accordingly; but in heaven's name give her a chance! Let the professions be open to her; let fifty years of college education be hers, and then we shall . . . be able to say what woman can and what she cannot do, and coming generations will know and be able to define more clearly what is "woman's sphere" than these benighted men who now try to do it. (*Letters* 189–90)

In *Little Men,* we recall, Jo viewed her mission—and that of her little women, Daisy, Bess, and Nan—as that of exerting a civilizing influence on little men. In *Jo's*

Boys, published fifteen and set ten years later, Jo and her girls seem to have achieved—or be preparing for—independent lives and to have abandoned the traditional notion of woman's moral superiority and edifying influence within her biologically ordained sphere, the home. Daisy Brooke, as might have been expected, is content to wait for Nat to prove himself worthy of her, but her younger sister, Josie, a mere toddler in *Little Men,* is an aspiring actress; her cousin Bess, as mentioned above, is a talented sculptor; and "naughty Nan" is fulfilling her dream of becoming a doctor.[2] Amy persists in the "artistic attempts" begun in *Little Women,* Meg is acting once more in amateur productions, and Jo herself has become a successful juvenile writer, who appears to believe, like her creator, that woman's sphere exists wherever she chooses to make it. Laurie's founding of coeducational Laurence College on the campus of formerly all-male Plumfield further contributes to our sense of a common sphere for men and women.

Despite its seeming emphasis on male adventure—Emil's voyage to the Far East, Nat's study in Europe, Dan's expeditions to the frontier, *Jo's Boys* is among Alcott's most overtly feminist works. Throughout the novel, Jo and the three girls most like her—Nan, Josie, and Laurence College student Alice Heath—support each other's enlightened views and challenge traditional male attitudes. During a discussion of "surplus women," Jo defends Nan's resolve to be a "useful, happy, and independent spinster" (15) and later vows to her son Rob that Nan's career "shall *not* be hampered by a foolish boy's fancy" (136). When the suffrage issue is debated, Nan argues that women should not pamper men, "making slaves of ourselves and tyrants of them. Let them prove what they can do and be before they ask anything of us, and give us a chance to do the same." Alice quickly chimes in, "Now we are expected to be as wise as men who have had generations of all the help there is. . . . I like justice, and we get very little of it" (96). Even fourteen-year-old Josie challenges Grandfather March: "must women always obey men and say they are wisest, just because they are the strongest?" (31) and to Laurie she insists "that a woman can act as well, if not better, than a man. . . . I'll never own that *my* brain isn't as good as his" (32). To a Plumfielder now at Harvard she argues, "you'll be much better off in all ways when [women] do get in, and keep you lazy things up to the mark, as we do here" (249–50). Jo adds that "girls who love study wish to be treated like reasonable beings, not dolls to flirt with" (252). The success of Laurence College's experiment with coeducation seems confirmed at Class Day when Alice delivers a speech on women's rights: "a slender white figure stood out against the background of black-coated dignitaries, and . . . spoke to them straight out of a woman's heart and brain concerning the hopes and doubts, the aspirations and rewards all must know, desire, and labor for" (276). Her male peers are described as "much fired by her stirring appeal to 'march shoulder to shoulder'" (277).

But the most protracted discussion of women's rights takes place within the March sisters' sewing circle, which extends to include female students at the college. Jo, at the center of the circle, gives "little lectures on health, religion, politics, and the various questions in which all should be interested, with copious extracts from Miss Cobbe's *Duties of Women,* Miss Brackett's *Education of American Girls,* Mrs. Duffy's *No Sex in Education,* Mrs. Woolson's *Dress Reform,* and many of the other excellent books wise women write for their sisters, now that they are waking up and asking, 'What shall we do?'" (262)[3] Students offer testimonials. One, in response to the surplus women problem, consoles herself that "Old Maids aren't sneered at half as much as they used to be, since some of them have grown famous and proved that woman isn't a half but a whole human being, and can stand alone" (263). Another admires spinsters because "they are so independent. My aunt Jenny can do just what she likes and ask no one's leave; but ma has to consult pa about everything" (265). A third girl claims to be "Stronger in body, and much happier in mind" since coming to college. Jo, in hearty approval, scoffs at "all [this] nonsense about girls not being able to study as well as boys. . . . we will prove that wise headwork is a better cure for . . . delicacy than tonics, and novels on the sofa, where far too many of our girls go to wreck nowadays" (266). When a visitor tells of Englishwomen's accomplishments—"Mrs. Cobbe's eloquent protest winning the protection of the law for abused wives; Mrs. Butler saving the lost"—Jo concludes, "our [English] sisters are in earnest, you see, and don't waste time worrying about their sphere, but make it wherever duty calls them" (270–71).

Jo's words to her sewing circle seem to echo those of Alcott to Maria Porter but admit of considerable ambiguity. Is she applauding Englishwomen for not allowing conventional notions of their sphere to prevent them from expanding it or for answering the call of duty within their traditional sphere rather than insisting on its expansion? For as Janet Horowitz Murray has pointed out, Josephine Butler's "sincere appeal [on behalf of prostitutes] to the 'weakness' of women, their loyalty to one another, their need of male protection, and the sacredness of their motherly functions, could all form a part of any hymn to the angel in the house" (13). And the very setting in which Jo exhorts her literal sisters and their daughters, as well as selected Laurence College students, is described as "the sweet privacy that domestic women love" (261). Ruth MacDonald, after identifying the novel's focus as women's rights and praising Alcott, with a touch of irony, for "preaching the feminist gospel" without "sugarcoat[ing] the sermon's pill," speculates that "she could be this frank because in other ways the book is quite conventional about woman's duties to her family" (1983, 41–42). This apparent conflict between the book's "feminist gospel" and its conventional code, a conflict that has led Martha Saxton to dismiss the former as mere "pap,"⁴ is epitomized by Jo in an earlier discussion of women's roles. After supporting Nan's decision to remain single so as to pursue her medical career, Jo responds to the news of her nephew Franz's engagement with a hearty "I'm glad to hear it. I do so like to settle my boys with a good wife and a nice little home. Now, if all is right, I shall feel as if Franz was off my mind" (15). Jo persists in believing that marriage settles a man and helps assure his successful career while a wife continues a mother's caretaking functions. As the surrogate mother of a dozen boys and the natural mother of two, Jo is anxious for them all to marry devoted, domestic women—women who feel that their first duty is to their husband and who are content within the confines of "a nice little home."

But *Jo's Boys* need not be read as an unconvincing effort to reconcile feminist with traditional values; indeed it counts the cost of such efforts. After Jo so blatantly contradicts herself—by urging careers on her girls, conventional marriage on her boys—she makes a startling confession: "I sometimes feel as if I'd missed my vocation and ought to have remained single; but duty seemed to point this way" (15–16). Viewed in this context, Jo's speech to the sewing circle takes on an ironic dimension. In applauding those who "don't waste time worrying about their sphere, but make it wherever duty calls," Jo identifies duty with one's calling as opposed to convention. But her confession reveals that if one has been indoctrinated in the notion of separate spheres, as Jo was indoctrinated by Marmee, one will be called by duty to conventional roles at the expense of one's vocation. Thus the novel implies that we *must* worry about our sphere—not about conforming to it but about redefining it, lest we fail to heed the call to any but domestic duty. Immediately before making her confession, Jo jokes that surplus women are "a merciful provision . . . for it takes three or four women to get each man into, through, and out of the world. You are costly creatures, boys" (15). Although half in jest, Jo at some level recognizes that men and boys *are* costly creatures, so costly that she cannot, in conscience, urge marriage upon her more ambitious girls or keep from regretting the sacrifices her own marriage has cost her.

The heavy price that Jo has paid for Professor Bhaer becomes increasingly clear despite her insistence to Meg, at the beginning of *Jo's Boys,* that her three girlhood wishes—"Money, fame, and plenty of the work I love" (2)—have come true. Jo, we learn, resumed writing when economic difficulties beset Plumfield and she, ill from overwork, was confined to her room. "A book for girls being wanted by a certain publisher, she hastily scribbled a little story describing a few scenes and adventures in the lives of herself and her sisters. . . . The hastily written story, sent away with no thought beyond the few dollars it might bring . . . came home heavily laden with an unexpected cargo of gold and glory" (38). Professor Bhaer, who in *Little Women* disapproved of Jo's writing, now encourages it, and Jo acknowledges that if "all literary women had such thoughtful angels for husbands, they would live longer and write more" (45). Yet that very afternoon Professor Bhaer returns to the house where his wife is warding off one interruption after another in a vain attempt to write and brings with him seventy-five mud-bespattered members of the Young Men's Christian Union, all of whom must be cheerfully supplied with refreshments and autographs. Jo's efforts to transform the domestic sphere into a workplace where she can satisfy the demands of her art are continually frustrated by such costly male incursions. Little wonder, then, that Jo's writing seems to her less like a true vocation than an extension of domestic duty, prompting her to characterize herself as "only a literary nursery-maid who provides moral pap for the young" (42).

The nautical metaphors used to describe Jo's literary career serve to contrast it with her sailor nephew Emil's. After the first success of her girls' book, "it was plain sailing, and she merely had to load her ships and send them off on prosperous trips, to bring home stores of comfort for all she loved and labored for" (38). The books travel, enter the public realm, but she does not; instead, her privacy becomes susceptible to invasion. As Emil prepares to leave on a voyage, Jo hints at her discontent: "I often wish I could go too, and someday I will, when you are captain and have a ship of your own" (108). Emil, as though he senses her frustration, responds, "I'd be a proud man to carry you round the world you've wanted to see so long and never could" (109). At a party in Emil's honor, Jo comments to Laurie, "The constant jollity of that boy is worth a fortune to him." Laurie, who knows Jo best, adds, "it's a blessing to be grateful for, isn't it? We moody people know its worth" (88). But Jo's moodiness, like Sylvia Yule's, is not so much a function of her nature as of her situation; excluded from Emil's masculine world of travel, exploration, and adventure, she is also deprived of the privacy and concentration that would help compensate for such exclusion. When Amy says of their generation, "We have only bloomed; and a very nice bouquet we make with our buds about us," Jo adds sourly, "Not to mention our thorns and dead leaves." The narrator comments that "life had never been very easy to her, and even now she had her troubles both within and without" (24).

These troubles are dramatized by Jo and Laurie in the Christmas theatricals they present at Plumfield. The main play, written by Jo in collaboration with Laurie, attempts to justify her submission to the claims of domestic duty; the final performance of the evening, a tableau created by Laurie, exposes the conflicts and compromises in such submission. The heroine of Jo's play, "a few scenes of humble life in which the comic and pathetic were mingled" (218), is an old woman who saves her grandson from his villainous father, her daughter from a wealthy but shallow suitor, and her son from death in an army hospital. The play ends with a Christmas toast to "Mother, God bless her!" (228). Thus Jo attempts to "prove that there's romance in old women also" (222) by transforming the humdrum mother's role, which she in life has chosen to play, into something more heroic. By casting as the heroine her sister Meg, nicknamed the "Pelican" because "for her precious children she would have plucked her last feather and given the last drop of her blood" (30), Jo further attempts to prove that domestic duty is not inconsistent with, can even lend itself to, artistic accomplishment. Yet the success of both Jo and Meg is, for Jo, a hollow one, serving only to remind her of the vocation she has sacrificed. As she exclaims to Meg between the acts, "Oh, why aren't you a real actress, and I a real playwright?" Meg's response—"Don't gush now, dear, but help me dress Josie . . . this is her best scene, you know" (224)—marks the difference between the sisters that Jo has long labored to obscure: that between the woman who aspires for herself and the one content to live through and for others.

The consequences of obscuring that difference are pointed up by Laurie's comic tableau "The Owlsdark Marbles." As Professor Owlsdark, he praises Nan as Minerva, "the strong-minded woman of antiquity," congratulates Professor

Bhaer as Jove upon "the brood of all-accomplished Pallases that yearly issue from his mighty brain," and mocks Jo as Mrs. Juno, "with her peacocks, darning needle, pen, and cooking spoon" (229–30). But Laurie, as the name Owlsdark implies, is wiser than he knows in assessing the causes and effects of Jo's plight as well as the potential plight of Plumfield's Pallases. In praising Nan, whose shield and scroll bear the words *Woman's Rights* and *Vote early and often,* Professor Owlsdark makes some "scathing remarks . . . upon the degeneracy of her modern sisters who failed to do their duty" (229). And in mocking Jo, he "alluded to her domestic infelicity, her meddlesome disposition, sharp tongue, bad temper, and jealousy, closing, however, with a tribute to her skill in caring for the wounds and settling the quarrels of belligerent heroes, as well as her love for youths in Olympus and on earth" (230). Instead of insisting, like Nan, on their right to participate in the larger world, the modern Pallases produced by still-patriarchal Plumfield may feel obliged, as did Jo, to create a peaceful, healing haven apart from it. But if they sacrifice the pen to the needle and spoon, or, like Jo, try unsuccessfully to combine them, they may suffer the same frustration and resentment that Jo so often displays and fail in their real duty to society and themselves. Having taken Laurie's mock scolding to heart, Jo, as in the past, resolves to treat the symptoms of repression and self-sacrifice rather than examine their underlying causes. We are assured that, "thanks to Professor Owlsdark's jest, Mrs. Jo made Professor Bhaer's busy life quite a bed of roses" (233), but those roses are doubtless paid for daily with the "thorns and dead leaves" Jo feels surrounded by.

Jo's internal struggle between self-assertion and self-sacrifice, artistic vocation and domestic duty, fullness of experience and conventional ideals of womanhood finds outward expression in concern for Amy and Laurie's daughter, Bess. Amy, as we recall from *Little Women,* was the most self-assertive, ambitious sister, determined to become a true artist, not merely a financially successful one. In *Jo's Boys,* Amy's studio and salon at Mount Parnassus, "Laurie's white-pillared mansion," seems living proof that "women can be faithful wives and mothers without sacrificing the special gift bestowed upon them for their own development and the good of others." And she "found her own art doubly dear as her daughter grew old enough to share its labors and delights with her" (19). But Jo, perhaps out of unconscious envy, disparages their work and subjects them to the kind of interruption that frustrates her. Bursting into "the studio where mother and daughter worked together" (19), she cries, "'My dear girls, stop your mud pies and hear the news!' Both artists dropped their tools and greeted the irrepressible woman cordially, though genius had been burning splendidly and her coming spoilt a precious hour" (21). Later when Laurie, perhaps jealous of their intimacy, expresses a wish to get Bess "away from this cold clay and marble into the sunshine, to dance and laugh as the others do" (22), Jo readily concurs. After Bess leaves the studio, Jo urges Amy to let her spend more time with her father, studying music and enjoying nature. "Now I advise you, Amy, to let Bess drop the mud pies for a time." Amy, under pressure from both Jo and Laurie, admits to having allowed Bess to overwork but explains that "I sympathize so deeply in it all, I forget to be wise" (23).

Amy's sympathy with her daughter's aspirations, however, does not prevent her from subtly undermining them or reinforcing the threat posed by Jo and Laurie. In *Little Women,* we recall, Amy concentrated on making herself her own most successful work of art. In *Jo's Boys,* she shares with Laurie an aesthetic appreciation of her daughter: "the beauty she had longed for seemed, to her fond eyes at least, to be impersonated in this younger self. Bess inherited her mother's Dianalike figure, blue eyes, fair skin, and golden hair, tied up in the same classic knot of curls. Also,—ah! never-ending source of joy to Amy—she had her father's handsome nose and mouth, cast in a feminine mold" (20–21). As the word *mold* indicates, Amy regards her daughter not only as a sculptor but as sculpture. Laurie too looks "at his tall girl as Pygmalion might have looked at Galatea; for he considered her the finest statue in the house." Yet Laurie, having observed that Bess "worked away with the entire absorption of the true artist," protests that "I want a flesh-and-blood girl, not a sweet statue in a pinafore, who forgets everything but her work" (20–21). Ironically, he fails to realize that his idealized conception of her as a work of art robs her of vitality whereas her absorption in her work is vitalizing. Laurie harbors no malign intent such as Bazil Yorke's in regard to Cecil; in fact, his conscious purpose is the opposite. Nonetheless, by molding Bess to conform to his ideal of womanhood, Laurie risks turning her into another marble woman, as he does in "The Owlsdark Marbles." There Bess appears as a "lovely Diana, who stood as white and still as the plaster stag beside her . . . quite perfect, and altogether the best piece of statuary in the show" (231).

Parnassus, then, rather than serving as a true haven for artists, perpetuates those values that would limit a woman's creative development. In the opening scene of *Jo's Boys,* Meg expresses regret that "dear Marmee, John, and Beth" (2) are not alive to share the sisters' content. Yet we find that they—and the self-denying values they represent—are enshrined on Parnassus, however inimical their spirit may be to the passionate self-absorption Bess needs in order to go beyond her aunt and mother to become a true artist. In an alcove of the summer parlor, "as became the founder of the house, hung the portrait of Mr. Laurence," who, by discouraging Laurie's passion for music, produced a patron of the arts rather than a performer. More significant than this portrait, or even Amy's busts of Beth and John, is the one that occupies the "place of honor." There, "with the sunshine warm upon it, and a green garland always round it, was Marmee's beloved face, painted with grateful skill by a great artist whom she had befriended when poor and unknown. So beautifully lifelike was it that it seemed to smile down upon her daughters, saying cheerfully, 'Be happy: I am with you still'" (25). Although Marmee may have aided a struggling male artist to realize his ambitions, we remember her telling Meg and Jo that to "be loved and chosen by a good man is the best and sweetest thing which can happen to a woman" (*Little Women* 123) and suffering much anxiety when Jo's "genius took to burning" (*Little Women* 331). As the sisters regard Marmee's portrait with the "tender reverence and the longing that never left them" (25), Laurie says, "I can ask nothing better for my child than that she may be a woman like our mother. Please God, she shall be, if I can do it." Just then they hear Bess singing "Ave Marie" as though she "unconsciously echoed her father's prayer for her as she dutifully obeyed his wishes. The soft sound of the air Marmee used to sing led the listeners back into the world again from that momentary reaching after the loved and lost" (26). Bess's "dutiful" rendering of Marmee's song suggests the danger that Laurie's aspirations for her, not her artistic aspirations for herself, will be realized. Still, Bess's song leads the listeners away from the shrine, out of their veneration of the past, into the world that, for all their nostalgia, is changing.

Two women in *Jo's Boys* seem harbingers of this changing world, and both help Josie, daughter of conservative Meg, to withstand the pressures brought to bear on her and Bess by the combined forces of Plumfield and Parnassus. One of course is Nan, the willful, headstrong girl of *Little Men,* now "a woman full of the energy and promise that suddenly blossoms when the ambitious seeker finds the work she is fitted to do well" (5). We are told that "she began to study medicine at sixteen," about Bess's age, and "never wavered in her purpose" (5), perhaps because, for all Jo's efforts to domesticate her, she had no mother, like Marmee, to enjoin self-sacrifice on her. Nan, unlike the rest of Jo's girls or Jo herself, is mobile and independent. Like Demi, Tommy, and other grown male Plumfielders, she moves freely back and forth between her practice in the town and recreation at rural Plumfield. We first see her "walking briskly along the pleasant road alone, thinking over a case that interested her," while Tommy, her erstwhile suitor, struggles to overtake her (6). Like Sarah Orne Jewett's female doctor, Nan Prince, Nan feels no conflict between the claims of duty and those of vocation, because she too is determined to "make many homes happy instead of one," whereas in marriage "a great share of [her] life . . . could not have its way, and could only hide itself and be sorry" (*A Country Doctor* 242). By casting her as Minerva in "The Owlsdark Marbles," Laurie is again wiser than he knows, for Nan is not simply a militant suffragist but, like Faith Dane in *Moods,* the Minerva side of woman that Margaret Fuller would see more completely developed. Nan, therefore, is an important role model for one like Josie, helping her over many hurdles just as, in the opening chapter, she extricates the younger girl from a hedge she has tried to leap, in pursuit of her cousin Ted.

Later Josie selects a mentor within her own field, one who represents what Jo might have become. Like Jo, the celebrated actress Miss Cameron has achieved fame, but she is able to enjoy the solitary concentration that Jo, as the center of a large family, has had to forgo. Secluded so as to "'create' a new part for the next season" (138), Miss Cameron is able to protect herself from the intrusions that continually disrupt Jo's day. Although a mere sketch in Alcott's gallery of women artists, Miss Cameron would seem to represent the woman who, unhampered by domestic duty within the private sphere, has sufficient privacy to realize her ambitions in the public one. Jo, as playwright, shares Miss Cameron's desire to transform the American stage, but she is unable to move beyond the modest Christmas play we see performed at Plumfield. After its success, she feels ready to "begin our great American drama . . . which, we may add, she did not write that year, owing to various dramatic events in her own family" (229). Miss Cameron is one who, while claiming the male prerogative of living "only for art" (147), withstands the temptation, so irresistible to Christie Devon, to neglect the claims of others. Unlike Christie, who found a stage career incompatible with her sense of solidarity with other women, Miss Cameron strives to make acting a less hazardous career for them and to remove the obstacles to their artistic fulfillment. Rather than fearing the competition of younger actresses, she seeks to befriend them. As she tells Josie, "It would be pleasant to me to know that when I quit the stage I leave behind me a well-trained, faithful, gifted comrade to more than fill my place" (150). When Miss Cameron fastens her own pin "like an order on Josie's proud bosom" (152), she becomes the true fairy godmother that Jo, in *Little Men,* tried in vain to play and provides Josie with a much more effectual talisman than Marmee was able to give her girls.

Josie is more fortunate than Bess, both in having such a mentor and in not being the only child of two adoring, artistic parents. True, Amy shares and supports Bess's artistic endeavors, whereas Meg, despite her love of acting, disapproves of Josie's theatrical ambitions. Yet Amy, who is determined to make a "gentlewoman" of her niece, is no less conventional than Meg in her attitude toward the theater, and she "guarded her daughter as a pearl of great price" (328) against any experience, however fruitful for her art, that might threaten her innocence. Moreover, Meg's overt opposition may even have the advantage of helping Josie define herself. More important, Josie has no charming, youthful father like Laurie to seduce her into conforming to his model of perfect womanhood, a model, as we have seen, based on her grandmother, Marmee. Also, Josie's older siblings, the twins Daisy and Demi, fulfill her mother's expectations (both continue to perpetuate the gender stereotypes they epitomized as infants), leaving Josie comparatively free to develop her own authenticity. Finally, Josie's rough-and-tumble relationship with Jo's high-spirited son, Ted—a relationship that, as their names imply, replicates the adolescent friendship of Jo and Laurie—and her admiration for her sailor cousin, Emil, serve to make her sturdy and self-reliant. Josie, then, is, like Nan, one of those rare women who can be trusted to make her way onto the larger stage without first suffering Christie Devon's paralyzing conflicts. Far more common, however, are women like Bess, driven to create but instilled with an even stronger desire to please. During a discussion of women's suffrage, Bess is asked to serve as arbiter and demurs, pleading that she is not wise enough. "And Bess took her place above them all as cool and calm as a little statue of Justice, with fan and nosegay in place of sword and scales" (97–98). Despite her diffidence, and real unpreparedness, Bess is, as Alcott indicates, the arbiter of her own fate and that of her sex, for she is the aspiring but feminine woman who must decide between the full exercise of her powers and a graceful, statuelike existence, the ultimate constriction of woman's sphere.

Bess and the other women at Plumfield are made to realize the narrowness of their sphere by Dan, the "firebrand" of *Little Men*. Dan, on his return to Plumfield after years in Latin America and the West, receives "a scolding from Josie for getting ahead of all the other boys and looking like a man first" (61). Not only has Dan become a man; he seems to breathe fresh air into the claustrophobic atmosphere of Plumfield and to give its residents a glimpse of wider possibilities. When Dan, with his horse and dog, performs at Plumfield, "It was a fine sight—the three wild things at play, so full of vigor, grace, and freedom that for the moment the smooth lawn seemed a prairie; and the spectators felt as if this glimpse of another life made their own seem rather tame and colorless." Jo, as she watches, wishes that she "were a girl again that she might take a gallop on this chained lightning of a steed" (79). Although Daisy admits that she is "still a little afraid of him," Nan admires him for his looks, his stories, his plans. "I like him very much; he's so big and strong and independent. I'm tired of mollycoddles and bookworms" (95). The night of the suffrage discussion, Jo and Laurie observe Bess listening spellbound to Dan's strange adventures. Laurie, amused, entitles the scene "Othello telling his adventures to Desdemona" (88), but Jo, feeling a vague premonition, confides, "I'm glad he's going away. He's too picturesque to have here among so many romantic girls" (88). Like Othello, Dan has the potential to widen woman's sphere, at least imaginatively, but, like Othello's, his own proves in some ways tragically limited.

The final chapters of *Jo's Boys,* devoted to Dan's recovery from a mining accident and expulsion from Plumfield, further expose Jo's frustration and its impact on Bess. During Dan's first visit, we are led to believe that, despite Jo's fears, he could have a salutary influence on Bess's art. For example, he presents her with a buffalo's head: "Thought it would do her good to model something strong and natural. She'll never amount to anything if she keeps on making namby-pamby gods and pet kittens" (70). Later Daisy confides to Nan that Bess "has been doing Dan's head. . . . I never saw her so interested in any work, and it's very well done" (95). But by the time Dan returns to Plumfield and his "Desdemona," he has undergone experiences—a killing in self-defense followed by a prison term—that he cannot impart to her innocent ears, though they enable Jo to live out the domestic drama of her Christmas play. After receiving "the wanderer like a recovered son" (308) and eliciting a full confession, Jo "put her arms about him, and lay the shorn head on her breast. . . . poor Dan clung to her in speechless gratitude, feeling the blessedness of mother love—that divine gift which comforts, purifies, and strengthens all who seek it" (311). Once Dan begins to recover, however, it becomes apparent, to Jo at least, that he has transferred much of his devotion to Bess, who, "at his special desire, set up a modeling stand in his parlor and began to mold the buffalo head he had given her" (315). Dan "faced Mrs. Jo's room, but never seemed to see her, for his eyes were on the slender figure before him, with the pale winter sunshine touching her golden head, and the delicate hands that shaped the clay so deftly" (317). Jo, on observing Dan's intensity of feeling, "caught up her workbasket and went to join her neighbors, feeling that a nonconductor might be needed" (318). And it is by acting as a nonconductor, by refusing to allow Dan to transmit his electricity to placid, genteel Bess, that Jo short-circuits her niece's creative potential just as, in *Little Women,* she short-circuited her own.

At first Jo would seem justified in her attempts to separate Dan and Bess, for Dan appreciates her less as artist than as art object, as Muse rather than as Minerva. On his earlier triumphant return to Plumfield, Dan first sees Bess "quite unconscious of the pretty picture she made standing, tall and slender, against the soft gloom of the summer night, with her golden hair like a halo around her head, and the ends of a white shawl blown out like wings by the cool wind sweeping through the hall" (59–60). The chastened Dan identifies Bess with the heroine of "Aslauga's Knight," who appeared "to her lover in hours of danger and trial . . . till she became his guide and guard, inspiring him with courage, nobleness, and truth, leading him to great deeds in the field, sacrifices for those he loved, and victories over himself by the gleaming of her golden hair" (320). Jo's "black sheep," as he is called, like the "black ram" Othello, would his "unhoused free condition / Put into circumscription and confine" (I.ii.26–27) by uniting with one free from the stains of his adventures but appreciative of them ("She lov'd me for the dangers I had pass'd; / And I lov'd her that she did pity them" [I.iii.167–68]). But in yearning to possess the vision of purity and innocence, and by doing so regain his own, Dan recapitulates Othello's error of ignoring Emilia's warning: "Let husbands know / Their wives have sense like them; they see and smell, / And have their palates both for sweet and sour / As husbands have" (IV.iii.91–94). Much as Dan has to offer Bess in knowledge of the larger world, he, the natural, freedom-loving man, prefers, like Othello and like Laurie, the eminently civilized one, to preserve her in marble or alabaster or between the covers of a sentimental tale.

Justified as Jo's intervention appears to be, her motives and her methods are suspect: her motives, as she dimly realizes, are compromised by her possessiveness of Dan, her methods by the muse or mother worship she perpetuates. When she discovers, during Dan's convalescence, that he indeed loves Bess, she immediately feels "how utterly hopeless such a longing was; since light and darkness were not farther apart than snow-white Bess and sin-stained Dan." Further, she conveniently assumes that Bess "was as cool and high and pure as her own marbles, and shunned all thought of love with maidenly reserve" (321). But having concluded all of this, Jo is oddly left feeling "like a thief who has stolen something very precious" (323). And when, on "yearning over" the sleeping Dan, she discovers Bess's photograph rather than her own in a little case inscribed "My Aslauga," she feels, as her eyes suddenly meet Dan's, "like a naughty child caught in mischief" (324). Jo could atone for her "mischief" by trying to help Dan see Bess, and himself, in a more realistic way, as complex human beings capable of complementing each other, but instead she destroys his already faint hopes by encouraging him in his idealization, knowing that from it she has nothing to fear. By urging him to let Bess "remain for you the high, bright star that leads you up and makes you believe in heaven" (326), Jo preserves Bess's sexual innocence and enjoins Dan to celibacy. Jo's unconscious purpose is not far to seek, for at the end of her discussion with Dan, she says, "remember, dear, if the sweet girl is denied you, the old friend is always here to love and trust and pray for you." We are told that "had she asked any reward for many anxieties and cares, she received it when Dan's strong arm came round her" and, in an echo of Jo's Christmas play, he pronounces the words "God bless her!" (327). Under the guise of protecting her niece from a too-powerful erotic and emotional experience, Jo reserves a portion of that experience for herself.

Jo's triumph in the book, like that of the mother in her play, is the dubious one long conceded to women—the triumph of influence. And Jo wields her influence—and appropriates Bess's—for the traditional purpose of curbing male passion and preserving female purity. True, Jo is capable of exercising influence in less traditional ways: she encourages vocation-minded girls like Nan and Josie, and she supports Nan's decision never to marry, a decision she occasionally regrets not having made herself. But she also uses her influence to deny Bess those things that she and other women artists have long been denied: single-minded dedication to their art and exposure to a larger world, including that of erotic experience. Jo has become a purveyor of "moral pap for the young" not only because traditional marriage, by its very nature, demands that women sacrifice vocation to duty, but because her passionless union with Professor Bhaer, as suggested by Laurie's tableau "The Owlsdark Marbles," has made of marriage an onerous obligation, stunting her emotional, and thus her artistic, growth. The wildness that the Jo of *Little Women* subdued in herself, and that the Jo of *Little Men* admired in Dan, could benefit Bess, as signified by his gift of the buffalo head. But Jo, as though to vindicate her own choice—that of a stable but passionless marriage and a financially successful but artistically bankrupt career—exerts her influence so as to destroy the possibility. She congratulates herself on having averted a tragic mismatch like that of Othello and Desdemona, whereas in fact she allows Dan to perpetuate Othello's mistake of blind idealization. To have allowed Bess and Dan a clearer view of each other would have constituted a true triumph of influence, one that would have expanded their spheres and her own.

Alcott, by having Jo separate Bess from Dan, the female artist from the energy and experience necessary for her self-knowledge and development, demonstrates how hard it is for even the most enlightened woman to relinquish the notion of separate spheres, together with its corollary—that men, by briefly entering woman's narrow sphere of influence, emerge purified and renewed for participation in their wider one. Jo can encourage Nan, applaud her professional ambitions, only because Nan has voluntarily committed herself to spinsterhood. Jo's limited feminism allows for the professional achievement of those women who can practice such self-denial, as spinsterhood in many cases is, but despite her own appearance of success (perhaps because of her half-acknowledged failure), she has no faith in the possibility of combining artistic achievement with personal fulfillment. Alcott's more thoroughgoing feminism, in *Jo's Boys* as in *Diana and Persis*, suggests that such self-denial, far from enabling the woman artist to succeed, can actually prevent her from doing so. Miss Cameron, the only fulfilled artist in the book, "lost her lover years ago" (147), but we are led to believe that it was not the loss but the having had something to lose that enabled her to become a great tragedienne. To return to the analogy between Alcott and Hawthorne's Dimmesdale, the overt feminism of *Jo's Boys* corresponds to the literal message of Dimmesdale's sermon, a message compromised by contradiction and concealment. But Alcott's more profound feminism corresponds to Dimmesdale's "deep, sad undertone of pathos" and is conveyed by the pathos of Jo's character and career, at once so like and unlike her creator's. Even the title, *Jo's Boys,* speaks eloquently, for instilled with Marmee's little-womanly values, Jo can only live through others, and those others are adolescent boys. As Alcott seems to have recognized, self-denial, whether it be the daily denial of self required in constantly administering to others or the denial of one's innermost feelings, condemns the aspiring artist, and her audience, to a diet of pap. Alcott was never called upon to deny herself more often than when writing *Jo's Boys*—the novel, like Dimmesdale's sermon, throbs with painful experience, but she somehow manages to provide sustenance for adults in the guise of moral pap for the young.

Given her own sufferings and those of her heroine, it is little wonder that Alcott shares her narrator's temptation "to engulf Plumfield and its environs so deeply in the bowels of the earth that no youthful Schliemann could ever find a vestige of it" (337). Instead, rather than "shock [her] gentle readers" (338), she approximates this act of violence by summarily disposing of her characters—most of them in conventional marriages. Dan's fate—he "never married, but lived, bravely and usefully, among his chosen people [a native American tribe] till he was shot defending them" (338)—has led critics to associate him with the exile and demise of Alcott's rebelliousness.[5] But another male character offers a more positive paradigm for her career. In summing up the fates of her characters, Alcott significantly reserves Jo's son Ted for last: "Teddy eclipsed them all by becoming an eloquent and famous clergyman, to the delight of his astonished mother" (338). Ted, who combines traits of the adolescent Jo and Laurie (or Teddy), seems like the offspring their union would have produced. Like Nan and Dan, he is well aware of the stuffiness of Plumfield, recognizes in Josie a kindred spirit, and shares her love of the theatrical, especially of the grand gesture and flamboyant costume. After Josie's impersonation of Peg Woffington, Ted declares, "Isn't she great fun? I couldn't stop in this dull place if I hadn't that child to make it lively for me. If ever she turns prim, I'm off; so mind how you nip her in the bud" (17). Running away, or the desire to, figures prominently, we recall, in both *Little Women* and *Little*

Men, and in *Jo's Boys* Ted not only threatens to "bolt" but does so, when, in defiance of his mother's orders, he goes west with Laurie to retrieve the injured Dan. As Dan's surrogate son in *Little Men,* Ted in *Jo's Boys* inherits his horse, the symbol of his wildness and freedom, when Dan returns to the West. Finally, Ted extracts from Dan the story of his violent past, the secret from which Jo would protect him, Bess, and other innocent Plumfielders. Ted's fate would indeed be "astonishing" were it not anticipated by the prank he pulls on Class Day, the day, as Jo tells him, "when we must all behave our best" (275). Observing the letter of the law, Ted appears in a "dress suit, bequeathed him by a dandy friend" (273), complete with handkerchief, gloves, cane, flowerlet, and "the little blond mustache he often wore when acting" (275). But the hilarity and horror that his "disguise" produces make a mockery of its spirit. Thus we can see in Teddy's clerical "eloquence" still another portrait of the artist who, while masquerading as a conservator of traditional values, preserved her own irreverent, iconoclastic voice.

Epilogue

Her final employment was to gather sea-weed, of various kinds, and make herself a scarf, or mantle, and a head-dress, and thus assume the aspect of a little mermaid. She inherited her mother's gift for devising drapery and costume. As the last touch to her mermaid's garb, Pearl took some eel-grass, and imitated, as best she could, on her own bosom, the decoration with which she was so familiar on her mother's. A letter,—the letter A,—but freshly green, instead of scarlet! The child bent her chin upon her breast, and contemplated this device with strange interest; even as if the one only thing for which she had been sent into the world was to make out its hidden import.

Nathaniel Hawthorne,
The Scarlet Letter (271)

Yet, with the slight fancy-work which we have framed, some sad and awful truths are interwoven.

Nathaniel Hawthorne,
"Fancy's Show Box" (455)

It is possible to see Louisa May Alcott's career as framed in several ways: by "A Whisper in the Dark" and *A Modern Mephistopheles*, with which it was finally bound; by *Little Women* and *Jo's Boys*; by the two editions of *Moods*; by "Psyche's Art" and *Diana and Persis*; or by "Patty's Patchwork," with which she concluded her first *Scrap-Bag* volume in 1872, and "Fancy's Friend," the last story of the final volume.¹ Although one of the latter is realistic, the other fantastic, both portray rebellious female children: Patty rebels against acquiring the feminine virtues represented by her patchwork; Fancy protests the masculine values that dictate the feminine virtues. In both cases the children appear to acquiesce—Patty to her Aunt Pen, Fancy to her Uncle Fact—and thus to signify Alcott's approval of those virtues and values. But, as we have seen, the quilt that Patty produces with the help of Aunt Pen, while seeming to exemplify and endorse the domestic virtues of neatness, patience, cheerful resignation, and quiet endurance actually continues, through its grime and puckers, to express their opposites. Similarly, in "Fancy's Friend," both the friend herself and the "moral" poem that she produces affirm the power of feminine fiction or "fancy" to subvert the patriarchal—or avuncular—values it would seem to support. Like Hawthorne's Pearl, who by fashioning a letter *A* for her "mermaid's garb," calls the whole system it represents into question, Alcott's Fancy and the creature of her imagination, Lorelei, confound the male power structure and contest its vision of reality. In Hawthorne's tale "Fancy's Show Box," a female "showman," Fancy, convicts a "venerable gentleman, one Mr. Smith, who had long been regarded as a pattern of moral excellence" (450), of forgotten or unrecognized crimes, not the least of which are crimes against women. Although "Fancy's Friend," like most of Alcott's sensational and domestic stories, may appear "slight fancy-work"—the product of a feverish imagination (a Helwyze or a Saul), on the one hand, or a piece of domestic trivia (Gladys's embroidery or Percy's still life), on the other—it interweaves among its light and shimmering threads those of a dark and sobering hue.

"Fancy's Friend" may have had its inspiration not only in *The Scarlet Letter*, in which Pearl contrives a mermaid costume for herself, but in Hawthorne's story "The Snow-Image," to which Alcott alludes in *A Marble Woman*. In Hawthorne's story a snow maiden, fashioned by two imaginative children, Violet and Peony, comes to life only to melt when their father, "an excellent but exceedingly matter-of-fact sort of man, a dealer in hardware" (1087), insists that she warm herself by the fire. In Alcott's story Fancy, while vacationing at the shore with her Aunt

Fiction and Uncle Fact, longs for a mermaid playmate and uses kelp and shells to outline one upon the sand. A wave carries the figure out to sea, but Fancy's mermaid returns in the form of Lorelei, a mysterious little girl. On accompanying Fancy home, Lorelei is greeted warmly by Aunt Fiction, suspiciously by Uncle Fact. Over the latter's objections, Fancy makes Lorelei her constant companion, and their friendship provides a kind of litmus test for members of their society: "It was curious to see the sort of people who liked both Fancy and her friend,—poets, artists; delicate, thoughtful children; and a few old people. . . . Dashing young gentlemen, fine young ladies, worldly-minded and money-loving men and women, and artificial, unchildlike children, the two friends avoided carefully" (222). Uncle Fact—even though Lorelei teaches Fancy a "moral song" that seems to support his values—cannot accept the stranger and finally persuades Fancy to give her up. At the moment he succeeds in doing so, Lorelei returns whence she came, leaving Fancy to mourn the loss of her friend.

Clearly, "Fancy's Friend" is a parable of the female imagination, aspects of which are represented by Fancy and her *two* friends, Lorelei and Aunt Fiction. From the opening paragraphs, Fancy is portrayed as different from other children: they dig holes and build sand castles; she creates a garden of seaweed and a castle of shells, tenanted by tiny water creatures. Fancy, who prefers to play alone and who "firmly believed" in mermaids, appears to live in a fantasy world, but she is in some ways more realistic than her peers. For she rejects their childish pretense that seals are mermaids and is much more inquisitive about the natural world: "she had friends and playmates among the gulls and peeps, and learned curious things by watching crabs, horseshoes, and jelly-fishes" (208). She is not only "dreamy"— "silly," as Uncle Fact calls her—but inventive, resourceful, willing to take pains and make sacrifices in order to realize her vision. When she finally despairs of encountering a real mermaid, she dismantles her garden and palace in order to create one, and the figure that she so ingeniously forms from kelp, marsh grass, seaweed, pebbles, and shells is as much an advance upon her previous play as that was upon the other children's. Lorelei, when Fancy asks if she is "really a mermaid," answers, "I am really the one you made," and convinces Fancy "it was her own work." She explains the miracle by reminding Fancy, "you believed in me, watched and waited long for me, shaped the image of the thing you wanted out of your dearest treasures, and promised to love and welcome me" (213). She then promises to remain with Fancy for as long as she continues to believe in her but warns that others will try to separate them. In order to retain her newfound power as well as access to its source, Fancy must make a firm commitment.

Fancy is at first supported in her commitment to Lorelei by Aunt Fiction, who serves as mentor and role model. Significantly, Fancy, when her mermaid is first washed out to sea, regrets not having had a chance to show her to Aunt Fiction, and the mermaid, on returning in the form of Lorelei, predicts that Fancy's aunt, unlike her uncle, will appreciate her. Indeed, Aunt Fiction takes an immediate interest "in the friendless child so mysteriously found" and places a hand upon her head "as if claiming her for her own." For Aunt Fiction, "a graceful, picturesque woman; who told stories charmingly, wrote poetry and novels, [and] was very much beloved by young folks," the very lack of information regarding the child is an advantage: "We can imagine all kinds of romantic things about her; and, by and by, some interesting story may be found out concerning her. I can make her useful in many ways" (217–18). As an artist herself, Aunt Fiction sees in Fancy's friend a gift like her own, a faculty not only useful but essential to creativity. But Aunt Fiction is undermined in her support for Fancy's friendship by her marriage to Uncle Fact, whose "keen eyes and powerful glasses" remind us of Professor Bhaer's "moral spectacles" and their destructive effect on Jo March's artistic vision. Uncle Fact, we are told, is in the process of compiling "a great encyclopedia" and believes that "Fancy is not to be relied on" (218).[2] When Aunt Fiction speculates that Lorelei has been washed ashore in a shipwreck, Uncle Fact points out that the bracelets she wears "are the ones you gave Fancy as a reward for so well remembering the facts I told her about coral" (219). The complex symbol of the bracelets suggests the common identity of Fancy and Lorelei, their dependence on Aunt Fiction, and the latter's enlistment in the service of Uncle Fact. As we have seen, bracelets and rings in Alcott's fiction often represent entrapment in patriarchal structures. Because Aunt Fiction, like Aunt Jo as wife of Professor Bhaer, is limited in her ability to help a younger artist, Fancy's aspirations are endangered.

Although Uncle Fact is scandalized that Lorelei cannot read, write, or "cipher," sew, or "tend babies," that she can only "play and sing, and comb [her] hair" (220), it is just her indifference to the one set of accomplishments and her devotion to the other that enables her to free Fancy and stimulate Aunt Fiction. Lorelei lulls Fancy to sleep with her voice, furnishes her with stories and marine lore (with which Fancy in turn charms Aunt Fiction and astonishes Uncle Fact), and dives "where no one else dared, to bring up wonderful plants and mosses," which she bestows upon Fancy and Aunt Fiction. In this way, and by having many people shun, neglect, or seem oblivious to Fancy and her friend, Alcott identifies Lorelei with the unconscious. Lorelei, who "didn't like tight clothes; but would have run about in a loose, green robe, with bare feet and flying hair, if Uncle Fact would have allowed it" (222), teaches Fancy how to use and enjoy her body: "Lorelei taught her to swim, like a fish; and the two played such wonderful pranks in the water that people used to come down to the beach when they bathed" (221). In "Fancy's Friend," as in *Jo's Boys,* where in a chapter entitled "Josie Plays Mermaid" Josie dives for Miss Cameron's bracelet, swimming and diving represent immersion in the creative element, what Jo March and Alcott both call falling into a vortex. As the result of her intimacy with Lorelei, Fancy causes "a great deal of talk" (221) and alienates some, but she attracts others and even acquires an audience, not only for her aquatic feats but for her "songs and stories" (222).

Lorelei, however, cannot thrive for long in an atmosphere dominated by Uncle Fact, who, like Sylvia Yule's father and Christie Devon's uncle, is ruled by the profit motive. Uncle Fact's scheme for exploiting her beautiful voice baffles Lorelei and saddens Fancy, who "thought singing for gold, not love, a hard way to get one's living" (221). Lorelei's utter lack of practicality—she refuses to sell the trinkets that she makes or the treasures that she brings up from the sea—violates Uncle Fact's utilitarian principles and commercial instincts. And despite his encyclopedic knowledge, Lorelei's mysterious past frustrates his passion for getting "to the bottom of everything" and classifying it. Like the governess Miss Fairbairn, who first interrogates Lorelei, Uncle Fact has no patience with myth and, by calling Fancy's friend Luly instead of Lorelei, attempts to domesticate it. As their summer at the shore draws to an end, and he comes no closer to solving the conundrum that she poses, Uncle Fact resolves to take Lorelei to "the Ragged Refuge, and see what they can make of her," but by that time she has already begun to suffer the effects of his skeptical scrutiny. As she tells Fancy, "I wish I could go home, and get you a string of finer pearls than these . . . but it is too far away, and I cannot swim now as I used to do" (223). Fancy, sensing her friend's unhappiness, longs "to tell people . . . who you really are," but Lorelei warns that, if they believed her, they would "put me in a cage, and make a show of me; and I should be so miserable I should die" (227).

As Lorelei realizes, Uncle Fact is merely representative of a culture that condemns female creativity as dangerous, freakish, even mad.

The crisis between Uncle Fact and Lorelei is anticipated, and perhaps even precipitated, by her song "The Rock and the Bubble," in which an audacious bubble confronts a "great rock [that] stood / Straight up in the sea" and bids it "make way" for her. The bubble, in a "rainbow-robe" and "crown of light," proclaims herself "queen / Of the ocean," but the rock tells her that he has "not stirred / This many a long day" and cannot be "overthrown." It is not only that he *will* not move, he informs her, but that he *cannot*. When the bubble accuses him of mocking her words and persists in her course, she is, predictably, dashed against the rock and broken. On observing her fate, the seabirds warn their young, "Be not like Bubble, / Headstrong, rude, and vain / Seeking by violence / Your object to gain," but "be like the rock, / Steadfast, true, and strong, / Yet cheerful and kind, / And firm against wrong" (224–26). As Lorelei, "laughing mischievously," tells Fancy, the song "has got what your uncle calls a moral to it," and the moral patently supports Uncle Fact against Lorelei. Yet the poem can be read as an assertion of female selfhood and a condemnation of male obduracy, of the way in which males, having for generations occupied a position of supremacy, confuse tenancy with right, even with necessity. It is perhaps no coincidence that Uncle Fact, on overhearing the song as well as Lorelei's disclosure of her identity, determines to separate her from Fancy at once for fear that "Luly will soon make Fancy as crazy as she is herself" (228).

Uncle Fact, in persuading Fancy to give up Lorelei, plays a role similar to Bazil Yorke's in causing Cecil to break her Cupid or Professor Bhaer's in prompting Jo to burn her manuscripts—that of denying the female artist access to the source of her creativity. While Aunt Fiction, whom he blames for letting Fancy "read too many fairy tales and wonderbooks," is away seeing "her publishers about a novel she had written" (228), Uncle Fact confronts his niece with Lorelei's claim to be a mermaid. Discrediting this story, he accuses Lorelei of being a "sly, bad child" and, as Joy A. Marsella points out (14), uses a favorite method of Bronson Alcott, Socratic questioning, to shake Fancy's faith in what she believes to be true. Forced to answer Uncle Fact's questions in the affirmative, Fancy finds herself seemingly with no choice but to agree with his conclusion, and her response to this dilemma is that of women unused to questioning male authority: "Fancy didn't answer; for she couldn't feel that it was so, though he made it seem so. When Uncle Fact talked in that way, she always got confused and gave up; for she didn't know how to argue. He was right in a certain way; but she felt as if she was right also in another way, though she could not prove it" (231), and like Bubble, who feels herself a queen but bursts on contact with the rock, Fancy's confidence in Lorelei founders on the rock of male logic and science. In surrendering her belief in Lorelei, Fancy forsakes the creative impulse at the core of her identity: "if you say there never were and never can be any [mermaids], I suppose I *must* give up my fancy" (230).[3]

In order to demolish Fancy's faith in Lorelei, Uncle Fact employs a battery of patriarchal weapons, including intimidation and ridicule, reason and logic, and, finally, an irresistible appeal to self-sacrificing love. Having reduced Fancy to tears at her inability to refute him, Uncle Fact takes her upon his knee and, after reminding her of how "the German Lorelei . . . lured people to death in the Rhine," tells Fancy that he loves her as a daughter and only wants to keep her safe and happy. When he then asks Fancy to give up Lorelei for his sake, "all the beauty seemed to fall away from her friend," who now appears as Uncle Fact portrays her—"treacherous," "naughty," "selfish." Uncle Fact's tenderness, following fast upon his severity, causes Fancy to see that her "uncle had been very kind to her all her life; and she loved him, was grateful, and wanted to show that she was, by pleasing him," even though "her heart clung to the friend she had made, trusted, and loved" (232). Little-womanly training triumphs over female instinct, and Fancy, begging Uncle Fact to "be kind" to Lorelei, agrees to give her up. But to entrust female creativity to masculine custody is to forfeit it entirely. On overhearing Fancy's words, Lorelei rushes to the sea and plunges in, leaving only the "mock mermaid"—"scattered pebbles, shells, and weeds"—upon the shore. Just as the father in Hawthorne's "The Snow-Image" matter-of-factly requests towels to mop up the remains of the snow maiden, so Uncle Fact insists that the mystery of Lorelei's disappearance "will be cleared up in a natural way" (233). Both are among the "wise men" that Hawthorne describes—those who fail to recognize any "phenomenon of Nature or Providence [that] transcend[s] their system" or to consider that what "has been established as an element of good to one being, may prove absolute mischief to another" (1102). Such "absolute mischief" is suffered by Fancy, who, "though she learned to love and value Uncle Fact as well as Aunt Fiction," cannot forget "her dearest playmate" (234) and each summer calls for her in vain.

Like many of Alcott's works, "Fancy's Friend," first published shortly before *Little Women,* appears to represent her capitulation—her betrayal of the fantastic and demonic imagination, of the sirenlike and subversive heroines of the sensation fiction, of her feminist and other feminine values in conflict with the dominant male culture, and, finally, of her artistic ambition. Fancy, with her devotion to Lorelei or Luly (or Lu, Lou, or Louy, as Alcott's family called her), would seem to represent the author as a young woman; Aunt Fiction, the successful author "much beloved by young folks." Uncle Fact, in addition to the patriarchal world and its taste for realistic, domestic fiction for young people, might well represent those to whom Alcott was in a sense married—her impecunious, dependent father and her entrepreneurial publisher. True, Uncle Fact is a shrewd and realistic businessman whereas Bronson Alcott was notoriously impractical, but they have more in common than their Socratic pedagogy. Uncle Fact, like Bronson, is a voluminous writer, though of encyclopedia entries rather than orphic sayings, and he is described as a lover of truth. In his devotion to his intellectual system and in the emotional distance he preserves, Uncle Fact, like other remote and unsatisfactory fathers in Alcott's fiction, would seem to resemble her own. Just as he resembles Bronson Alcott, whose inability to provide for his family forced his daughter into the role of breadwinner, so Uncle Fact resembles Thomas Niles, with whom, at the time of the story's first publication, Alcott was beginning a long and fruitful collaboration. Niles, as sharp-sighted as Uncle Fact and nearly as literal minded, was largely responsible for Alcott's commercial success and for what many have taken to be her artistic failure. That Fancy is persuaded to forsake Lorelei during Aunt Fiction's visit to her publisher, especially when we remember that Niles may have discouraged the publication of *Diana and Persis,* supports Joy A. Marsella's view of "Fancy's Friend" as a "rationalization" for Alcott's artistic "silence."[4] When we think of Alcott bound to an Uncle Fact in the form of a dependent and subtly demanding father, however loving, and of an opportunistic publisher, however genial, we can easily imagine that Alcott as an Aunt Fiction was unable to indulge her fancy, fall into the vortex of her imagination, or call upon more than a mockery of her muse.

Rather than rationalizing Alcott's artistic "silence," however, "Fancy's Friend" can enable us to hear her muted voice. First, the story, while it appears to advocate the yielding of fancy to fact, is itself a fantasy. And by adopting as her heroines Fancy and a mermaid, Alcott allies herself with two subversive traditions and thereby signals the subversive nature of her art. As Cheryl Walker has demonstrated, nineteenth-century American women poets not only used a free bird to symbolize their poetic aspirations but used Fancy as a code word for their distinctive genius and as a central figure in what she calls their "power-fantasy" poems.[5] And as Nina Auerbach writes, Victorian art "slithered" with images of mermaids, who, unlike angels ("pious emblems of a good woman's submergence in her family"), "submerge themselves not to negate their power, but to conceal it" (1982, 7). When Fancy's friend submerges herself, she anticipates what Alcott is about to do in writing *Little Women,* and when she reemerges from between the covers of *Aunt Jo's Scrap-Bag,* she calls attention to what her creator has accomplished. Alcott's fancy may have been increasingly at the disposal of Uncle Fact, in the form of father, publisher, and public. But she continued to exercise the "woman's power"—what Auerbach calls the "disruptive capacity for boundless transformation" (1982, 55)—possessed by Hawthorne's Pearl and Alcott's actress heroines. Submerging herself in anonymous or domestic fiction, Louisa May Alcott, like Lorelei, left traces from which the reader, like the uncorrupted Fancy, can construct a figure and even bring it to life. This figure proves not to be the well-known "friend" of Victorian childhood and family life but the feminist familiar of modern women.

Notes

Introduction

1. *Hospital Sketches* (1863) was reprinted in 1960, *Transcendental Wild Oats* (1873) in 1975; two editions of *Work* (1873) appeared in 1977, the previously unpublished *Diana and Persis* in 1978. But it was not until 1991 that Alcott's first novel, *Moods* (1864), became available.

   Alcott indicates in her journal that she found the opportunity to write an adult novel welcome relief from "providing moral pap for the young" (*Journals* 204). All references to Alcott's journals are to *The Journals of Louisa May Alcott*, edited by Joel Myerson and Daniel Shealy. Portions of the journals appeared previously in Ednah D. Cheney's *Louisa May Alcott*.

2. Stern reprinted nine tales, seven of them originally published anonymously or pseudonymously, under the titles *Behind a Mask* (1975) and *Plots and Counterplots* (1976). In 1984 she brought all nine together in a single volume entitled *The Hidden Louisa May Alcott*, and in 1988 she reprinted an additional five tales under the title *A Double Life*. Finally, in 1991, Daniel Shealy reprinted six more of Alcott's "unknown thrillers" in *Freaks of Genius*. (See Stern's introductions to all of these volumes for an account of the tales' discovery and publishing history.) In 1987 two editions of Alcott's one full-length sensation novel, *A Modern Mephistopheles* (1877), appeared, and in 1988 Elaine Showalter brought together *Hospital Sketches, Transcendental Wild Oats, Diana and Persis,* and other selections under the title *Alternative Alcott*.

3. The subtitle of Ednah Cheney's memorial tribute.

4. At the risk of oversimplifying their positions, I would place such scholars as Ann Douglas, Judith Fetterley, Karen Halttunen, Eugenia Kaledin, and Martha Saxton in the first category, Sarah Elbert, Alfred Habegger, Joy A. Marsella, Ruth MacDonald, and Charles Strickland in the second. Ann B. Murphy's 1990 essay "The Borders of Ethical, Erotic, and Artistic Possibilities in *Little Women*" provides a useful discussion of recent Alcott criticism.

5. For an account of Alcott's contributions to *The Woman's Journal* and her political activity in Concord, see Madeleine Stern's "Louisa Alcott's Feminist Letters."

6. Modern readers do see it as a program. For example, see Claudia Mills's "Choosing a Way of Life: *Eight Cousins* and *Six to Sixteen*." In fact Mills's discussion of Alcott's *Eight Cousins* and the British writer Juliana Horatio Ewing's *Six to Sixteen* epitomizes the attitude of many toward Alcott's children's fiction: "*Eight Cousins* and *Six to Sixteen* can be seen as typifying the theories, if not the practice, of their time, rather

than offering a challenge to them. Together they provide a snapshot of enlightened opinion about child nurture and about the appropriate scope and reach of woman's sphere in the last half of the nineteenth century" (74).

7. Joy A. Marsella's detailed summary and characterization of "Patty's Patchwork" first alerted me to its paradigmatic possibilities. Elaine Showalter, in her essay "Piecing and Writing," also comments on the story: "While the discipline of the pieced quilt itself represents women's confinement within the grid of nineteenth-century feminine domestic morality, it also offers the potential creative freedom of textuality and design" (232–33). For a detailed analysis of the story that differs somewhat from my interpretation, see Angela M. Estes's dissertation, "An Aptitude for Bird: Louisa May Alcott's Women and Emerson's Self-Reliant Man." Quilter Radka Donnell-Vogt captures the dual nature of Patty's quilt and Alcott's domestic fiction when she speculates that a quilt may serve either as "an instrument of liberation" or as "the ultimate placebo" (48).

8. Stern, in her introduction to the *Journals,* argues that "lack of complete privacy did not inhibit Louisa's analysis of self. On the contrary, it probably spurred her on, for she was already becoming a writer in search of an audience" (5).

9. Stern has shown that "The Witch's Curse" is a composite of Alcott's youthful melodramas. See "Louisa Alcott, Trouper."

10. Karen Halttunen, in *Confidence Men and Painted Women,* also sees a connection between sculpture or painting and tableaux vivants: "The parlor performer was . . . virtually sculpted into genteel propriety. In fact, many tableaux did feature human sculptures or portraits" (184). A literary example is Lily Bart's performance as Sir Joshua Reynolds's Mrs. Lloyd in Edith Wharton's *The House of Mirth.*

11. In portraying Kitty's dilemma, Alcott may have again been drawing on her own or her sisters' experience. Caroline Ticknor, biographer of Alcott's sister May, suggests that Bronson Alcott may have played the role of headmistress. In reproducing the eight-year-old May's letter to her mother, who was visiting in Waterford, Connecticut, Ticknor comments, "The writing seems to be in Mr. Alcott's hand, to whom the letter was evidently dictated" (27). The letter itself concludes, "This is a long letter; longer a great deal than I wanted to write, but Father kept asking me more and more questions, till it seemed as if he would never be done, and so filled this letter—I am glad he has got through" (29). Although May "dictates" to her father, who serves as her amanuensis, his questions determine the contents of her letter, and he decides when she has said enough.

12. Although she does not deal explicitly with Alcott, Susan K. Harris, in "'But is it any good?': Evaluating Nineteenth-Century American Women's Fiction," professes her faith in the ability of these writers to challenge "the public definition of 'women's place'" so as to communicate with like-minded readers. Angela Estes and Kathleen Lant's essay "The Feminist Redeemer" provides a reading of Alcott's *Work* that, like my own, demonstrates how Alcott managed to convey this challenge.

Chapter 1. "The Wrongs of Woman": "A Whisper in the Dark"

1. As Angela Estes writes of another Alcott sensation story, "Perilous Play," "Even in an adult thriller, Alcott's solution to the 'woman problem' is so radical and revolutionary that it must be sugar-coated with a patriarchal surface narrative" (1985, 103).

2. See Alfred Habegger's "Precocious Incest: First Novels by Louisa May Alcott and Henry James." Habegger writes of Alcott's sensation fiction: "The problem is, the secret fantasy the books express is not liberation from male supremacy but bondage made satisfying. . . . Her heroines are either submissive girls who grow up to share ecstasy with their stern fathers, or they are sirens and femme fatales who are obsessed with revenge; either way, men are the one thing on their mind" (236).

3. Susan K. Harris writes in "'But is it any *good?*'" that nineteenth-century American women writers, in order "to achieve their 'subversive' objects, . . . had to find a form that would embody . . . dual, and often contradictory, ideas. There are a number of ways this can be done: . . . the plot can outweigh the narrator's interpretive gestures or the dense 'flowery' rhetoric can hide heretical phrases and clauses; . . . the narrator can play more than one role (in which case the text risks being labeled 'confused')" (53). Alcott uses all of these strategies in "A Whisper in the Dark."

4. "A Whisper in the Dark" recalls Wilkie Collins's *The Woman in White,* published three years earlier. Sybil's uncle resembles the fortune hunter Sir Percival Glyde; Sybil combines traits of his victim, Laura Fairlie, and his antagonist, Laura's resourceful half sister, Marian Halcombe. Dr. Karnac corresponds to Glyde's accomplice, Count Fosco, who is also a doctor, and Sybil's mother resembles the enigmatic "woman in white." Alcott's tale also bears some resemblance to Charles Reade's *Hard Cash,* published the same year. But in that sensation novel a young man is committed to a madhouse by his father, and its female director becomes one of his persecutors.

5. This scene would seem to support Habegger's theory that a "dominance-submission incest-fantasy" characterizes Alcott's sensation stories (236). Instead, I would argue that Alcott saw in father-daughter incest the ordinary state of male power and female powerlessness writ large.

6. It is significant that Collins's unconventional heroine, Marian Halcombe, never questions Mr. Fairlie's right, before his death, to promise Laura to Sir Percival. Later, however, Laura herself rebels when, like Sybil, she is confronted with a legal document. She too is confined first in her room, then in a madhouse.

7. For a recent study of women's madness and its treatment see Elaine Showalter's *The Female Malady.* In her chapter "The Rise of the Victorian Madwoman," Showalter writes, "In a society that not only perceived women as childlike, irrational, and sexually unstable but also rendered them legally powerless and economically marginal, it is not surprising that they should have formed the greater part of the residual categories of deviance from which doctors drew a lucrative practice and the asylums much of their population" (73).

8. Similarly, Laura Fairlie's transformation from blooming girl to pathetic creature is anticipated by her physical resemblance to the mad "woman in white," Anne Catherick, who dared to defy Sir Percival.

9. See, for example, Sandra M. Gilbert and Susan Gubar's *The Madwoman in the Attic* (361). Jean Rhys's *Wide Sargasso Sea,* the story of Rochester's marriage from the perspective of his wife, Antoinette Mason, also implies that men deprive insubordinate women of their sanity. Antoinette's husband, on learning of her mother's madness (also the result of patriarchal oppression), deprives her of the name she shares with her mother (he insists on calling her Bertha), the home she loves, and the mirror that confirms her identity. Antoinette, placed under Grace Poole's care in England, reflects:

"Names matter, like when he wouldn't call me Antoinette, and I saw Antoinette drifting out of the window with her scents, her pretty clothes and her looking-glass. There is no looking-glass here and I don't know what I am like now. . . . What am I doing in this place and who am I?" (180).

10. In her defacement of the asylum walls, Sybil anticipates the heroine of "The Yellow Wallpaper," who, deprived of other forms of self-expression, resorts to interpreting, recreating, and finally destroying the wallpaper's grotesque pattern. "A Whisper in the Dark" also anticipates Alcott's own "A Modern Mephistophiles," an unpublished sensation story (not to be confused with the published novel *A Modern Mephistopheles*) written three years later. In this longer story Alcott also describes a woman incarcerated in a madhouse for insubordination—this time for her defiance of the man she believed to be her husband until her discovery of a prior and undissolved marriage. Having been drugged, the heroine, Rosamond, awakens in a madhouse, ironically called The Refuge. The doctor, like Dr. Karnac, is "an unscrupulous skilful charlatan, who made money by lending his house for any illegal imprisonment for inconvenient people." "Books were denied her, also pen or needle. . . . Tempest [her "husband"] proved his wit in leaving her no employment." But unlike Sybil, Rosamond is not allowed to remain in the relative comfort of solitary confinement. Instead, she is moved into a wing where she is "surrounded by lunatics." Still hoping for a reconciliation, Tempest is at last con-strained by the "dread of making her a mad-woman in dreadful earnest" and enables her to escape. He becomes indignant when he finds that the doctor "exceeded orders; I bade him break her spirit & he has destroyed her health."

11. Hair figures prominently in many of Alcott's works as a symbol of women's strength, their vulnerability, or, as when Jo sells her hair in *Little Women,* both.

   Sybil's mother combines the functions of Bertha Rochester, Jane's mad double, and Jane's mother, whose spirit warns her to flee Thornfield. Having learned of Rochester's marriage to Bertha, Jane watches the moon rise "as though some word of doom were to be written on her disk. She broke forth as never moon yet burst from cloud: a hand first penetrated the sable folds and waved them away; then, not a moon, but a white human form shone in the azure, inclining a glorious brow earthward. It gazed and gazed and gazed on me. It spoke to my spirit: immeasurably distant was the tone, yet so near, it *whispered* in my heart—'My daughter, flee temptation'" (281, my emphasis).

12. Guy is an ambiguous figure throughout the tale. As his father's creature he is an instrument of patriarchal oppression, but in his powerlessness he also resembles a woman under patriarchy.

   The ending of "A Whisper in the Dark" resembles that of a later sensation story, "The Skeleton in the Closet," in which a young woman, the victim of an arranged marriage, is linked to a husband who has degenerated into an imbecile. When, after her husband's death and her remarriage, she removes the iron bracelet that had symbolized her former union and proclaims herself "free at last," her new husband replaces it with a slender gold chain, telling her that she is "captive still, not to duty but to love, whose thralldom shall be as light as the fetter I now bind you with" (534). As Jeanne F. Bedell has commented, "Alcott's diction here implies that woman's freedom is illusory and that marriage, however loving the husband, is a form of bondage" (11).

13. See Lynette Carpenter's essay "'Did They Never See Anyone Angry Before?'" for a discussion of the sibylline theme in "A Whisper in the Dark."

14. In contrast, Tania Modleski cites "A Whisper in the Dark" as an example of a prevailing pattern in Gothic fiction by women: "The imprisoned woman . . . is presented not as a rebel, but almost wholly as a victim, even a self-victimizer . . . and it is against assuming the victim's role that the heroine desperately struggles" (1982, 72).

15. As Moira Ferguson observes, Maria's account, together with that of her attendant, Jemima, "stands as a fictional corollary to *A Vindication of the Rights of Woman*" (6).

16. Claire Kahane discusses how both in the "paradigmatic Gothic novel," *The Mysteries of Udolpho,* and in *Jane Eyre* the heroine flees the temptation to merge "with a mother imago who threatens all boundaries between self and other" and escapes to "a space that she seemingly controls," though that control is based "on social withdrawal and psychological repression, on an ultimate submission to patriarchal constructs of the feminine" (340–41).

17. I am indebted to the anonymous reviewers of *Legacy* for helpful comments on a version of this chapter. I am also grateful to Lynette Carpenter for her reading of a later version.

Chapter 2. *"Woman in the Nineteenth Century":* Moods

1. James's review of *Moods* appeared in the *North American Review* 101 (July 1865): 276–81, and is reprinted in the Rutgers University Press edition of *Moods,* from which this quotation is taken. See Alfred Habegger's essay "Precocious Incest" for a discussion of James's response to *Moods.* Years later Alcott got revenge on James. In *A Garland for Girls* (1887), the heroine of "Pansies" tells her friends, "I never read Richardson, but he couldn't be duller than Henry James, with his everlasting stories, full of people who talk a great deal and amount to nothing" (92).

2. A discussion of *Moods* is complicated by its existence in two different versions. Its original publisher, A. K. Loring, demanded that Alcott shorten the novel, and by her own account she deleted ten chapters. In her preface to the 1882 edition, Alcott claimed to have restored much of the deleted material and explained why she was now altering the ending. Ruth K. MacDonald, in "*Moods,* Gothic and Domestic," and Sarah Elbert, in her introduction to the Rutgers University Press edition, agree that it is impossible to know which scenes added to the 1882 edition were cut from the 1864 edition. MacDonald and Elbert also agree that the changes emphasize the centrality of the heroine, Sylvia, and make the novel less sensational. The Rutgers reprint, to which I will refer, includes the entire text of the 1864 edition as well as an appendix of chapters and passages added to or revised in the 1882 edition.

3. All references to Alcott's letters, unless otherwise specified, are to *The Selected Letters of Louisa May Alcott,* edited by Joel Myerson and Daniel Shealy. The letter I quote from here is addressed simply to a Mr. Ayer.

4. Alcott could write more candidly to Moncure Daniel Conway, who had recommended that she publish *Hospital Sketches* in *The Commonwealth.* Her allusion in this letter to "unmated pairs" anticipates Charlotte Perkins Gilman's term "moral miscegenation"— the mismatch of powerful and powerless, master and servant. At the end of *Women and Economics* (1898), Gilman writes, "So we may trace from the sexuo-economic relation of our species not only definite evils in psychic development, bred severally in men and women, and transmitted indifferently to their offspring, but the innate perversion of

character resultant from the moral miscegenation of two so diverse souls,—the unfailing shadow and distortion which has darkened and twisted the spirit of man from its beginnings" (339).

5. For an account of Bronson and Abba Alcott's conflict at Fruitlands, see Madelon Bedell's *The Alcotts,* chap. 15.

6. For one of many discussions of Fuller as Zenobia, see Paula Blanchard's *Margaret Fuller: From Transcendentalism to Revolution,* 189–95.

7. In August 1850, eighteen-year-old Louisa wrote in her journal: "Reading Mrs. Bremer and Hawthorne. The 'Scarlet Letter' is my favorite. . . . I fancy 'lurid' things, if true and strong also" (63). In April 1864, while *Moods* was going the rounds of publishers, Alcott wrote: "Read Oliver Twist, Cecil Dreeme & Scarlet Letter again & like them all better than ever" (129). Elbert, in her introduction to *Moods,* alludes to the influence of *The Scarlet Letter* as well as *Jane Eyre* on Alcott's novel.

8. The following paragraph summarizes the action of the 1864 edition of *Moods.* I will discuss major differences between the two editions at the end of this chapter.

9. Readers have identified Warwick with Thoreau, whom Alcott much admired, and Moor, who inhabits the Old Manse, with Emerson. See Marie Olesen Urbanski's "Thoreau in the Writing of Louisa May Alcott," as well as Elbert's introduction. Allusions to the Old Manse further suggest Alcott's indebtedness to Hawthorne.

10. As Elbert points out in her introduction, Faith Dane appeared earlier as the heroine of Alcott's Civil War story "My Contraband" (1863).

11. In the 1882 version Moor has composed a song entitled "Waiting" (228).

12. See Stern's introduction to *The Hidden Louisa May Alcott* (xxviii).

13. Like so many of Alcott's heroines, both Priscilla and Zenobia are connected with the stage and theatricality. Priscilla, before coming to Blithedale, gave public performances as a trance medium, "the Veiled Lady"; Westervelt, her manager and Zenobia's former lover, marvels, "What an actress Zenobia might have been!" (841). According to Coverdale, her amateur performances "made one feel it an intolerable wrong to the world, that she did not at once go upon the stage" (725). As many have observed, *The Blithedale Romance* is filled with references to the theater, and the Blithedale experiment itself is likened to a masquerade and a tragedy.

14. Instead of interpreting her apocalyptic dream as a harbinger of her own death, Sylvia, in the 1882 edition, interprets it as a premonition of Warwick's and as a promise of their reunion in the hereafter.

15. A similar sentence appears in the 1864 edition, but not at the very end in connection with the painting (213).

16. While the novel may have germinated in Alcott's adolescence, it is the fruit of her early maturity. In a letter (tentatively dated Feb. 1864 by Myerson and Shealy) to James Redpath, publisher of *Hospital Sketches,* Alcott wrote, "Now about 'Moods'—it is a big thing, thirty chapters long—rather odd, sentimental, & tragical—written for my own amusement at various spare times during the last three years. . . . It is done except the last Chap" (103). And in her letter to Ayer, a censorious reader, she explains that her treatment of the characters was carefully considered: "as the book has been underway for six years there has been no occasion for haste any where" (109).

17. In the 1864 edition Sylvia's death occurs in the final chapter, which, according to her letter to Redpath, in 1864 (when she was thirty-two) remained to be written.

18. Hawthorne writes, "These characters, he [the author] feels it right to say, are entirely fictitious. It would, indeed, (considering how few amiable qualities he distributes among his imaginary progeny,) be a most grievous wrong to his former excellent associates, were the Author to allow it to be supposed that he has been sketching any of their likenesses" (634).

Chapter 3. *"The Seduction of Daughters"* or *"The Sins of the Fathers"*: A Marble Woman or The Mysterious Model

1. Alcott was early fascinated with the Pygmalion story. In "The Inheritance," an unpublished manuscript inscribed "my first novel written at seventeen," the heroine, Edith, plays Galatea in a tableau vivant opposite her suitor, who plays Pygmalion.
2. See Nancy Cott's essay "Passionlessness." Cott sees the nineteenth-century emphasis on female passionlessness as having some advantages for women. But in the following passage Cott's use of the word *immobilize* recalls Alcott's "marble woman": "The ideology of passionlessness, conceived as self-preservation and social advancement for women, created its own contradictions: on the one hand, by exaggerating sexual propriety so far as to immobilize women and, on the other, by allowing claims of women's moral influence to obfuscate the need for other sources of power" (236).
3. Veronica Bassil, in "Eros and Psyche in 'The Artist of the Beautiful,'" has demonstrated the enthusiasm with which the transcendentalists embraced the Psyche myth. As Bassil mentions, Bronson Alcott wrote two essays entitled "Psyche or the Breath of Childhood" (1836) and "Psyche as Evangele" (1838) (4). He also called his daughter Elizabeth "Psyche."
4. See Neumann's *Amor and Psyche: The Psychic Development of the Feminine*. According to Neumann's commentary on the myth, Psyche is the "principle of encounter and individuation" engaged in a struggle with Venus, the "principle of fascinating attraction and the fertility of the species" (89). Prompted by her sisters, who represent "the matriarchal powers," Psyche rejects her unconscious sensual bliss with Amor, a form of "imprisonment in the patriarchate" (132).
5. Tania Modleski, in *Loving with a Vengeance,* writes that "the most typical plot of female Gothics . . . is one in which the lover plays 'the father,' and the heroine either suspects him of having killed his first wife or else fears that her own relationship with him will be a repetition of one which occurred in the past" (76). Elizabeth MacAndrew, in *The Gothic Tradition in Fiction,* argues that as Gothic villains became more human "their inner conflicts split them in two. Then, in the doubles figures, two separate characters appear, an ordinary but basically good man who is confronted with his own evil self" (79). She then speculates that "an assault against a daughter or sister seems to epitomize the self-destructive struggle within the evil mind" (85).
6. In "Passionlessness," Cott cites Howard Gadlin, who believes that men "wanted to desexualize relationships to maintain their domination." According to Cott, "female passionlessness was a keystone in men's construction of their own self-control" (235).
7. Paradoxically, the desexualization of relationships that men perceived as enabling them to maintain domination was perceived by women as limiting it (Cott 235). Although desexualization may have had some advantages for women in a patriarchal society, patriarchy was responsible for imposing it.

8. In another Alcott sensation story, "Perilous Play" (1869), the heroine, Rose St. Just, experiments with hashish because "I hoped it would make me soft and lovable, like other women. I'm tired of being a lonely statue" (589). Like Cecil, Rose resents the passionlessness that has been imposed upon her. She, like Cecil, views herself as an exceptional rather than a normal woman, but Alcott implies that both are more typical than they believe themselves to be.

9. Of relevance to this discussion is the following observation by Frederick Crews in *The Sins of the Fathers*: "Art theory in *The Marble Faun* is not really separable from Hawthorne's omnipresent brooding about sex. As its title implies, the book deals in an oxymoronic marriage of marble and faun, of cold artistic stasis and the raw passion which it imprisons" (236).

10. Modleski would see the conclusion of *A Marble Woman* as typical of female Gothics except that Cecil is accepted not by one father figure but by two, one of whom actually *is* her father: "In most cases, the feared omnipotent male is shown to have unsuspected reserves of tenderness and love. . . . Thus the admired male—the 'father'—who had formerly been perceived as remote and rejecting, finally accepts the heroine, releasing her from the uncomfortable identification with the mother and simultaneously supplying the strength the heroine lacks" (1982, 80–81).

11. Alcott contracted typhoid fever while serving as a Union army nurse. Her hallucinations are recorded in her 1863 journal. Of these Martha Saxton writes, "Tamed, these fantasies were material for stories. Untamed, they were expressions of Louisa's deepest sexual and emotional horrors" (284). Sandra Gilbert and Susan Gubar have contended that "the madwoman in literature by women is not merely, as she might be in male literature, an antagonist or foil to the heroine. Rather, she is usually in some sense the *author's* double, an image of her own anxiety and rage" (78). Germain, like his female counterparts, including Sybil's mother, can also be seen as the author's double.

12. Other vengeful heroines in Alcott's sensation fiction include Pauline Valary in "Pauline's Passion and Punishment," Virginie Varens in "V. V. or Plots and Counterplots," and Sybil Varna in "Taming a Tartar."

Chapter 4. "The Second Sex": Behind a Mask or A Woman's Power

1. While Polly Milton, the eponymous heroine of Alcott's *An Old-Fashioned Girl* (1870), is out sledding with her cousin Tom, his sister Fanny, Polly's fashionable foil, is described as having been "curled up for an hour or two, deep in 'Lady Audley's Secret'" (42).

2. Alcott may have been inspired by a long passage in *Lady Audley's Secret* on women at the tea table. Lady Audley is described as looking "very pretty and innocent, seated behind the graceful group of delicate opal china and glittering silver. Surely a pretty woman never looks prettier than when making tea. The most feminine and most domestic of all occupations imparts a magic harmony to her every movement, a witchery to her every glance. . . . To do away with the tea-table is to rob woman of her legitimate empire. . . . Better the pretty influence of the tea cups and saucers gracefully wielded in a woman's hand than all the inappropriate power snatched at the point of the pen from the unwilling sterner sex" (146–47). Surely this is an ironic comment from one who went on to write "about eighty books under her own name, half-a-dozen pseudonymously" (xiii).

3. Winifred Hughes, writing of Lady Audley, agrees that the cultural emphasis on women's passionlessness served to immunize them against the very feelings that would ensure the unselfish use of influence. Like Halttunen, Hughes believes that Victorian women's "childishness, self-suppression, [and] talent for pleasing"—qualities that, ironically, were cultivated while professed to be natural—both armed women and disarmed men in what remained an unequal battle between the sexes (124).

4. Fetterley points out that the Coventrys are chagrined upon unmasking Jean to find that she has treated the men as commodities rather than allowing herself to be so treated (1983).

5. Alcott's unpublished early novel "The Inheritance" contains a scene very similar to the one in which Jean plays Judith. During an evening of tableaux taken from portfolio pictures, Edith, the heroine, plays Rebecca-at-the-Stake, and a friend comments, "how strongly [strangely?] proud & stately Edith looks. I thought she was too gentle to look scornful even in play." Edith's scorn is directed at those among her audience who have taken advantage of her dependent position to exploit, insult, and sexually harass her.

6. Jean is a female artist after Hawthorne's heart, for he praised his contemporary Fanny Fern for writing "as if the devil was in her" (quoted in introduction to *Ruth Hall*, xxxv).

7. I refer here to Judith Fetterley, Karen Halttunen, Jeanne Bedell, and Eugenia Kaledin, among others. Bedell, though she believes that the sensation fiction "reveals an understanding of the relationship between subterfuge and powerlessness not found in the domestic novels" (9), does admit at the outset of her essay that the latter reflect a feminist sensibility. Rena Sanderson has recently argued that Alcott's writings "both moral and subversive, were not truly her own, but merely conditioned responses to patriarchal pressures" (50). Only in *A Modern Mephistopheles* does Sanderson see Alcott escaping "the Faustian bargain imposed on her by the contradiction between her own inclinations and her world's expectations" (51).

Chapter 5. "Portrait(s) of the Artist": Little Women

1. Although at first reluctant to undertake the task, Alcott was actually well prepared to do so. As the editor of the children's magazine *Merry's Museum* and as a writer of occasional verse and fairy tales for children, she was familiar with the juvenile literary market. Her May 1868 journal entry reads: "Father saw Mr. Niles about a fairy book. Mr. N. wants a *girls' story,* and I begin 'Little Women.' Marmee, Anna, and May all approve my plan. So I plod away, though I don't enjoy this sort of thing. Never liked girls or knew many, except my sisters; but our queer plays and experiences may prove interesting, though I doubt it" (165–66).

2. In "Louisa Alcott, Trouper," Madeleine Stern identifies an earlier sketch for *Little Women,* "The Sisters' Trial" (1856) (195). Still another is the fantasy story "The Rose Family" (1864), in which the three oldest daughters all suffer from some character flaw: Moss is indolent, Briar is passionate and willful, and Blush is vain. They are sent to a fairy, Star, who gives each a talisman—a drop from a magic fountain in which, no matter where they are, they can see their mother's face. Thus the drops function much like the notes from Marmee that Meg and Jo fasten inside their clothes. Each rose is then forced, like Psyche, to perform labors until, aided by the talisman drop, she is

ready to return home, cured of her indolence, passion, or vanity.

3. Bronson Alcott kept a journal on the growth of each of his daughters. His journal for his third daughter, Elizabeth, was entitled "Psyche, or The Breath of Childhood" (M. Bedell 1980, 101). Janice Alberghene, in "Alcott's Psyche and Kate," believes it possible to read "Psyche's Art" as "a specific response to Elizabeth's death" but prefers to "see the story as a more general expression of Alcott's view of the artist's proper balancing of her relationship to her art and to her family" (38).

4. For a discussion of this pattern see Veronica Bassil's "The Artist at Home: The Domestication of Louisa May Alcott." Still another example in *Little Women* is Amy March, who at the end of the book is modeling a bust of her frail daughter, Beth, with the encouragement of her husband, Laurie. Also, in "Patty's Patchwork" Aunt Pen encourages Patty to finish the quilt as a tribute to the baby sister who has just died.

5. In *Little Women* Mr. March tells Amy that "though I should be very proud of a graceful statue made by her, I shall be infinitely prouder of a lovable daughter, with a talent for making life beautiful to herself and others" (275).

6. Psyche's sculpture recalls the jeweled butterfly in Hawthorne's story "The Artist of the Beautiful." In contrast to Psyche, Hawthorne's artist produces through minute observation and exhaustive analysis a "mechanism" of metallic brilliance. Eventually it is destroyed by a malevolent child, but one wonders if it was not the bitterness of the artist's nature, projected onto the child, that doomed his art. Although Psyche actually molds only the chrysalis, her love for the child who holds it succeeds in creating the illusion of "airy life." In fact, by portraying only the chrysalis, Psyche solves on a small scale the problem Hawthorne attributed to sculpture—that of rendering life and motion through the lifeless immobility of stone.

7. Alcott was no stranger to the conflict that Psyche experiences. For example, she wrote to her sister Anna some years earlier, "You ask what I am writing. Well, two books half done, nine stories simmering, and stacks of fairy stories moulding on the shelf. I can't do much, as I have no time to get into a real good vortex. It unfits me for work, worries Ma to see me look pale, eat nothing, and ply by night. These extinguishers keep genius from burning as I could wish. . . ." (59).

8. As one would expect, critical opinions of *Little Women* vary widely. Eugenia Kaledin, Judith Fetterley, Karen Halttunen, Beverly Lyon Clark, and Lynda Zwinger believe that the book, by advocating women's self-abnegation (or at least the semblance of it), marked the end of Alcott's attempt to subvert traditional values for women; Elizabeth Langland and Nina Auerbach see an unacknowledged conflict between "female self-realization in marriage to a man" and "female fulfillment in a community of women" (Langland 112); Sarah Elbert sees the novel as a feminist utopia in which women's traditional values are celebrated and promise to transform the world. Different as their opinions are, all of these feminist critics, with the possible exception of Kaledin, recognize with Madelon Bedell that *Little Women* is "not about 'being good,' nor even about growing up, but about the complexities of female power and the struggle to maintain it in a male-dominated society" (1983, xv). For a brief but comprehensive survey of the last twenty years of *Little Women* scholarship, see Ann Murphy's "The Borders of Ethical, Erotic, and Artistic Possibilities in *Little Women*."

9. For extended discussions of the theater in Alcott's life and art see Madeleine Stern's "Louisa Alcott, Trouper," Nina Auerbach's afterword to *Little Women*, and Karen Halttunen's "The Domestic Drama of Louisa May Alcott." As early as 1943 Stern gave

a detailed account of Alcott's youthful dramatic activities in Walpole, between 1855 and 1857, and in Concord, between 1857 and 1860. Stern perceived that the "thrillers that she launched across the pages of the penny dreadfuls had their source in the writer's early dramatic career" (194) and observed that "Whenever she wrote a story that contained any autobiographical elements, one theme was sure to concern the drama" (195). Auerbach and Halttunen both comment on how theatricals frame the March novels—*Little Women, Little Men,* and *Jo's Boys.* As Auerbach puts it, "The March trilogy begins with a play; once it produces an actress, it can let 'the curtain fall forever on the March family'" (465). Halttunen argues that Bronson Alcott encouraged theatricals as a means of teaching children "how to control every aspect of their self-expression" (237), but that Louisa Alcott's melodramas "not only moved beyond Bronson's use of allegorical drama, but actually subverted it" (238). She believes, however, that in *Little Women* Alcott "left behind not only her Gothic period, but also her use of theatricality to undermine the cult of domesticity" (242). Sharon O'Brien, in "Tomboyism and Adolescent Conflict," sees Alcott's adolescent plays as foreshadowing her inability to reconcile "the energetic, assertive self represented by her tomboy period with an adult female identity" (365).

10. In an early scene the March girls sacrifice their Christmas breakfast to an impoverished family. The narrator's editorial emphasis seems to be on the goodness of the girls, called "angelkinder" by the Hummel children, and their satisfaction in self-sacrifice. But the stark description of the Hummels' living conditions—"A poor, bare, miserable room . . . with broken windows, no fire, ragged bed-clothes, a sick mother, wailing baby, and a group of pale, hungry children cuddled under one old quilt, trying to keep warm" (23–24)—reveals the helplessness of women who have lost or been abandoned by their men. Significantly, Mrs. March believes that they too would be "lonely and helpless" should anything happen to Mr. March (57).

11. In an argument similar to Sarah Elbert's, Anne Dalke, in "'The House-Band': The Education of Men in *Little Women,*" discusses how the feminine sphere, represented by the March women, transforms the men who are allowed to enter it.

12. As Fetterley points out in "Alcott's Civil War," female anger in the novel produces, or threatens to produce, dire consequences for its female subject, whereas male anger threatens its female object (376, 380).

13. Auerbach argues in *Communities of Women* that Marmee allows "her girls a great freedom . . . the freedom to remain children and, for a woman, the more precious freedom *not* to fall in love" (62). But how can the girls appreciate the latter freedom if, as Marmee implies, it means missing out on the most fulfilling experience a woman can know?

14. Anne Hollander, in "Reflections on *Little Women,*" views the younger Amy as unlike the other March girls in that she is unpleasant, selfish, and genuinely bad.

15. Fetterley remarks that Amy's accident is part of a "pattern of maximum possible consequences for a minimal degree of self-absorption and selfishness" (1978, 381).

16. Jane Van Buren sees Alcott's "suffusion of florid prose" as recommending an "idealized version" of marriage (297–98).

17. Carolyn Heilbrun writes in *Reinventing Womanhood,* "Perhaps only in America, with its worship of 'manliness,' could boy-girl twins, elsewhere universally a literary phenomenon characterized by their resemblance to one another, be so sharply defined and differentiated by sex roles" (191).

18. See note 7, above.
19. Alcott's contemporary, Elizabeth Stuart Phelps, has the heroine of *The Story of Avis* wonder, "Was that what the work of women lacked?—high stimulant, rough virtues, strong vices, all the great peril and power of exuberant, exposed life?" (79). As we have seen, Hawthorne praised Fanny Fern for writing "as if the devil was in her." He goes on to say that "Generally women write like emasculated men, and are only distinguished from male authors by greater feebleness and folly; but when they throw off the restraints of decency, and come before the public stark naked, as it were—then their books are sure to possess character and value" (xxxv).
20. Cheri Register, in "Letting the Angel Die," views Beth as Jo's "shadow," but argues that "Jo does not really come into her own until she learns how to practice Beth's patience, kindness, and self-forgetfulness" (3). On the other hand, Angela Estes and Kathleen Lant see Jo as stretched to the snapping point between her "independent impulses" and "her need to be a proper member of the female community of 'little women.'" Alcott, in order to disguise "the final snap of her experimental creation," replaces the "corpse" of the "self-celebratory Jo . . . with the self-effacing Beth" (115).
21. Fetterley writes in "Alcott's Civil War," "Good writing for women is not the product of ambition or even enthusiasm, nor does it seek worldly recognition. Rather it is the product of a mind seeking solace for private pain, that scarcely knows what it is doing and that seeks only to please others and, more specifically, those few others who constitute the immediate family. Jo has gone from burning genius to a state where what she writes isn't even hers" (374). Lynda Zwinger adds, "Jo's relation to her text is now neither physical nor direct. She may have written it, but she can't read it" (56). Beverly Lyon Clark identifies the chastened Jo with her creator: "Alcott may have espoused women's rights, including suffrage, but in her books as in her life the greatest good was not individual rights and self-fulfillment but loyalty and service to the Family" (93).
22. Patricia Meyer Spacks contends that Amy's desire to paint is "narcissistic" (126), but Hollander discerns that Amy is artistically more ambitious than Jo; Jo wants to be successful and to make money, whereas Amy wants to achieve greatness (33).
23. Much of the material in this chapter previously appeared in my essay "'The Most Beautiful Things in All the World'? Families in *Little Women*" and is reprinted here by kind permission of the Macmillan Company.

Chapter 6. "The Anxiety of Influence": Little Men

1. For example, Charles Strickland writes in *Victorian Domesticity* that "the bulk of her fiction subscribed to the idea that cultured women hold an obligation peculiar to themselves to promote the moral regeneration of society through their influences as wives and mothers, which is to say that Alcott saw a reformed family as the key to a reformed society. This 'domestic feminism,' as one historian has called it, was a form of Utopianism, but of a kind characteristic of the Gilded Age. Like the sentimental writers of the Jacksonian period, Alcott confined her hopes for a better world to the boundaries of the domestic circle" (145). For a counterargument, see my essay "'Playing Puckerage,'" in which I use "Cupid and Chow-Chow" as a test case.
2. See especially Elbert's *Hunger for Home* and MacDonald's *Louisa May Alcott*. MacDonald, however, recognizes a darker side to Plumfield.

3. Ironically, Alcott wrote *Little Men* in response to the death of her brother-in-law, John Pratt, the model for John Brooke. Madeleine Stern writes in *Louisa May Alcott*, "Out of her love she drew another book, so that John's death would not leave Anna and her children in want" (214).

4. The young Brookes and Bhaers also burn a wooden village, of which William Blackburn writes in "'Moral Pap for the Young'?": "It would perhaps be perverse to suggest that the children consciously think of the soldiers as their fellow students, of the village as Plumfield, or of the 'little churn-shaped lady' as Mrs. Jo" (104). Alcott's Kitty-mouse resembles Mary Austin's Snockerty in *A Woman of Genius* (1912). Even more striking is the resemblance between the burning of the doll Annabella and Paul Morel's burning of his sister Annie's doll Arabella in D. H. Lawrence's *Sons and Lovers* (1913). All three episodes anticipate the childish savagery we find in William Golding's *Lord of the Flies*.

5. Bess is not so named for the intruder on the three bears but for the heroine of an older story, Madame d'Aulnoy's "La Belle aux Cheveux d'Or" or "Pretty Goldilocks." Andrew Lang's rendition of the story begins, "Once upon a time there was a princess who was the prettiest creature in the world, and because her hair was like the finest gold, and waved and rippled nearly to the ground, she was called Pretty Goldilocks. She always wore a crown of flowers, and her dresses were embroidered with diamonds and pearls, and everybody who saw her fell in love with her" (*Blue Fairy Book* 202).

6. When Dan returns after having run away, Jo makes a similar plea: "I may keep him, Fritz?" (160).

7. This episode resembles the one in which Tom Sawyer and Becky Thatcher get separated from their party while exploring the caves. But whereas Tom encounters Injun Joe, finds his own way out of the caves, and returns to town a hero, Nan encounters a cow, falls asleep, and is discovered by Jo and Dan. After a brief hour of glory, she finds herself ignominiously tied to the sofa.

8. In a piece entitled "Sketch of Childhood, by herself," Alcott confesses that "Running away was one of the delights of my early days; and I still enjoy sudden flights out of the nest to look about this very interesting world, and then go back to report." She then recounts one childhood adventure that ended with her being "tied to the arm of the sofa to repent at leisure" (Cheney 1980, 27–28). In "Poppy's Pranks" (1868), it is Papa who ties Poppy to the sofa as punishment for running away. Although his language is almost identical to Jo's in disciplining Nan, Papa does not tie Poppy loosely within view of the window and her humiliation seems much greater. Niki Alpert McCurry argues that Jo, by tying Nan so loosely, enables her to achieve self-control through self-realization (94).

9. See Anne Sexton's "Cinderella" in *Transformations*.

Chapter 7. "The Quest for Identity": Work: A Story of Experience

1. All references are to Sarah Elbert's edition of *Work*.

2. See Madeleine Stern, *Louisa May Alcott* 103–4. The hero of *Work*, David Sterling, is thought, like Adam Warwick, to have been modeled on Thoreau. See Marie Olesen Urbanski's "Thoreau in the Writing of Louisa May Alcott."

3. For example, see Elizabeth Langland's "Female Stories of Experience: Alcott's *Little Women* in Light of *Work*."

4. Jean Fagan Yellin, in "From *Success* to *Experience*: Louisa May Alcott's *Work*," argues

that Alcott loses her social focus in the second half of the book, concentrating instead on Christie's moral development; as a result, Christie becomes a more conventional heroine and the book suffers a loss of vitality. "Success" was Alcott's initial title for *Work.*

5. The gender-specific treatment of fairy-tale heroes and heroines has become axiomatic. Alcott's British contemporary George MacDonald, in *The Light Princess,* objected to it: "forests are very useful in delivering princes from their courtiers, like a sieve that keeps back the bran. Then the princes get away to follow their fortunes. In this they have the advantage of the princesses, who are forced to marry before they have had a bit of fun. I wish our princesses got lost in a forest sometimes" (23–24). Ellen Cronan Rose observes that even when fairy-tale princesses *do* get lost in the woods, they "are rescued from their plights by kind woodsmen, good fairies, and handsome princes" (210). Modern writers have both satirized and attempted to revise fairy-tale models. For example, in "Petronella" by Jay Williams, the heroine startles her parents by insisting on setting out to seek her fortune like her two older brothers: "If you think . . . that I'm going to sit at home, you are mistaken. I'm going to seek my fortune, too" (55).

6. In a performance similar to Christie's as Amazon, Ida Jex, the heroine of an uncompleted Alcott story "The Amber Amulet," saves a prince by taming a den of lions. Just as a lion prepares to devour him, Ida flings "a golden chain over the beast who crouched submissively at her feet as if that light fetter possessed an irresistible spell to conquer him. Dancing airily in & out among the beasts she wove a network of golden chains about them till all were bound in her magic bonds while the baffled enemies looked on in powerless dismay." Later we learn that the lion Ida defies on stage is actually "old, toothless, heavily drugged" by her lover-partner, a true lion tamer, who contends that woman is the creature "hardest to subdue." Thus while Ida may find an outlet on-stage for her passionate nature, it is contained and directed by her lover offstage and on.

7. Christie, in repudiating Fletcher, seems to be abandoning Jane Eyre's model, but her impassioned speech is similar to the one in which Jane declares her equality with Rochester.

8. In fact, as Daniel Shealy has recently revealed in *Freaks of Genius,* an early version of the Helen Carrol episode, entitled "A Nurse's Story," appeared in *Frank Leslie's Chimney Corner* at the height of Alcott's career as a writer of sensation stories (Dec. 30, 1865, and Jan. 6, 1866). In "A Nurse's Story" the narrator, Kate Snow (an allusion to Charlotte Brontë's Lucy Snowe, the heroine of *Villette?*), is hired as a companion for Elinor Carruth, but the tale is more complicated and sensational than the episode in *Work,* for Kate engages in a battle of wills with Elinor's mysterious half brother, Robert Steele.

9. In contrast to my reading of Mr. Power, Angela Estes and Kathleen Lant, in "The Feminist Redeemer: Louisa Alcott's Creation of the Female Christ in *Work,*" argue that "the force that Mr. Power represents is the hierarchical, patriarchal power which Christie previously shunned" (244).

10. Estes and Lant read this scene very differently: "into this green 'paradisiacal' (288) garden Mr. Power intrudes repeatedly, and his attempts to coerce Christie into the heterosexual world, to make her surrender her virginity and independence, trouble her. . . . although a representative of traditional Christianity, he is a Satanic figure who continually tempts

Christie out of her 'homosocial' female community and into the heterosexual realm" (245).

11. Estes and Lant view David as "a *failed* Christ," guilty of Hawthorne's "'unpardonable sin' . . . of cutting himself off from humanity" (246). But in condemning his initial harshness to Letty, they tend to discount his later benevolence.

12. In Marie Howland's novel *The Familistere*, first published in 1874 (a year after *Work*) under the title *Papa's Own Girl*, two women, having been devastated by unhappy love relationships, rebuild their lives by establishing a nursery business, which in turn becomes the basis of a utopian community.

Chapter 8. *"An Identity 'Other' Than Their Own":* A Modern Mephistopheles

1. Alcott's epigraph from Goethe reads: "The Indescribable, / Here it is done: / The Woman-Soul leadeth us / Upward and on!" All references to *A Modern Mephistopheles* will be to the edition introduced by Madeleine Stern, who writes that in the novel both of Alcott's "selves are welded, the sensational is joined with the ethical. . . . The result is an interesting and often brilliant amalgam completely uncharacteristic of the author of that domestic novel, *Little Women*" (xxxiv).

2. In November 1876 Alcott recorded in her journal that "My new task gets on slowly" (201). Whether at this time she was trying to revise the earlier "A Modern Mephistopheles" or making abortive attempts to begin something entirely new is unclear. In the Houghton Library at Harvard University I found two versions of the early story, neither of which appears complete: the longer, and clearly the original, version, is entitled "A Modern Mephistophiles [*sic*] or The Fatal Love Chase" and shows signs of editing; the shorter version is entitled "Fair Rosamond." Alcott could have edited the longer version and written the shorter in the 1860s in the hope that, by compressing the story and eliminating some sensational elements, she could get it published. Yet the change of a chapter title in "A Modern Mephistophiles" from "The Rose in Bloom" to "Rocabella" suggests a later date for at least that revision. Since Alcott's juvenile novel *Rose in Bloom* was published in November 1876, the chapter title would have provided a clue to the identity of Niles's anonymous author.

   If Alcott did undertake a revision, she must soon have abandoned it, for Niles wrote in December, "I did hope you might turn in your old story." Early in the new year, Alcott recorded with satisfaction in her journal: "Went for some weeks to the Bellevue, and wrote 'A Modern Mephistopheles' for the No Name Series. It has been simmering ever since I read Faust last year. Enjoyed doing it, being tired of providing moral pap for the young" (204). In February, Niles, after reading at least part of the manuscript, reiterated that "I have had in view the idea that you would revamp an old story wh. you wd. never publish in any other way." He went on to explain that the series was bringing the firm more "notoriety" than money and to express his fear that her story would not be popular. Apparently Alcott was demanding more money for a new story than Niles had expected to pay for an old, unmarketable one. But possibly Alcott hoped to salvage its theme and title for the No Name Series, *then* perform a major rescue operation, in which case it would be necessary to obliterate the few remaining connections between the two works. By canceling the first part of the title, "A Modern Mephistophiles," on the longer of the two early manuscripts and by canceling all allusions to Faust or Mephistopheles in the text itself, Alcott appears to have been trying to cover her traces.

While *A Modern Mephistopheles* bears little obvious resemblance to "A Modern Mephistophiles," it strongly resembles another Alcott sensation story, "The Freak of a Genius," published anonymously in *Frank Leslie's Illustrated Newspaper* in October and November 1866. As Madeleine Stern points out in her introduction to *Freaks of Genius,* the latest collection of Alcott's sensation fiction, "The Freak of a Genius" and *A Modern Mephistopheles* both involve a Faustian pact between an aging man and his young protégé as well as their relationships with the women who love them. The recent rediscovery of "The Freak of a Genius," first published so soon after the rejection of "A Modern Mephistophiles" and resembling *A Modern Mephistopheles* so closely, further suggests that in 1866 Alcott decided to write an entirely new story on the Faust theme rather than revise the rejected manuscript, briefly revisited that manuscript in 1876, then, confident that Niles would know nothing of the story published anonymously ten years earlier, decided to rework that one instead for the No Name Series. Stern finds "more morality" in *A Modern Mephistopheles* than in "The Freak of a Genius," but the earlier story, with its noble rather than diabolic hero, is far tamer. The more sensational elements and darker implications of *A Modern Mephistopheles* seem closer to those of the unpublished manuscript despite their very different plots.

For further discussion of "A Modern Mephistophiles" see Stern's introduction to *A Modern Mephistopheles* and Madelon Bedell's introduction to *Little Women.* Stern gives a clear and accurate account of "A Modern Mephistophiles" but does not mention the "Fair Rosamond" variant. Bedell sets forth the relationships among all three works. Neither Bedell nor Stern shares my preference for the published novel. Bedell argues that *A Modern Mephistopheles* lacks "the narrative power of the earlier stories" (liii), including "A Modern Mephistophiles" (lii). Stern asserts that "Unlike the published version, the rejected story is strongly and elaborately plotted" (xiv) and that "Unlike the vague never-never land of the revision, the earlier settings are realistically drawn" (xv). Although she does not compare the 1866 and 1877 versions, Rena Sanderson, in "*A Modern Mephistopheles:* Louisa May Alcott's Exorcism of Patriarchy," sees the novel as "a work of the author's maturity," which "deserves attention as a *Künstlerroman* that takes as its subject matter the doubleness of subversive and conformist creativity" (41).

3. Burlingame's review appeared in the *North American Review* 125 (Sept. 1877): 316–18, and is reprinted in *Critical Essays on Louisa May Alcott.*

 Alcott's "psychological quadrilateral" not only looks back to works by one of her acknowledged mentors (one thinks particularly of *The Blithedale Romance* and *The Marble Faun* as well as of *The Scarlet Letter,* to which it alludes) but forward to one who condescendingly reviewed her (one thinks especially of *The Portrait of a Lady, The Sacred Fount,* and *The Golden Bowl*).

4. Earlier Helwyze is described as offering "the last temptation of this young Eve, whom he was beguiling out of the safe garden of her tranquil girlhood into the unknown world of pain and passion, waiting for womankind beyond" (73). Felix and Gladys are frequently compared to Adam and Eve as well as to Ferdinand and Miranda.

5. The main connecting link between Alcott's unpublished Faustian tale and *A Modern Mephistopheles* is the demonic villain-hero who, as the result of his obsession, destroys

himself and the woman he loves. In the early version, the modern Mephistopheles is Phillip Tempest, who abducts, then marries in a mock wedding ceremony, a young girl, Rosamond Vivian, whom he has won from her grandfather in a game of chance. Interestingly, however, Alcott originally conceived her Faust as a woman. In "A Modern Mephistophiles," Rosamond tells Tempest on first meeting him that she is willing to sell her soul for a year of liberty. Although coerced into marriage, Rosamond seems to find with Tempest the liberty she craves until the appearance of his real wife. Still half in love, Rosamond flees to Paris, where she is befriended by two women, including the actress Mademoiselle Honorine, and by Tempest's son, Lito, whom she had formerly believed to be his servant. Dressed as a boy, Rosamond flees Paris with Lito, finally taking refuge in a convent. There Tempest, impersonating a priest, almost entraps her, but with the aid of another priest, Rosamond escapes again. Befriended by a count, Rosamond is persuaded to marry him for protection, but Tempest manages to convince him that she is mad and has her imprisoned in a madhouse. Tempest himself finally enables her to escape and attempts to revive her love, but Rosamond, under the influence of her friend Father Ignatius, resists him, and, traveling as father and daughter, they make their way to England and the home of Mrs. Tempest. The narrative breaks off with Mrs. Tempest, Rosamond, Ignatius, and Lito united against the further machinations of Tempest, but a separate page briefly describes the death of Rosamond, Ignatius's grief, and Tempest's suicide.

Although there are gaps in the shorter version, "Fair Rosamond," her death is described more fully there. In a final chapter, entitled "The Vision Verified," Alcott describes how Tempest, in pursuit of the fleeing Rosamond, runs down a small craft, drowning its occupants. Only later does he find that Rosamond, not Ignatius as he expected, is among the drowned. The "vision" of the chapter title refers to an early scene in both versions in which Tempest tells Rosamond how he once saw his fate in a magic mirror—"a lovely dead woman, an old man mourning over her & myself standing near with an expression of remorse and despair."

6. Sanderson also comments that "the master-slave relationship between Helwyze and Felix is associated with prominent homosexual imagery. In other words, Helwyze has manipulated Felix into compromising his morality, his sexuality, and his writing" (47).

7. Stern recognizes the tableaux, what she considers Alcott's version of Goethe's Walpurgis Night, as the novel's crucial episode, and she sees its "two elements"—opium and "the innocent *tableaux vivants* of her youth" (xxiii)—as representing Alcott's "two identities . . . mingled to produce a devastating effect" (xxix). Sanderson, like me, sees the tableaux themselves as representing a split identity (47–48).

8. Tennyson critic William Buckler points out that "Elaine is a slight Edenic figure frozen, like a diamond, in a paradise of simplicity who chooses to die rather than grow up and wend her way, like the first humans [and like Enid], into the trials and tribulations and successes of an ontologically moral life" (116).

9. Rozsika Parker explains how the lily of the Annunciation, a symbol of Mary's fertility in the medieval period, came to represent purity and asceticism, in accordance with the Victorian ideal of womanhood (37).

10. Niles added, perhaps unconsciously, to Alcott's irony in *A Modern Mephistopheles* by placing on the title page, beneath the heading "No Name Series," a quotation from George Eliot's *Daniel Deronda* (published in *Harper's* between Feb. and Sept. 1876): "Is the gentleman anonymous? Is he a great unknown?" The implication, of course, is that

the authors in the No Name Series, like authors in general, are "gentlemen"—an implication doubly ironic in that the author of the quotation, as well as the author of this volume and others in the series, was a woman. The epigraph could not have been Alcott's choice because, according to her journal, she did not read Eliot's novel until March 1879 (214). Alcott was grateful to Niles for launching her career as a children's writer. In the autobiographical poem "The Lay of a Golden Goose," she describes "poor goosey" searching "many wide unfruitful fields" until "At length she came into a stream / Most fertile of all *Niles*" (Cheney 1980, 205). While Niles appreciated the market value of her work and enjoyed reading it, he seems to have had little appreciation of its subtleties, as Alcott hints at the end of *A Modern Mephistopheles* where Felix tells of having to undeceive his publisher.

11. In the afterword to her edition of *Little Women,* Nina Auerbach writes that Alcott "deplored writing for the market, enforcing nursery pieties she did not believe in, relinquishing her adult ambitions and instead becoming 'the children's friend.' Her anonymous novel, *A Modern Mephistopheles,* may be inspired by her own sense that, like Faust, she had sold her soul, though in her case the buyer was virtue rather than vice" (469–70). Octavia Cowan, in the introduction to her edition of *A Modern Mephistopheles,* also sees Felix's collaboration with Helwyze as Alcott's way of confessing to a kind of literary prostitution. She observes that the "abundance and diversity of literary allusion . . . points to Alcott's identification with her character Felix Canaris. . . . he, like Alcott, sells his soul, his freedom, in exchange for literary success. Canaris's wife and his public audience love him not for who he is, but for the person reflected in his poetry; just as Alcott's audience loved her, not for her fierce independence, or her campaigning for women's suffrage, but for her juvenile literature" (xi). Finally, Sanderson speculates that "Like Felix, Alcott may have felt the need to admit, '"I am a living lie"' (257), to escape the duplicity of her public and hidden selves, and to discover a legitimate artistic autonomy free of compromises. Alcott, indeed, may have suspected that her own writings, both moral and subversive, were not truly her own, but merely conditioned responses to patriarchal pressures—in other words, that she originated or authored nothing herself" (50).

12. Sanderson comments that this scene "is important because (a) it grants a female character editorial power over a script produced by a male conspiracy and (b) the female character uses that editorial power to revise her own role in the Faustian script into that of a woman savior" (48–49).

13. See Mary Kelley's *Private Woman, Public Stage: Literary Domesticity in Nineteenth-Century America.* Kelley's view of nineteenth-century women writers is of course more complex than my discussion of Gladys in this paragraph would indicate.

14. Parker writes in her foreword to *The Subversive Stitch* that the "art of embroidery has been the means of educating women into the feminine ideal, and of proving that they have attained it, but it has also provided a weapon of resistance to the constraints of femininity." Gladys—and Alcott, like the needlewomen Parker describes—"managed to make meanings of their own in the very medium intended to inculcate self-effacement" (215).

15. Cowan goes so far as to argue that Helwyze's "intellectual seduction" of Gladys is Alcott's "metaphor for an actual physical sexual encounter. . . . By transferring the site of sexual union from the body to the mind, Alcott maintains decorum and also obscures

the identity of the man responsible for Gladys's pregnancy. . . . Gladys believes that Canaris is the father of her child, but Helwyze appears to think differently" (x). She then speculates that "Alcott's identification with Helwyze, a manipulative male character who spiritually rapes an ideally feminine woman, underscores her ambivalence toward her own gender; the dark extrapolation of her circumstances reveals a woman deeply disturbed by her extraordinary, in many ways unsatisfactory, success" (xii).

16. Still another link between the plots of Alcott and of Helwyze is the inspiration both find in *Faust:* as mentioned earlier, Alcott recorded that *A Modern Mephistopheles* had been "simmering ever since I read Faust last year"; Helwyze tells Olivia, "the accidental reading of my favorite tragedy . . . gave me a hint which has afforded amusement for a year" (36).

Chapter 9. *"Paradoxes of the Woman Artist":* Diana and Persis

1. Niles's letter was written in December 1878; in her journal that same month Alcott recorded having begun "an art novel, with May's romance for its thread" (211). In January 1879 May herself recorded that "Louisa is at the Bellevue writing her art story in which some of my adventures will appear." They did not appear, however, until 1978, when Sarah Elbert first edited and gave a title to the manuscript. Ten years later Elaine Showalter reedited the text, reversing chapters 3 and 4, which were incorrectly numbered in the Houghton Library manuscript, and correcting errors in Elbert's transcription. The return of chapters 3 and 4 to their original order makes the work read less like the fragment of a novel and more like a completed—or nearly completed—novella. All my references will be to Showalter's edition in *Alternative Alcott.*

    Alcott's comment on May's marriage, at thirty-eight, to the much younger Ernest Nieriker, suggests a literary as well as autobiographical donnée for *Diana and Persis:* "May says—'To combine art & matrimony is almost too much bliss.' I hope she will find it so & prove 'Avis' in the wrong" (*Letters* 228). Elizabeth Stuart Phelps's *The Story of Avis,* published like *A Modern Mephistopheles* in 1877, recounts the tragic story of a talented female painter, who finds it impossible to combine painting with marriage and motherhood. May herself later read *Avis* and found it "wanting much to make it . . . really artistic," but one wonders if her judgment wasn't swayed by the heroine's haunting resemblance to herself. Although May's letters from Paris, where the newlyweds had settled, are indeed blissful, her journal sometimes reflects Avis's disenchantment. For example, she juxtaposes her reference to Louisa working at the Bellevue with the lament, "These are rather lonely, gloomy days for me & I think I am not so well as usual for being so many hours left entirely to my own thoughts." For an illuminating discussion of the relationship between May and Louisa and its portrayal in *Diana and Persis,* see "Artists and Daughters in Louisa May Alcott's *Diana and Persis,*" by Natania Rosenfeld.

2. See Elbert's introduction (33), Showalter's introduction to *Alternative Alcott* (xxxviii), and Rosenfeld (8). May died in December 1879, a few weeks after giving birth to a daughter, Louisa May Nieriker. She seems to have had a foreboding of disaster, for she wrote on August 1: "I am very well & happy living in a rosy dream from which I hope there will be no sudden awakening." And her last journal entry, dated November 7,

reads, "I long to have the illness over & a baby of my own in my arms, for I experience many sad days & my mind is filled with doubts as to the future of our little family."

3. Mrs. Alcott quotes extensively from May's letters in the journal that she kept from September 1876 until shortly before her death in November 1877. Caroline Ticknor, in turn, quotes "Marmee's Journal" in *May Alcott: A Memoir*. A comparison of Ticknor's chapters 6 through 8 with chapter 2 of *Diana and Persis* reveals just how much of May's experience and even language Alcott appropriated. An examination of the Houghton Library manuscript of the novella suggests that, in response to Niles's strictures, Alcott attempted to edit out some of the less important detail that she had borrowed from May.

4. Chapter 3 proved prophetic, for in June the pregnant May, having attended an exhibit, records in her journal, "Each visit fires me with a short lived desire to paint but I do not seem to find the energy to begin & so the days pass without a touch of the brush being accomplished." But she goes on, as though to reassure herself, that "no woman's life [is] complete without children, even tho she may have a pursuit like Art or Music to partly compensate for the absence of husband & children."

5. Niles, after criticizing the first two chapters, wrote, "The 3rd chapter I did not have but skipping to the 4th I dipped at once into romance & was delighted. The baby drops in quite in the order of nature & I trust is an episode with more fact than fiction." Because we do not know at what point chapters 3 and 4 became confused, and because the child Nino "drops in" to chapter 4, which hints at a future romance between Diana and his father, Niles could have been referring to either the third or the fourth chapter.

6. Certainly it is that of Jo March Bhaer, who found that she could not sustain her artistic flights (achieve "fame") without a nest ("the praise of those she loved"), then found the nest a prison from which she could not escape. And it is that of Phelps's Avis Dobell, whose nobility of spirit gives wings both to her artistic flights and to an exalted passion that finally grounds her in self-sacrificing familial love.

Diana and Percy's debate about the skylark painting echoes passages in *Moods* and *Little Women* as well as in *The Story of Avis*. In the 1882 edition of *Moods,* Warwick warns Sylvia to "keep to the happy, wholesome places in life, and leave the melancholy sea, the wandering winds, and craggy peaks to those who are made for them" (239), and in both editions Faith Dane tells her that to marry Warwick would be "like a woodbird mating with an eagle, straining its little wings to scale the sky with him, blinding itself with gazing at the sun, striving to fill and warm the wild eyrie which becomes its home, and perishing in the stern solitude the other loves" (181). Percy, in response to Diana's exhortation, seems to see herself as a Sylvia, Diana as a Warwick. Addressing Diana as "my eagle," she protests, "however high I go I shall find you before me, for you can look at the sun with unwinking eyes and your wings never tire; while I can only twitter up a little way and tumble down again all out of breath" (391). In *Little Women,* Beth compares Jo to a gull, "strong and wild, fond of the storm and wind, flying far out to sea, and happy all alone. Meg is the turtle-dove, and Amy is like the lark she writes about, trying to get up among the clouds, but always dropping down into its nest again. Dear little girl! she's so ambitious, but her heart is good and tender, and no matter how high she flies, she never will forget home" (461). Although Amy and Percy are both based on May Alcott, the experience of watching larks go up, which Alcott attributes to Amy (389) and Percy (387), was actually Alcott's (*Journals* 151).

Phelps's Avis, as her name leads us to expect, is consistently associated with birds, including those that destroy themselves beating against the lighthouse, the injured bird that dies while sheltered in her future husband's breast, and the sphinx that is her masterpiece. And her mother, once an aspiring actress, is likened to the female robin imprisoned by her nest. Thus both Phelps and Alcott ally themselves with a tradition of nineteenth-century women poets, for as Cheryl Walker has pointed out in *The Nightingale's Burden,* the "free bird poem" was the paradigm of that tradition. Analyzing a poem by Elizabeth Oakes-Smith, Walker observes, "Inherent in these lines is a suggestion that a woman must choose between love and poetry, that commitment to both is somehow impossible" (47).

7. Both Elbert and Showalter identify Percy with May Alcott, Diana with Louisa. According to Showalter, Diana's coldness, and that of the statues she creates, "represented [Alcott's] own imprisonment. Persis/May, however, represents a generation of women artists who no longer feel obliged to hide behind a mask, and who are not stifled by ideals of feminine self-sacrifice" (xxxix). Rosenfeld, on the other hand, concludes that Alcott "blended the characters and careers of May and herself in each of the two protagonists of *Diana and Persis*" (20).

8. The works of May Alcott attributed to Percy in this chapter—the Moor, the legs in muddy boots, the still life—all hang in Orchard House, the Alcott family home in Concord, where they may be seen.

9. May Alcott's description of her still life on Varnishing Day reveals her to have been a hardier soul than Percy. Like Percy's, May's painting is surrounded by enormous canvases, "but it held its own surprisingly well being good, strong, vigorous painting, simple in its subject and unaffectedly treated. The great frames round it made a superb edge of gold making the neat little frame look like a mere inner panel and proved most becoming" (Ticknor 198). Percy sees her still life as basking in reflected glory from the larger paintings; May sees them as simply making an elaborate and flattering outer frame for her own. By altering May's words in this instance, Alcott points up how Percy, unlike May, has been overawed by her Paris experience.

   Significantly, the same year that May Alcott's still life was selected for the Salon, Mary Cassatt had two pictures rejected, prompting her to exhibit instead with the Impressionists. May described Cassatt's work as "exceedingly strong and fine, but perhaps it's too original a style for these fogies to appreciate" (Ticknor 194–95).

10. Rose Peckham's portrait of May Alcott, which was not completed in time for the 1877 Salon where May's still life was exhibited, also hangs at Orchard House. For a description of it and of Mrs. Alcott's reaction to it, see Ticknor (185–88, 228–29). In her journal for December 1876, Alcott describes what must have been a preliminary sketch: "Miss P. sends us a pretty oil sketch of May,—so like the dear soul in her violet wrapper, with yellow curls piled up, and the long hand at work. Mother delights in it" (201).

11. Rosenfeld comments on the erotic implications of Percy and Diana's collaboration: "Onto this scene of *jouissance,* the august father intrudes, clearly threatened by the spectacle of his wife 'hard at it' with another woman. Diana and Percy have been, in effect, creating a baby together: a female Cupid who revels in pre-lapsarian immodesty" (15).

12. Showalter also comments that Percy's "musician husband resembles pictures of Shelley, as if to imply that now he has taken over the role of artist" (xl).

13. Showalter observes that "Alcott presents the idyll of Percy's family life in the language of romance" and that "We see Percy through Diana's eyes in ways that suggest that Diana's sexual awakening has become the center of the novel" (xl).

14. This symbolic use of gloves recalls their significance in *Little Women*. To Meg and Marmee fresh gloves, like a clean pocket-handkerchief, are the marks of a real lady (36–37). In order to attend the Gardiners' party, Jo has to force her large hand into Meg's tight glove.

15. Alcott's manuscript reads "like the stroke upon the rock," not "upon the sack" (Showalter 429) or "upon the clock" (Elbert 91). I also believe that "draught" makes more sense in this context than "drought," the word that appears in both editions. Alcott is clearly alluding here to Exodus 17:6: "Behold, I will stand before thee there upon the rock in Horeb; and thou shalt smite the rock, and there shall come water out of it, that the people may drink. And Moses did so in sight of the elders of Israel."

16. Stafford is generally acknowledged to have been modeled on the American sculptor William Wetmore Story, Diana in part at least on his fellow sculptor Harriet Hosmer, whose most famous works include a Saul and a Puck (see Elbert [13], Showalter [xli], and Rosenfeld [8, 18]). Alessandra Comini, in her essay on Hosmer and Elisabet Ney, notes that although "marriage was not for Hosmer, she was enthusiastic godmother to Cornelia Crow Carr's daughter, who was named after her" (25). Rosenfeld goes on to identify Diana with Margaret Fuller, whose child by the Italian Ossoli was named Nino. She also draws parallels between May Alcott, as well as Percy, and Fuller (19–20).

17. Rosenfeld also sees the collaboration of Diana and Stafford as "Perhaps the most ideologically meaningful, as well as idealistic, passage in *Diana and Persis*. . . . Stafford shares 'mastery' with Diana instead of exerting it over her. Together, the two sculptors, making a baby out of clay, represent not merely mother and father but Creatrix and Creator. Like the husband and wife Margaret Fuller described in her vision of ideal marriage, they 'work together for a common purpose . . . with the same implement'" (19).

    Complicated connections can also be made between *Diana and Persis* and "Cupid and Chow-Chow," a children's story I have analyzed elsewhere. Cupid, whom Nino strongly resembles, suffers a series of symbolic emasculations, including one—the covering of his dimple (which Chow-chow calls an "ugly hole") with court plaster—that suggests a denial of female sexuality. In "Cupid and Chow-Chow," as in *Diana and Persis,* a cherubic boy seems to serve as alter ego for the heroine, but whereas Chow-chow, by feeding Cupid her share of a pie, surrenders her "puckerage" (which I interpret not only as the rights demanded by the suffrage movement but also as the claim to mature sexuality), Diana, in feeding Nino, or Puck, claims hers. That Stafford will support her claim is clear from his contribution to her sculpture, for in supplying Nino's missing dimple, he acknowledges the existence of what Chow-chow would deny and thus restores "his fingers" to more than artistic "mastery."

18. For example, Alcott, apparently responding to a question about her writing process, wrote: "chapters go down word for word as they stand in my mind & need no alteration. I never copy, since I find by experience that the work I spend the least time upon is best liked by critics & readers. . . . Materials for the children's tales I find in the lives of the little people about me, for no one can invent anything so droll, pretty or pathetic as the sayings & doings of these small actors, poets & martyrs" (*Letters* 307).

19. To the journal entry describing the casual inception of *Little Women* and expressing her "doubt" that it "may prove interesting" (see chap. 5, note 1), Alcott later appended a comment similar to Percy's on the success of her still life: "[Good joke.—L. M. A.]".

Chapter 10. A Voice of One's Own: Jo's Boys

1. As we have seen, Alcott's journal indicates that she found writing *A Modern Mephistopheles* a welcome relief from "providing moral pap for the young" (chap. 8, note 2). Doubtless Alcott chafed against the constraints of her genre, and comments on and in *Jo's Boys* reveal frustration, impatience, and self-deprecation. To Thomas Niles she expressed a desire to "finish off these dreadful boys" (*Letters* 298). At the end of the novel, the narrator confesses to "a strong temptation . . . to close the present tale with an earthquake which should engulf Plumfield and its environs" (337). In her journal, after completing the last two chapters, she describes having "gladly corked [her] inkstand" (277). And in her preface to the novel, she explains that having "been written at long intervals during the past seven years, this story is more faulty than any of its very imperfect predecessors." Family cares and failing health interfered with the writing of the book and probably colored Alcott's attitude toward it. But the obstacles she confronted may well have contributed to her remarkable gallery of women artists—incipient, frustrated, and manqué—in *Jo's Boys*.

2. Alcott's Nan is one of several women doctors portrayed in American fiction of the 1880s. Others are Grace Breen in Howells's *Doctor Breen's Practice* (1881), Zaidee Lloyd in Phelps's *Doctor Zay* (1882), and Nan Prince in Jewett's *A Country Doctor* (1884). In his afterword to the Feminist Press edition of *Doctor Zay*, Michael Sartisky compares Alcott's three predecessors but makes no reference to *Jo's Boys*. Jewett's Nan, like Alcott's, chooses to remain a spinster, whereas Doctor Zay, like Phelps's Avis, succumbs to an importunate suitor.

3. Anna C. Brackett's *The Education of American Girls* and Eliza Bisbee Duffey's *No Sex in Education: Or, An Equal Chance for Both Girls and Boys,* both published in 1874, were answers to Dr. Edward Clarke's misleadingly entitled *Sex in Education; or, A Fair Chance for the Girls* (1873). Jo, too, dismisses as "nonsense" Clarke's theory that rigorous study endangers a girl's mind and body, especially her reproductive system. For a discussion of Clarke's argument and contemporary reactions to it, see the first chapter of Rosalind Rosenberg's *Beyond Separate Spheres*.

4. Saxton finds that in *Jo's Boys* the "varieties of pap are several, including lectures of [*sic*] temperance, plain-living, honesty, independence, and self-sacrifice. There is, of course, a speech on the value of spinsters, whose lot has been improved by some who have become famous" (412). Madelon Bedell concurs: "There is something for everybody in *Jo's Boys,* including its central figure, Josephine Bhaer, who, having finally achieved literary fame, broods over her nest with a serenity that her creator Louisa Alcott never achieved. We do not believe it" (1983, xlviii).

5. For example, Ann Douglas writes, "In the late and flawed *Jo's Boys,* the last of the March family sagas, Alcott, tired as she clearly was, . . . nonetheless permitted a character congenial to her own violent nature to enter the solitary life of adventure she had craved and sacrificed" (xxiii–xxiv). Bedell similarly finds in the "symbol-laden conclusion to Dan's story . . . the hidden end of the *Little Women* legend. The 'large

and hungry soul' that was Josephine March, with all her ambitions, passions, and excesses of character, has no place in the civilized world into which she was born" (1983, xlix).

Epilogue

1. "Fancy's Friend" actually represents three stages in Alcott's career. It contains a poem, "The Rock and the Bubble," which first appeared in 1858 in *The Little Pilgrim*. The story itself first appeared in *Morning Glories and Other Stories,* published in 1868 shortly before *Little Women.* Finally, "Fancy's Friend" was given pride of place in the last *Scrap-Bag* volume, *An Old-Fashioned Thanksgiving,* published in 1882. Joy A. Marsella's *The Promise of Destiny* includes a useful appendix, "The Publication Record of 'Scrap-Bag' Stories."

2. Uncle Fact is reminiscent of Dickens's Thomas Gradgrind, Lorelei of Sissy Jupe, and Fancy of Louisa Gradgrind in *Hard Times* (1854).

3. The opposition between Lorelei and Uncle Fact, the bubble and the rock, can also be interpreted as a struggle between Fancy's "inner voice," her "subjective knowledge," and the voice of authority and reason, especially as it encourages a mode of knowledge divorced from feeling. According to Mary Field Belenky and her collaborators in *Women's Ways of Knowing,* the goal of female development should be "constructed knowledge"—an integration of what women feel intuitively to be personally important with knowledge they gain from others (134). Constructive knowers move beyond the "either/or thinking" and "hypothetico-deductive inquiry" employed by Uncle Fact (137, 139).

4. Marsella, who begins and ends her book on the *Scrap-Bag* stories with discussions of "Fancy's Friend," explores several levels of meaning to support her view that Alcott acknowledged the superiority of fact and thus rationalized her choice of "the didactic mode" (147).

5. In Frances Osgood's "A Flight of Fancy," for example, "the forces of the patriarchy and its supporters . . . try to jail her and make Reason her keeper. But true to the power-fantasy form, she escapes" (Walker 40).

Works Cited

Works by Louisa May Alcott

Alternative Alcott. Edited by Elaine Showalter. American Women Writers Series. New Brunswick: Rutgers Univ. Press, 1988.

"The Amber Amulet: A Tale of India and England." MS. 104 pp. 59M-309, no. 24. Houghton Library, Harvard Univ.

Aunt Jo's Scrap-Bag. 6 vols. Boston: Roberts, 1872–82.

"Behind a Mask or A Woman's Power." In *The Hidden Louisa May Alcott.* Edited by Madeleine Stern, 3–104. New York: Avenel, 1984.

Behind a Mask: The Unknown Thrillers of Louisa May Alcott. Edited by Madeleine B. Stern. New York: Avenel, 1975.

"Cupid and Chow-Chow." In *Works of Louisa May Alcott.* Edited by Claire Booss, 690–704. New York: Avenel, 1982.

"Diana and Persis." MS. 138 pp. 59M-309, no. 21. Houghton Library, Harvard Univ.

Diana and Persis. Edited by Sarah Elbert. New York: Arno, 1978.

"Diana and Persis." In *Alternative Alcott,* 383–441.

A Double Life: Newly Discovered Thrillers of Louisa May Alcott. Edited by Madeleine B. Stern with Joel Myerson and Daniel Shealy. Boston: Little, Brown, 1988.

"Fair Rosamond." MS. 74 pp. 59M-309, no. 19. Houghton Library, Harvard Univ.

"Fancy's Friend." In *An Old-Fashioned Thanksgiving, Etc.,* 208–34. Vol. 6 of *Aunt Jo's Scrap-Bag.* Boston: Roberts, 1882.

"The Freak of a Genius." In *Freaks of Genius: Unknown Thrillers of Louisa May Alcott.* Edited by Daniel Shealy with Joel Myerson and Madeleine B. Stern, 115–191. Introduction by Stern. Contributions to the Study of Popular Culture, no. 28. New York: Greenwood, 1991.

The Hidden Louisa May Alcott: A Collection of Her Unknown Thrillers. Edited by Madeleine Stern. New York: Avenel, 1984.

Hospital Sketches. Edited by Bessie Z. Jones. Cambridge, Mass.: Harvard Univ. Press, 1960.

"The Inheritance." MS. 166 pp. bMS Am 1817.2 (22). Houghton Library, Harvard Univ.

Jo's Boys. New York: Grosset, 1949.

The Journals of Louisa May Alcott. Edited by Joel Myerson and Daniel Shealy with Madeleine B. Stern. Introduction by Stern. Boston: Little, Brown, 1989.

"The Lay of a Golden Goose." In *Louisa May Alcott,* by Ednah D. Cheney, 204–7. Introduction by Ann Douglas. American Men and Women of Letters Series. New York: Chelsea House, 1980.

Little Men. New York: Grosset, 1947.

Little Women. Introduction by Madelon Bedell. New York: Modern Library, 1983.

"Mamma's Plot." In *Works of Louisa May Alcott.* Edited by Claire Booss, 784–89. New York: Avenel, 1982.

"A Marble Woman or The Mysterious Model." In *The Hidden Louisa May Alcott,* 407–511.

"A Modern Cinderella; or, The Little Old Shoe." In *Hospital Sketches and Camp and Fireside Stories,* 257–94. Boston: Roberts, 1869.

A Modern Mephistopheles and Taming a Tartar. Introduction by Madeleine B. Stern. New York: Praeger, 1987.

"A Modern Mephistophiles [*sic*] or The Fatal Love Chase." MS. 287 pp. 59M-309, no. 18. Houghton Library, Harvard Univ.

Moods. Edited by Sarah Elbert. American Women Writers Series. New Brunswick: Rutgers Univ. Press, 1991.

"A Nurse's Story." In *Freaks of Genius*, 29–114.

An Old-Fashioned Girl. Orchard House edition. Boston: Little, Brown, n.d.

"Pansies." In *A Garland for Girls*, 79–105. New York: Grosset, n.d.

"Patty's Patchwork." In *My Boys, Etc.*, 193–215. Vol. 1 of *Aunt Jo's Scrap-Bag*. Boston: Roberts, 1872.

"Pauline's Passion and Punishment." In *The Hidden Louisa May Alcott*, 105–52.

"Perilous Play." In *The Hidden Louisa May Alcott*, 579–89.

Plots and Counterplots: More Unknown Thrillers of Louisa May Alcott. Edited by Madeleine B. Stern. New York: Avenel, 1976.

"Poppy's Pranks." In *Morning Glories and Other Stories*, 89–107. Boston: Fuller, 1868.

"Psyche's Art." In *Alternative Alcott*, 207–26.

"The Rose Family." In *Morning Glories and Other Stories*, 45–71. Boston: Fuller, 1868.

Rose in Bloom. The Plumfield edition. New York: Grosset, n.d.

The Selected Letters of Louisa May Alcott. Edited by Joel Myerson and Daniel Shealy with Madeleine B. Stern. Introduction by Madeleine B. Stern. Boston: Little, Brown, 1987.

"The Skeleton in the Closet." In *The Hidden Louisa May Alcott*, 515–34.

Transcendental Wild Oats and Excerpts from the Fruitlands Diary. Cambridge, Mass.: Harvard Common Press, 1975.

"V. V. or Plots and Counterplots." In *The Hidden Louisa May Alcott*, 315–403.

"A Whisper in the Dark." In *The Hidden Louisa May Alcott*, 537–75.

Work: A Story of Experience. Introduction by Sarah Elbert. New York: Schocken, 1977.

Work: A Story of Experience. Introduction by Elizabeth Hardwick. New York: Arno, 1977.

Other Works Cited

Alberghene, Janice M. "Alcott's Psyche and Kate: Self-Portraits, Sunny-side Up." In *Proceedings of the Eighth Annual Conference of the Children's Literature Association*, 37–43. Univ. of Minnesota, Mar. 1981. Boston: Children's Literature Association, 1982.

Alcott (Nieriker), Abigail May. Diary, MS. bMS Am 1817.2 (15). Houghton Library, Harvard Univ.

Auerbach, Nina. Afterword to *Little Women*, by Louisa May Alcott. Toronto: Bantam, 1983.

———. *Communities of Women*. Cambridge, Mass.: Harvard Univ. Press, 1978.

———. *Woman and the Demon: The Life of a Victorian Myth*. Cambridge, Mass.: Harvard Univ. Press, 1982.

Bassil, Veronica. "The Artist at Home: The Domestication of Louisa May Alcott." *Studies in American Fiction* 15 (1987): 187–97.

———. "Eros and Psyche in 'The Artist of the Beautiful.'" *Emerson Society Quarterly* 30 (1984): 1–21.

Baym, Nina. *Woman's Fiction: A Guide to Novels by and about Women in America, 1820–1870*. Ithaca: Cornell Univ. Press, 1978.

Beauvoir, Simone de. *The Second Sex*. Translated and edited by H. M. Parshley. New York: Bantam, 1961.

Bedell, Jeanne F. "A Necessary Mask: The Sensation Fiction of Louisa May Alcott."
  Missouri Philological Association Publications 5 (1980): 8–14.
Bedell, Madelon. *The Alcotts: Biography of a Family*. New York: Potter, 1980.
———. Introduction to *Little Women*, by Louisa M. Alcott. New York: Modern Library, 1983.
Belenky, Mary Field, et al. *Women's Ways of Knowing: The Development of Self, Voice, and
  Mind*. New York: Basic, 1986.
Bernikow, Louise. *Among Women*. New York: Harper, 1980.
Blackburn, William. "'Moral Pap for the Young'? A New Look at Louisa May Alcott's *Little
  Men*." In *Proceedings of the Seventh Annual Conference of the Children's Literature
  Association*, 98–106. Baylor Univ., Mar. 1980. New Rochelle, N.Y.: Children's
  Literature Association, 1982.
Blanchard, Paula. *Margaret Fuller: From Transcendentalism to Revolution*. Radcliffe
  Biography Series. New York: Delacorte, 1978.
Braddon, Mary Elizabeth. *Lady Audley's Secret*. Introduction by Norman Donaldson. New
  York: Dover, 1974.
Brontë, Charlotte. *Jane Eyre*. Edited by Richard J. Dunn. Norton Critical Edition. New
  York: Norton, 1971.
Buckler, William E. *Man and his Myths: Tennyson's* Idylls of the King *in Critical Context*.
  New York: New York Univ. Press, 1984.
Burlingame, Edward R. Review of *A Modern Mephistopheles*. In *Critical Essays on Louisa
  May Alcott*. Edited by Madeleine B. Stern, 204–5. Boston: Hall, 1984.
Carpenter, Lynette. "'Did They Never See Anyone Angry Before?': The Sexual Politics of
  Self-Control in Louisa May Alcott's 'A Whisper in the Dark.'" *Legacy* 3 (1986): 31–41.
Cheney, Ednah D. *Louisa May Alcott*. Introduction by Ann Douglas. American Men and
  Women of Letters Series. New York: Chelsea House, 1980.
———. *Louisa May Alcott: The Children's Friend*. Boston: Prang, 1888.
Clark, Beverly Lyon. "A Portrait of the Artist as a Little Woman." *Children's Literature* 17
  (1989): 81–97.
Cogan, Frances B. *All-American Girl: The Ideal of Real Womanhood in Mid-Nineteenth-
  Century America*. Athens: Univ. of Georgia Press, 1989.
Comini, Alessandra. "Who Ever Heard of a Woman Sculptor? Harriet Hosmer, Elisabet
  Ney, and the Nineteenth-Century Dialogue with the Three-Dimensional." In *American
  Women Artists 1830–1930*. Edited by Eleanor Tufts, 17–25. Washington, D.C.:
  National Museum of Women in the Arts, 1987.
Cott, Nancy. "Passionlessness: An Interpretation of Victorian Sexual Ideology, 1790–1850."
  Signs 4 (1978): 219–36.
Cowan, Octavia. Introduction to *A Modern Mephistopheles*, by Louisa May Alcott.
  Toronto: Bantam, 1987.
Crews, Frederick. *The Sins of the Fathers: Hawthorne's Psychological Themes*. New York:
  Oxford Univ. Press, 1966.
Critical Essays on Louisa May Alcott. Edited by Madeleine B. Stern. Boston: Hall, 1984.
Dalke, Anne. "'The House-Band': The Education of Men in *Little Women*." *College English*
  47 (1985): 571–78.
Donnell-Vogt, Radka. "Memoir." In *Lives and Works: Talks with Women Artists*. Edited by
  Lynn F. Miller and Sally S. Swenson, 37–56. Metuchen, N.J.: Scarecrow, 1981.
Douglas, Ann. Introduction to *Louisa May Alcott*, by Ednah D. Cheney. American Men and
  Women of Letters Series. New York: Chelsea House, 1980.

Elbert, Sarah. *A Hunger for Home: Louisa May Alcott and* Little Women. Philadelphia: Temple Univ. Press, 1984.

———. Introduction to *Diana and Persis,* by Louisa May Alcott. New York: Arno, 1978.

———. Introduction to *Moods,* by Louisa May Alcott. American Women Writers Series. New Brunswick: Rutgers Univ. Press, 1991.

Estes, Angela M. "An Aptitude for Bird: Louisa May Alcott's Women and Emerson's Self-Reliant Man." Diss., Univ. of Oregon, 1985.

Estes, Angela M., and Kathleen Margaret Lant. "Dismembering the Text: The Horror of Louisa May Alcott's *Little Women.*" *Children's Literature* 17 (1989): 98–123.

———. "The Feminist Redeemer: Louisa Alcott's Creation of the Female Christ in *Work.*" *Christianity and Literature* 40 (1991): 223–53.

Ferguson, Moira. Introduction to *Maria or The Wrongs of Woman,* by Mary Wollstonecraft. New York: Norton, 1975.

Fern, Fanny. *Ruth Hall and Other Writings.* Edited by Joyce W. Warren. American Women Writers Series. New Brunswick: Rutgers Univ. Press, 1986.

Fetterley, Judith. "Impersonating 'Little Women': The Radicalism of Alcott's *Behind a Mask.*" *Women's Studies* 10 (1983): 1–14.

———. "*Little Women:* Alcott's Civil War." *Feminist Studies* 5 (1979): 369–83.

Fuller, Margaret. *Woman in the Nineteenth Century.* Introduction by Bernard Rosenthal. The Norton Library. New York: Norton, 1971.

Gilbert, Sandra M., and Susan Gubar. *The Madwoman in the Attic: The Woman Writer and the Nineteenth-Century Literary Imagination.* New Haven, Conn.: Yale Univ. Press, 1979.

Gilligan, Carol. *In a Different Voice: Psychological Theory and Women's Development.* Cambridge, Mass.: Harvard Univ. Press, 1982.

Gilman, Charlotte Perkins. *Women and Economics: A Study of the Economic Relation Between Men and Women as a Factor in Social Evolution.* Edited by Carl N. Degler. American Perspectives. New York: Harper, 1966.

———. *The Yellow Wallpaper.* Afterword by Elaine Hedges. Old Westbury, N.Y.: Feminist Press, 1973.

Gordon, Mary. "Mary Cassatt." In *Good Boys and Dead Girls,* 156–59. New York: Viking, 1991.

Greer, Germaine. *The Obstacle Race: The Fortunes of Women Painters and Their Work.* New York: Farrar, 1979.

Habegger, Alfred. "Precocious Incest: First Novels by Louisa May Alcott and Henry James." *Massachusetts Review* 26 (1985): 233–62.

Halttunen, Karen. *Confidence Men and Painted Women: A Study of Middle-class Culture in America, 1830–1870.* Yale Historical Publications, Miscellany, 129. New Haven, Conn.: Yale Univ. Press, 1982.

———. "The Domestic Drama of Louisa May Alcott." *Feminist Studies* 10 (1984): 233–54.

Harris, Susan K. "'But is it any *good?*': Evaluating Nineteenth-Century American Women's Fiction." *American Literature* 63 (1991): 43–61.

———. *19th-Century American Women's Novels: Interpretative Strategies.* Cambridge, Mass.: Cambridge Univ. Press, 1990.

Hawthorne, Nathaniel. *Novels.* The Library of America. New York: Viking, 1983.

———. *Tales and Sketches.* The Library of America. New York: Viking, 1982.

Heilbrun, Carolyn G. *Reinventing Womanhood.* New York: Norton, 1979.

———. *Writing a Woman's Life.* New York: Norton, 1988.

Herman, Judith, and Lisa Hirschman. "Father-Daughter Incest." In *The* Signs *Reader:*

Women, Gender and Scholarship. Edited by Elizabeth Abel and Emily K. Abel, 257–78. Chicago: Univ. of Chicago Press, 1983.

Hollander, Anne. "Reflections on *Little Women.*" *Children's Literature* 9 (1981): 28–39.

Howland, Marie Stevens. *The Familistere*. Philadelphia: Porcupine, 1975.

Hughes, Winifred. *The Maniac in the Cellar: Sensation Novels of the 1860s*. Princeton: Princeton Univ. Press, 1980.

James, Henry. "Miss Alcott's 'Moods.'" In *Moods*, by Louisa May Alcott. Edited by Sarah Elbert, 219–24. American Women Writers Series. New Brunswick: Rutgers Univ. Press, 1991.

Jewett, Sarah Orne. *A Country Doctor*. Introduction by Joy Gould Boyum and Ann R. Shapiro. New York: New American Library, 1986.

Kahane, Claire. "The Gothic Mirror." In *The (M)other Tongue: Essays in Feminist Psycho-analytic Interpretation*. Edited by Shirley Nelson Garner, Claire Kahane, and Madelon Sprengnether, 334–51. Ithaca: Cornell Univ. Press, 1985.

Kaledin, Eugenia. "Louisa May Alcott: Success and the Sorrow of Self-Denial." *Women's Studies* 5 (1978): 251–63.

Kelley, Mary. *Private Woman, Public Stage: Literary Domesticity in Nineteenth-Century America*. New York: Oxford Univ. Press, 1984.

Keyser, Elizabeth Lennox. "'The Most Beautiful Things in All the World'? Families in *Little Women.*" In *Stories and Society: Children's Literature in Its Social Context*. Edited by Dennis Butts, 50–64. London: Macmillan, 1992.

———. "'Playing Puckerage': Alcott's Plot in 'Cupid and Chow-Chow.'" *Children's Literature* 14 (1986): 105–22.

Kolbenschlag, Madonna. *Kiss Sleeping Beauty Good-Bye: Breaking the Spell of Feminine Myths and Models*. Toronto: Bantam, 1981.

Lang, Amy Schrager. "Slavery and Sentimentalism: The Strange Career of Augustine St. Clare." *Women's Studies* 12 (1986): 31–54.

Lang, Andrew. "The Story of Pretty Goldilocks." In *Blue Fairy Book*. Edited by Brian Alderson, 202–16. New York: Viking, 1975.

Langland, Elizabeth. "Female Stories of Exerience: Alcott's *Little Women* in Light of *Work.*" In *The Voyage In: Fiction of Female Development*. Edited by Elizabeth Abel, Marianne Hirsch, and Elizabeth Langland, 112–27. Hanover, N.H.: Univ. Press of New England, 1983.

Lubin, David M. *Act of Portrayal: Eakins, Sargent, James*. Yale Publications in the History of Art, no. 32. New Haven, Conn.: Yale Univ. Press, 1985.

MacAndrew, Elizabeth. *The Gothic Tradition in Fiction*. New York: Columbia Univ. Press, 1979.

McCurry, Niki Alpert. "Concepts of Childrearing and Schooling in the March Novels of Louisa May Alcott." Diss., Northwestern Univ., 1976.

MacDonald, George. *The Light Princess and Other Fantasy Stories*. Grand Rapids, Mich.: Eerdman's, 1980.

MacDonald, Ruth K. *Louisa May Alcott*. Twayne United States Authors Series, no. 457. Boston: Twayne, 1983.

———. "*Moods*, Gothic and Domestic." In *Critical Essays on Louisa May Alcott*. Edited by Madeleine B. Stern, 74–78. Boston: Hall, 1984.

Marsella, Joy A. *The Promise of Destiny: Children and Women in the Short Stories of Louisa May Alcott*. Contributions to the Study of Childhood and Youth, no. 2. Westport, Conn.: Greenwood, 1983.

Mills, Claudia. "Choosing a Way of Life: *Eight Cousins* and *Six to Sixteen*." *Children's Literature Association Quarterly* 14 (1989): 71–75.

Modleski, Tania. *Loving with a Vengeance: Mass-Produced Fantasies for Women.* Hamden, Conn.: Archon, 1982.

———. "Rape versus Mans/laughter: Hitchcock's *Blackmail* and Feminist Interpretation." *PMLA* 102 (1987): 304–15.

Murphy, Ann B. "The Borders of Ethical, Erotic, and Artistic Possibilities in *Little Women*." *Signs* 15 (1990): 562–85.

Murray, Janet Horowitz. *Strong-Minded Women and Other Lost Voices from Nineteenth-Century England.* New York: Pantheon, 1982.

Neumann, Erich. *Amor and Psyche: The Psychic Development of the Feminine: A Commentary on the Tale by Apuleius.* Translated by Ralph Manheim. New York: Pantheon, 1956.

Niles, Thomas. Letters to Louisa May Alcott, MS. 1868-1886. 59M-310, no. 1–142. Houghton Library, Harvard Univ.

O'Brien, Sharon. "Tomboyism and Adolescent Conflict: Three Nineteenth-Century Case Studies." In *Woman's Being, Woman's Place: Female Identity and Vocation in American History.* Edited by Mary Kelley, 351–72. Boston: Hall, 1979.

Oliphant, Margaret. *Hester.* Introduction by Jennifer Uglow. New York: Penguin, 1984.

Parker, Rozsika. *The Subversive Stitch: Embroidery and the Making of the Feminine.* London: The Women's Press, 1984.

Parker, Rozsika, and Griselda Pollock. *Old Mistresses: Women, Art and Ideology.* New York: Pantheon, 1981.

Phelps, Elizabeth Stuart. *Doctor Zay.* Afterword by Michael Sartisky. New York: Feminist Press, 1987.

———. *The Story of Avis.* Edited by Carol Farley Kessler. American Women Writers Series. New Brunswick: Rutgers Univ. Press, 1985.

Register, Cheri. "Letting the Angel Die." *Hurricane Alice* 3, no. 2 (1986): 1–4.

Reynolds, David S. *Beneath the American Renaissance: The Subversive Imagination in the Age of Emerson and Melville.* New York: Knopf, 1988.

Rhys, Jean. *Wide Sargasso Sea.* New York: Norton, 1982.

Rose, Ellen Cronan. "Through the Looking Glass: When Women Tell Fairy Tales." In *The Voyage In: Fiction of Female Development.* Edited by Elizabeth Abel, Marianne Hirsch, and Elizabeth Langland, 209–27. Hanover, N.H.: Univ. Press of New England, 1983.

Rosenberg, Rosalind. *Beyond Separate Spheres: Intellectual Roots of Modern Feminism.* New Haven, Conn.: Yale Univ. Press, 1982.

Rosenfeld, Natania. "Artists and Daughters in Louisa May Alcott's *Diana and Persis*." *New England Quarterly* 64 (1991): 3–21.

Rowe, Karen. "To Spin a Yarn: The Female Voice in Folklore and Fairy Tale." In *Fairy Tales and Society: Illusion, Allusion, and Paradigm.* Edited by Ruth B. Bottigheimer, 53–74. Philadelphia: Univ. of Pennsylvania Press, 1986.

Sanderson, Rena. "*A Modern Mephistopheles*: Louisa May Alcott's Exorcism of Patriarchy." *American Transcendental Quarterly* 5 (1991): 41–55.

Sartisky, Michael. Afterword to *Doctor Zay,* by Elizabeth Stuart Phelps. New York: Feminist Press, 1987.

Sarton, May. *Mrs. Stevens Hears the Mermaids Singing.* Introduction by Carolyn G. Heilbrun. New York: Norton, 1975.

Saxton, Martha. *Louisa May: A Modern Biography of Louisa May Alcott.* New York: Avon, 1978.

Sexton, Anne. "Cinderella." In *Transformations,* 53–57. Preface by Kurt Vonnegut, Jr. Boston: Houghton Mifflin, 1971.

Showalter, Elaine. *The Female Malady: Women, Madness, and English Culture, 1830–1980.* New York: Pantheon, 1985.

———. Introduction to *Alternative Alcott.* Edited by Elaine Showalter. American Women Writers Series. New Brunswick: Rutgers Univ. Press, 1988.

———. "Piecing and Writing." In *The Poetics of Gender.* Edited by Nancy K. Miller, 222–47. Gender and Culture. New York: Columbia Univ. Press, 1986.

Spacks, Patricia Meyer. *The Female Imagination.* New York: Avon, 1972.

Spender, Dale. *Women of Ideas (And What Men Have Done to Them).* London: Ark, 1983.

Stanton, Elizabeth Cady. *Eighty Years and More: Reminiscences 1815–1897.* Introduction by Gail Parker. Studies in the Life of Women. New York: Shocken, 1971.

Stern, Madeleine B. Introduction to *Freaks of Genius: Unknown Thrillers of Louisa May Alcott.* Edited by Daniel Shealy with Joel Myerson and Madeleine B. Stern. Contributions to the Study of Popular Culture no. 28. New York: Greenwood, 1991.

———. Introduction to *The Journals of Louisa May Alcott.* Edited by Joel Myerson and Daniel Shealy with Madeleine B. Stern. Boston: Little, Brown, 1989.

———. Introduction to *A Modern Mephistopheles and Taming a Tartar,* by Louisa May Alcott. New York: Praeger, 1987.

———. "Louisa Alcott, Trouper: Experiences in Theatricals, 1848–1880." *New England Quarterly* 16 (1943): 175–97.

———. "Louisa Alcott's Feminist Letters." In *Studies in the American Renaissance.* Edited by Joel Myerson, 429–52. Boston: Twayne, 1978.

———. *Louisa May Alcott.* Norman: Univ. of Oklahoma Press, 1950.

Strickland, Charles. *Victorian Domesticity: Families in the Life and Art of Louisa May Alcott.* Foreword by Robert Coles. University: Univ. of Alabama Press, 1985.

Tennyson, Alfred Lord. "Idylls of the King." In *The Poems of Tennyson.* 3 vols. Edited by Christopher Ricks, 3:255–561. Annotated English Poets. Berkeley: Univ. of California Press, 1987.

Ticknor, Caroline. *May Alcott: A Memoir.* Boston: Little, Brown, 1928.

Urbanski, Marie Olesen. "Thoreau in the Writing of Louisa May Alcott." In *Critical Essays on Louisa May Alcott.* Edited by Madeleine B. Stern, 269–74. Boston: Hall, 1984.

Van Buren, Jane. "Louisa May Alcott: A Study in Persona and Idealization." *Psychohistory Review* 9 (1981): 282–99.

Walker, Cheryl. *The Nightingale's Burden: Women Poets and American Culture before 1900.* Bloomington: Indiana Univ. Press, 1982.

Williams, Jay. "Petronella." In *Don't Bet on the Prince: Contemporary Feminist Fairy Tales in North America and England.* Edited by Jack Zipes, 55–61. New York: Methuen, 1986.

Wollstonecraft, Mary. *Maria or The Wrongs of Woman.* Introduction by Moira Ferguson. New York: Norton, 1975.

———. *Vindication of the Rights of Woman.* Edited by Miriam Brody Kramnick. Baltimore: Penguin, 1975.

Woolf, Virginia. *A Room of One's Own.* New York: Harcourt, n.d.

Yellin, Jean Fagan. "From *Success* to *Experience*: Louisa May Alcott's *Work.*" *Massachusetts Review* 21 (1980): 527–39.

Zwinger, Lynda. *Daughters, Fathers, and the Novel: The Sentimental Romance of Heterosexuality.* Madison: Univ. of Wisconsin Press, 1991.

Index

Alcott, Abigail May (Abba), xvi, 13, 16, 44, 192n, 196n, 199n, 210n, 211n

Alcott (Nieriker), Abigail May, xii, 59, 145–46, 160, 161, 163–64, 192n, 199n, 209–12n; journals, 209–10n; journals quoted: 192n, 209n–10n; letters, 145, 149, 152, 209–11n; letters quoted: 211n

Alcott, Anna, xvii, 59, 199n, 200n, 203n

Alcott, Bronson, xii, xvii, xviii, 13, 16, 29, 59, 186, 188, 192n, 196n, 197n, 199n, 200n, 201n; Fruitlands, xvi, 87, 196n; journal quoted: 13; *see also* Fruitlands

Alcott, Elizabeth, 59, 197n, 200n

Alcott, Louisa May

—career, xi, xii, 3, 29–31, 101, 119–20, 161–62, 182, 199n

—childhood, xvi–xvii, xviii, 13, 16, 203n

—Civil War nursing experience, xi–xii, 101, 102, 119, 198n

—feminism, xiii, xiv, 3–4, 47, 57, 75, 85–86, 87–88, 121, 142–43, 164, 167, 178–79, 188, 189, 191n; *see also* Alcott, Louisa May—writing—themes and motifs in—Women's Rights

—health, 44, 198n, 213n

—parents, xvi–xvii, xviii, 13, 16, 44, 196n; *see also* Alcott, Abigail May (Abba), and Alcott, Bronson

—theater in the life of, xvii–xviii, 101, 119, 200–1n

—transcendentalism, 18, 21, 197n; *see also* Alcott, Louisa May—writing—allusions in and influences on—Emerson, Ralph Waldo, and Thoreau, Henry David

Alcott, Louisa May—writing—allusions in and influences on

—Aeschylus, 27

—Amazon, 103–4, 114, 120, 204n

—Amor, 32, 197n; *see also* Alcott, Louisa May—writing—allusions in and influences on—Psyche

—Andersen, Hans Christian: "Marchën," 111

—Apollo, 22, 23

—Aulnoy, Madame d': "Pretty Goldilocks," 203n

—Bible, and Biblical characters, 73; Adam, xviii, 206n; Christ, 205n; Eve, 154, 206n; Exodus, 212n; Jael and Sisera, 44; John the Baptist and daughter of Herodias, 44; Judith and Holofernes, xvii, 44, *55*, 57, 59, 87, 103, 199n; Mary, 207n; Satan, 204n; Saul and David, xviii, 149, 157, 158, 159, 161, 182

—Bluebeard, 128

—Boadicea, 104

—Brackett, Anna C: *The Education of American Girls*, 166, 213n

—Braddon, Mary Elizabeth, xii; *Lady Audley's Secret* 46, 48, 198–99n

—Bremer, Fredrika, 196n

—Britomart, 104

—Brontë, Charlotte, 122; *Jane Eyre*, 4, 5, 8, 12, 47–48, 51–53, 101, 105–7, 112, 114, 120, 193n, 194n, 195n, 196n, 204n; *Villette*, 204n

—Bunyan, John: *Pilgrim's Progress*, xviii, 63, 118

—Butler, Josephine, 166–67